Credit Scoring for Risk Managers

The Handbook for Lenders

Elizabeth Mays
Bank One

THOMSON
™
SOUTH-WESTERN

Australia · Canada · Mexico · Singapore · Spain · United Kingdom · United States

CREDIT SCORING FOR RISK MANAGERS: THE HANDBOOK FOR LENDERS
Elizabeth Mays

Vice President/ Editorial Director:
Jack Calhoun

Vice President/ Editor-in-Chief:
Dave Shaut

Acquisition Editor:
Steve Momper

Channel Manager, Retail:
Chris McNamee

Channel Manager, Professional:
Mark Linton

Production Editor:
Darrell Frye

Production Manager:
Tricia Matthews Boies

Manufacturing Coordinator:
Charlene Taylor

Compositor:
Edgewater Editorial Services

Editorial Associate:
Michael Jeffers

Production Associate:
Barbara Evans

Printer:
Phoenix Book Technology
Hagerstown, MD

Sr. Design Project Manager:
Michelle Kunkler

Cover Designer:
Beckmeyer Design
Cincinnati, OH

Cover Images:
PhotoDisc, Inc.

DEDICATION

To Ed Irmler.

I miss your wisdom and your friendship.

CONTENTS

ABOUT THE AUTHOR

Elizabeth Mays is Director of Retail Risk Modeling and Analytics at Bank One. Her unit is responsible for building risk models for a variety of consumer loan products, including home equity, auto, and small business loans as well as demand deposit accounts. She is a well-known expert in credit scoring and has 15 years of experience building risk management models for financial institutions. Among her previous books are *The Handbook of Credit Scoring, Credit Modeling: Design and Application,* and *Interest Rate Risk Models: Theory and Practice.* Dr. Mays holds a Ph.D. in economics from the University of Cincinnati.

CONTRIBUTORS

Mark A. Beardsell is Director of Home Equity Modeling in the Consumer Asset Division of Citigroup. His area is responsible for building credit risk, prepayment, and valuation models to support risk management of first and second lien mortgages. Before joining Citigroup in 2001, Dr. Beardsell spent two years with Hibernia National Bank as a small business loan portfolio risk manager and three years as a quantitative portfolio analyst at Fleet Financial Group. While at Fleet, he created a residential mortgage valuation model that integrated loan level prepayment, default, and loss severity models. His expertise also includes credit value-at-risk and economic capital models for large corporate loans and mortgages. He holds a Ph.D. in economics from Brown University.

Gary Chandler, President of GGC Consulting, Inc., has proven expertise in credit scoring, consulting, and the impact of federal credit regulations on scoring systems. He has served the credit industry as a leading researcher, author, and educator for more than 30 years. He is currently an adjunct research scholar at the Credit Research Center of Georgetown University and a member of the Center's Advisory Council and Research Council. For over 15 years Dr. Chandler was a member of the Advisory Council and a faculty member of the American Bankers Association's School of Bank Card Management.

In 1976, Dr. Chandler co-founded Management Decision Systems, Inc. (now Experian, formerly CCN-MDS Division), which became the second largest credit-scoring firm in the world. He has earned a B.S. in physics, an M.S. in industrial administration, and a Ph.D. in finance from Purdue University and has taught at Purdue University, the University of Southern California, and Georgia State University.

Elaine Fortowsky is a Director of Fair Lending Modeling at Wells Fargo Home Mortgage. Before joining Wells Fargo, she worked in mortgage modeling for Citimortgage, Greenpoint, and Donaldson, Lufkin and Jenrette. She earned her Ph.D. in economics from Rice University.

Michael LaCour-Little joined Wells Fargo Home Mortgage in November 2000 as a Vice President in the Risk Management Division and currently manages a group responsible for fair lending, including compliance with the Home Mortgage Disclosure Act and the Community Reinvestment Act. Before joining Wells Fargo, he was Director of Financial Research at CitiMortgage, the mortgage subsidiary of Citigroup, where he built and implemented its first loan-level prepayment models. He is also adjunct professor of real estate finance at the John M. Olin School of Business at Washington University in St. Louis, where he has taught M.B.A. courses in real estate finance and mortgage-backed securities.

Dr. LaCour-Little earned his Ph.D. at the University of Wisconsin, Madison, and undergraduate and master's degrees at the University of California. He is on the editorial boards of several academic journals and his research has appeared in *Real Estate Economics,* The Journal of Real Estate Finance and Economics, The Journal of Real Estate Research, The Journal of Real Estate Literature, The Journal of Housing Research, The Journal of Housing Economics, The Journal of Fixed Income, Mortgage Banking, and elsewhere.

Philip Nuetzel is a Senior Economist in the Risk Modeling Department of the Citigroup Real Estate Group. He builds predictive models of credit risk for clients within Citigroup, as well as financial models used to value credit risks. Dr. Nuetzel's work includes creating origination scorecards for default or delinquency risk, behavior scores, and prepayment models. Before joining Citigroup in April of 2000, he was an economist with SBC

Communications, where he prepared economic and financial studies and forecasts, building and using predictive models of customer demand and customer value.

Dr. Nuetzel earned a Ph.D. in economics from Northwestern University. Formerly an economist with the Federal Reserve Bank of St. Louis, he has also taught graduate and undergraduate courses in economics and finance at Northwestern University, the University of Missouri, the University of Texas, and St. Louis University.

Rhonda Sicilia is an Assistant Vice President and Managing Consultant at Equifax Decision Solutions, where she manages the U.S. Decision Solutions Consultants that provide analytic and consulting solutions spanning the customer lifecycle for clients of Equifax.

Before joining Equifax, Ms. Sicilia was national credit risk manager at Avco Financial Services Inc., credit consultant at Southern California Edison, and a research analyst at the U.S. Agency for International Development, the University of Southern California, and California State University, Fullerton. Ms. Sicilia has expertise in building and implementing scorecards in distributed branch network systems and centralized systems, credit strategy and policy, marketing, econometric analysis, and modeling. She has earned a B.A. and an M.A., both in economics, from California State University, Fullerton.

Dana Wiklund, Vice President of Equifax, has spent 11 years with the company and presently manages the Decision Solutions organization. Before rejoining Equifax in 1998, Dana served as Assistant Vice President, credit score strategies in FleetBoston Financial Group's consumer lending business and a credit risk manager in Consumer Finance for BankBoston. Previously he had been a database manager for Equifax.

Mr. Wiklund is an expert in credit risk data, scorecard development, and designing score-driven risk management and marketing response strategies. He has managed many scoring projects for Equifax, ranging from origination and account management risk to attrition, response, and profitability projects. He has published white papers on such topics as project management for scoring, risk model performance on low-income populations, and the impact of an economic recession on consumer debt service. Mr. Wiklund has earned a B.S. in finance and economics from Massachusetts College of Liberal Arts and a Certificate of Special Studies in Administration and Management from Harvard University.

Jean Yuan is Director of Prepayment Modeling with CitiMortgage's Mortgage Analytics group, where she builds prepayment models and pipeline fallout models for hedging purposes. Previously she was with the Risk Modeling group within Citigroup's Consumer Assets and Consumer Finance Division, where her main responsibilities were to build risk models and develop portfolio loss forecasts for prime first mortgages. She also built models in various other businesses, such as subprime first and second mortgages.

Before joining Citigroup in 1999, Dr. Yuan was with the Credit Card Division at Mellon Bank, where she worked on building models to support collections efforts. Previously she taught university statistics and mathematics courses. She earned a Ph.D. in statistics from York University

PREFACE

This book was written for bankers and other consumer lenders who need a clear understanding of how to use credit scoring effectively to manage credit risk throughout the loan life cycle. In the last two decades, credit scoring has come to be used by virtually all lenders in every facet of consumer lending. That makes it vitally important that lending institutions—especially the risk managers of those institutions—understand how to manage and monitor scores, how to set policies for their use, and how to use scores in making decisions on loan applications, pricing loans according to risk, and forecasting future losses.

Credit Scoring For Risk Managers is divided into three sections, each devoted to an important aspect of credit scoring. In the introductory section we discuss the many ways lenders use credit scoring today in loan approval decisions, risk-based pricing, managing delinquency and default, and loss forecasting. The section describes recent advances in credit scoring, including the move to profitability modeling and the incorporation of economic effects into score development and scorecard policies. It also provides a complete list of credit scores in the public domain. We discuss credit bureau data in detail and describe its importance in lenders' decision making.

The second section is devoted to scorecard development and validation. We provide a nontechnical description of how scorecards are developed, emphasizing how scorecard weights are derived, reasons why scorecard point weights may not always reflect the actual impact of a characteristic on the outcome variable, and what can be done to minimize this problem. The most popular measures of scorecard performance are discussed in detail, along with pitfalls risk managers must be aware of when using these measures. We discuss the common practice of excluding indeterminate accounts from scorecard development and describe a study that tested the benefit of this practice. One chapter describes how to improve loss forecasts by incorporating credit scores into forecasting models. Credit scoring and the fair lending issue of disparate impact on protected borrower classes is also covered. We describe how to test scorecards for disparate impact and how scorecard developers can modify their practices to minimize its effect.

The third section covers important aspects of scorecard implementation, monitoring, and management. We describe how to monitor scores to avoid costly mistakes and explain a detailed set of scorecard monitoring reports. These reports enable risk managers to monitor their scorecards for maximum effectiveness. One chapter discusses scorecard policies and details the steps necessary to set cutoff scores properly, limit lending parameters, and set policies for overriding scorecards.

It is hoped that this book will guide lenders in how to use credit scores to their greatest advantage in all facets of loan origination and portfolio management. A solid understanding of the best practices in scorecard development, management, and monitoring will give lenders a clear advantage in the rapidly evolving environment in which financial services companies find themselves.

I am grateful to the credit scoring experts who wrote chapters for this book. Their expertise, knowledge, and insights are very much appreciated. Thanks also go to Keith Krieger, Jay Huling, and Scott Humphreys, who provided helpful suggestions on drafts of several chapters. To my friends and associates John Watkins and Jeff Polkinghorne—I hope we got everything right this time.

I am grateful as well to South-Western for their support, and to Barbara Evans—as always, you are a pleasure.

Elizabeth Mays

Section One
INTRODUCTION

Chapter 1
THE ROLE OF CREDIT SCORES IN CONSUMER LENDING

Elizabeth Mays
Director of Retail Risk Modeling and Analytics
Bank One

INTRODUCTION

In the last 10 to 15 years there has been a revolution in the financial services industry—lenders have rushed to embrace automated decision-making and modeling to speed loan decisions and manage credit risk.

Although credit scoring has been used by lenders since the 1950s, in the last decade it has become pervasive throughout the consumer lending arena, expanding into areas like residential mortgages and small business loans. Mester[1] describes a 1997 Federal Reserve survey in which 70 percent of large banks responded that they use credit scoring in their small-business lending. Credit scoring has become the standard method for evaluating the credit quality of residential mortgages since automated decisioning technologies were introduced by the government-sponsored enterprises (GSEs) Freddie Mac and Fannie Mae in the mid-1990s.

Mester notes several benefits from credit scoring. First, it promotes great efficiencies and time-savings in the loan approval process. While the traditional approval process for small business loans reportedly can take

---

[1] See Mester, Loretta J. (1997). "What's the Point of Credit Scoring?" *Business Review.* Federal Reserve Bank of Philadelphia, September/October.

from 12.5 hours to as long as two weeks, credit scoring can reduce this to under an hour.

A second benefit of credit scoring is that it reduces subjectivity in the loan approval process. With traditional underwriting, the standards to which applications are held can vary depending on the decision maker, and human judgment is affected by past experiences. With credit scoring, lenders can ensure they are applying the same standards to all applicants, regardless of race, gender, or other applicant characteristics.

Hand[2] notes another benefit of credit scoring over traditional under-writing: Score models permit the loan decision to take into account more factors than could a human making the decision judgmentally.

U.S. Federal Reserve Chairman Alan Greenspan stated in an October 2002 speech to the American Bankers Association that "credit scoring technologies have sharply reduced the cost of credit evaluation and improved the consistency, speed, and accuracy of credit decisions."[3] The benefits of credit scoring apply not just to the loan acquisition process but also to credit scores used to manage accounts. Using credit scores for decisions about loan collection and modification, line management, and loss recovery strategies can speed these decisions, eliminate bias, and help lenders make the right decisions.

In the same speech, Chairman Greenspan noted that:

> *"[The use of credit scoring technologies] has expanded well beyond their original purpose of assessing credit risk. Today they are used for assessing the risk-adjusted profitability of account relationships, for establishing the initial and ongoing credit limits available to borrowers, and for assisting in a range of activities in loan servicing, including fraud detection, delinquency intervention, and loss mitigation. These diverse applications have played a major role in promoting the efficiency and expanding the scope of our credit-delivery systems and allowing lenders to broaden the populations they are willing and able to serve profitably."[4]*

In the next section we discuss in more detail how lenders are using scores today and talk briefly about the latest methods for building and using credit scores.

---

[2] Hand, David J. (2001). "Modeling Consumer Credit Risk." *IMA Journal of Management Mathematics,* 12: 139-55.

[3] *http://www.federalreserve.gov.*

[4] Ibid., p. 4.

USE OF SCORES IN LOAN ACQUISITION

Today many lenders—certainly the vast majority of large lenders—have their own proprietary custom acquisition scores. A custom score is one built for a specific product using a lender's own data. Often, a custom score will contain characteristics based on data from the loan application, such as borrower income or debt-to-income ratio; generic scores are based only on credit bureau data.

Because generic scores are built on a wide array of consumer credit data, they do not focus on a specific loan product or a specific type borrower. The best-known example is the FICO score,[5] which is based on models built by a leading scorecard developer, Fair Isaac Company. It is designed to rank the likelihood that an applicant will go 90 days delinquent on any consumer credit loan or account within the next two years. Chapter 2 details the differences between generic and custom scores; it also lists scores in the public domain.

Chapter 3 describes how credit data is used in consumer lending. Lenders who use custom scores may also use generic credit scores to make quick decisions about the highest credit quality customers. In this case, the generic score is reviewed, often in combination with other data provided by the applicant, to get a preliminary risk assessment. If the borrower appears to pose very low risk, the loan may be funded with little or no further review. If the generic score leaves any question about the risk, more information is obtained so that the custom score can be calculated. For instance, many indirect auto lenders will commit to fund a borrower's loan on the basis of a high FICO score as long as certain other lending parameters are not exceeded. For applicants with lower FICO scores, the custom score is calculated and used to name the decision.

For residential mortgages, the GSEs use scoring to determine the amount of documentation the borrower must provide to certify income and liquid assets. If the credit risk is considered low, applicants need less documentation of their income and assets.

In addition to supporting credit decisions on individual loan applications, the generic credit score is a standard requirement for lenders bidding on loan packages. Credit rating agencies like Fitch IBCA and Standard & Poor's require that lenders wanting to securitize consumer loan packages provide credit scores along with other data elements before a package can be rated.

---

[5] The FICO score is called the BEACON score at Equifax and EMPIRICA at TransUnion.

Credit scores are often used to set prices for loan packages and individual loans. Even prime lenders who lend to borrowers with generally good credit histories often segment their populations into tiers and set prices based on credit quality. In an article detailing the use of credit scores, Makuch says, "The value of a loan is nothing more than its expected future cash flows discounted appropriately to incorporate the uncertainty and volatility of cash flow."[6] The most complex pricing models specify all expected future cash inflows and outflows and the timing of each. Scores or score-based models can be used to predict the incidence of credit losses. We discuss score-based loss forecasting systems in Chapter 8, where we describe a score-based loss forecasting system for residential mortgages. In Chapter 14, we describe an income statement approach to risk- based pricing that uses scores.

ACCOUNT MANAGEMENT SCORING

Scores are used at each stage in the life cycle of a consumer loan. Behavior or account management scores are distinguished from acquisition scores because they include characteristics representing the borrower's own payment pattern on the loan. The number of times a borrower has gone delinquent, the seriousness of the delinquency, and even the point during the month when payments are typically received are all very predictive of future behavior. Because they include variables related to the borrower's demonstrated willingness and ability to pay on the loan under consideration, behavior scores tend to be even more predictive than acquisition scores, which, of course, are based only on data available when the loan is originated.

For nondelinquent loans, behavior scores are often used to set limits for credit card products and home equity lines of credit. Thomas and colleagues note that a typical strategy for setting overdraft limits is to use a matrix where behavior score ranges form the rows and average balance forms the columns.[7] Overdraft limits are then set for each cell in the matrix in an attempt to control not just the likelihood of delinquency or default as measured by the behavior score but also overall profitability, which is related to both default incidence and the amount of loss if there is a default.

Behavior scores are also used for streamlined residential mortgage refinancing programs. Borrowers who have shown a pattern of paying on time

---

[6] Makuch, William M. (2001). "Scoring Applications," in Elizabeth Mays, ed., *Handbook of Credit Scoring.* Chicago: Glenlake Publishing, pp. 3-22.
[7] Thomas, Lyn, David Edelman, and Jonathan Crook (2002). *Credit Scoring and Its Applications.* Philadelphia, PA: Society for Industrial and Applied Mathematics.

and have excellent behavior scores may be eligible to refinance without having to provide the income and asset documentation that is typically required.

Behavior scores are also used to cross-sell products to existing borrowers. For example, a lender may use a behavior score generated for its mortgage portfolio to select borrowers for a favorable offer on a credit card.

One of the most important uses of behavior scores is in collecting delinquent accounts. Borrowers with poor behavior scores are contacted earlier in the month and the method of contact (phone calls versus letters, etc.) may be varied with the score. Often collections strategies use scores in combination with outstanding balance (or loan amount minus expected collateral value if the loans are secured) to decide whom to contact and how often.

Champion and challenger strategies became common in the collections area in the 1990s. They begin by designating a given score or score strategy as the "champion," the accepted way of doing things. New, untried strategies, the challengers, are tested on a sample of loans. The performance of the sample is then compared to the performance of the loans to which the champion strategy was applied. If a challenger strategy is found to beat the champion, it becomes the new champion strategy.

Behavior scores are also used to determine strategies for handling seriously delinquent accounts. Scores that predict the likelihood a borrower can recover from serous delinquency may be used to select loans for modification programs or other special treatment.

Loss forecasting is another area in which scoring is being used more and more. Acquisition scores may be used to generate loss forecasts for accounts that have not been on the books long (say, less than a year). For accounts that have a long enough payment history, a forecast can be generated using behavior scores that reflect the borrower's payment pattern. Score-based loss forecasting is discussed in Chapter 8.

Finally, another type of behavior scoring, the recovery score, is used to estimate the likelihood that all or some portion of a bad debt will be recovered. After an account has gone seriously delinquent or even been charged off, recovery scores can be generated to rank accounts by the likelihood that some of the debt will be collected. Recovery scores help lenders make sound decisions about which accounts to retain and attempt to recover on themselves and which to sell to debt collection agencies or other third parties.

NEW CREDIT SCORING METHODS AND APPLICATIONS

In the last several years, many techniques for building credit scores have been tested. In Chapter 4 we describe the technique of logistic regression, a statistical technique that is very popular in building scorecards. Thomas and colleagues describe a range of other techniques, including nonstatistical methods like neural networks, genetic algorithms, and linear programming.[8]

A number of studies have been undertaken to determine if any of these techniques make scorecards more powerful. Though most methods have been found to produce acceptable results, none has proven to be a clear winner as far as ranking borrower credit risk is concerned.

Certain techniques may have advantages over others, depending on the situation. For example, regression techniques have an advantage over neural networks because they make it easier to interpret and explain the effect of characteristics on the outcome variable; since it is easy to determine the incremental effect of a given change in each characteristic, generating adverse action reasons for rejected applications is straightforward. Neural networks, on the other hand, have become fairly common in fraud modeling, where such interpretability is not as important.

Credit scores are now being used to forecast portfolio default rates and credit losses and even to estimate the profitability of an individual loan. Historically, credit scores have been used to rank the relative risk that borrowers would go seriously delinquent or default. A model's ability to assign lower scores to loans that eventually went bad than to loans with good outcomes was the main concern among developers and users of scores. Although some attention was paid to the default odds of various score ranges when the score cutoff was set, scores were not typically used to predict the default rate for a given set of loans, or to estimate the likelihood that a given loan would default.

As is discussed in Chapters 4 and 8, scores are no longer being used just as risk-ranking tools. The logistic regression technique described in Chapter 4 can be used to generate for each loan the predicted probability that an event, such as default, will occur. These probabilities can be used to generate loss estimates at the loan level that can be used for loss forecasting and provisioning, as well as for estimating the potential credit losses that must be covered by the price set for the loan at origination.

---

[8] Ibid., Chapter 5; see also Gruenstein, John M. (2001). "Optimal Use of Statistical Techniques," in Elizabeth Mays, ed., *Handbook of Credit Scoring*. Chicago: Glenlake Publishing, pp. 149-184.

The emphasis in risk management at financial services companies has changed over the last several years from loss avoidance to profit maximization. Lenders are willing to take on more risk and offer products they may have avoided in the past as long as they feel comfortable that they understand the risks. Understanding the risks requires that lenders estimate risk-adjusted profitability.

The Thomas monograph discusses two techniques for estimating loan-level profitability that have been applied in other fields but that are relatively new to the credit-scoring world.[9]

The first is *Markov chain models,* which the authors consider as both an alternative to behavior scoring models and as a way to estimate the profitability of a single loan. The Markov model predicts the likelihood that a loan will transition from a particular status to another status in each future period of time. For consumer loans, the statuses include being current on the loan, being one, two, three, or four cycles delinquent, paying off the loan, or defaulting.

To build the models, we would use data on the borrower's current delinquency state and risk characteristics. To generate the forecast a transition matrix is estimated that contains the probability that a loan in each state will transition to each of the other states over the next period. Numerous transition matrices are produced for different portfolio segments.

The idea is to segment the portfolio into homogeneous groups of loans with similar risk characteristics so that the likelihood of rolling to a particular state is the same for all loans in the group. Certainly, loans should be segmented by their current delinquency status but other important drivers of future performance may be found by using decision trees.[10]

The transition matrix for each homogeneous group can be estimated simply by using the most recent transition rates observed. The entries in the matrix are the estimated probability that the loan will transition to each of the states mentioned in each future month. Because these probabilities represent the likelihood the lender will receive cash flows from the borrower, they can be used to generate dollar estimates of profit. Besides being used as an input to loan level profitability models, the probabilities can be aggregated for all loans in the portfolio to support estimates of the number of delinquent and defaulted loans and thus plan the resources needed for collections and recovery.

---

[9] Thomas et al., op. cit., no. 7, Chapter 6, Section 12.7
[10] See Scallan, G. "Bad Debt Projection Models: An Overview of Modeling Approaches." *http://www.Scoreplus.com.*

The second technique that can be useful in profitability estimation is *survival analysis.* Survival analysis has had wide applications in other fields, including the bio-medical field. It is a regression technique like logistic regression but instead of predicting the likelihood that an event will occur, it predicts the time until the event will occur. With this approach, the probable performance of loans is predicted in each future period (typically monthly) from the origination up until some given point in time.

From a survival model we derive the probability that the stated event will happen at each future point in time. For loans, an obvious event of interest is default. The survival model tells us the probability that the borrower will default on the loan in each future month of the loan's life. These probabilities are important inputs into profitability models because they tell us the likelihood of receiving each future payment. Unlike Markov models, survival models predict only the point at which loan payments are likely to cease for good (default); they do not generate predictions about interim delinquencies from which the loan cured before default. These would have to be estimated separately and incorporated into the profitability analysis.

The Thomas group notes that survival analysis has a number of advantages over logistic regression models for building score models. One is that it avoids the instability caused by having to choose a fixed period like 18 months to measure whether a loan is good or bad. Certain characteristics may dominate a scorecard in the first 18 months of the life of a loan while others may have greater influence later in the loan term.

With survival analysis the model can also incorporate the effect of changes in the economy over the life of the loan. In addition to borrower characteristics, economic variables can be very significant predictors of the rate at which loans go bad. These variables may be included as *time varying covariates*—variables whose values can change during the period that loan performance is observed. As we discuss in Chapter 4, incorporating variables that measure changes in economic conditions over time may reduce any bias in scorecard point weights resulting from omitting variables from the model that in fact have an important effect on what we are trying to predict.

Removing this bias may make scorecards more robust across economic environments. Also, the regression coefficients for economic variables like the unemployment rate in a geographic region or market interest rates provide estimates of how the bad rate will vary when economic conditions are changing. This may help us manage scorecard policies. For example, cutoff scores might be raised in states where the unemployment rate is rising.

Other methods have been used to attempt to incorporate into credit scoring models and underwriting methods the effect of economic conditions on loan performance. Thomas[11] summarizes some of the approaches that have been examined. One option is to build separate scorecards for good economic times and bad. The lender could presumably use the scorecards in different regions depending on economic conditions in each region, or could switch from one scorecard to the other as economic conditions changed. The drawback of this is that building such scores would likely require the use of data that are at least a few and perhaps several years old. Such data may no longer represent the lender's current product mix or current market conditions.

Zandi[12] suggests using the credit score in combination with an economic score based on leading economic indicators for the region where a customer is located. Economic factors would not be incorporated into the credit score directly but would be used separately, for example, to adjust credit score cutoffs.

More and more studies are looking at incorporating economic variables directly into scoring-type models along with traditional scorecard characteristics.[13] The advantage over matrixing the credit score with economic variables is that the exact effect of an economic variable on the loan's outcome can be estimated in the presence of the other variables typically included in scorecards. Because there may be correlations between the economic variables and traditional scorecard characteristics (borrowers in high unemployment regions may have somewhat poorer credit histories), this may be a better way to measure the effect of economic variables on the outcome.

These studies used the survival model approach so that the effect on loan performance of changing economic conditions over time might be estimated. Variables like unemployment rate, market interest rates, and property values have all been found to be important predictors in these models.

---

[11] Thomas, Lyn C. (2000). "A Survey of Credit and Behavioral Scoring; Forecasting Financial Risk of Lending to Consumers." *International Journal of Forecasting,* 16: 149-172

[12] Zandi, Mark (1998). "Incorporating Economic Information into Credit Risk Underwriting," in Elizabeth Mays, ed., *Credit Risk Modeling: Design and Application.* Chicago: Glenlake Publishing, pp. 155-168.

[13] See Heitfield and Sabarwal. "What Drives Default and Prepayment on Subprime Auto Loans?" Paper presented at the 2002 Subprime Lending Symposium sponsored by the Georgetown University Credit Research Center, Washington, D.C., and Deng and Quigley. "Woodhead Behavior and the Pricing of Residential Mortgages." Working paper presented at the Institute of Business and Economic Research, Berkeley Program on Housing and Urban Policy, 200.

If a lender is to implement such a model as an acquisition scorecard, a number of issues need to be worked out. First, the lender must decide if it actually wants to assign applicants points based on economic variables. If so, an applicant would be penalized for, say, living in a region where the unemployment rate is increasing. An alternative would be to neutralize the point weights for economic variables in the scorecard itself but use the point weights to adjust score cutoffs by appropriate amounts depending on the values of the economic variables. For example, a 1 percent increase in the regional unemployment rate may imply that the cutoff score would need to be increased by 10 points to maintain the same expected good/bad odds as before the chane in the unemployment rate.

Another issue lenders may face with such a model would be assigning a predicted value to economic variables, which would be necessary if it is found (as is likely to be the case) that economic conditions *after* loan origination have the greatest effect on loan performance rather than just economic conditions at the time of loan origination. Lenders may be uncomfortable predicting the future course of economic variables like the unemployment rate and property values.

It should be noted that the expected odds for each score generated using the traditional logistic regression approach depends on the economic conditions prevailing during the outcome period of the loans used to estimate the odds; thus within the expected odds is an assumption that the same economic conditions will prevail in the future as were present before. The risk manager may be no worse off and possibly could be much better off using a scorecard based on survival analysis and explicitly recognizing the effect of economic conditions on loan performance. That way, he is positioned to act on informed economic projections rather than simply accepting this implicit assumption.

THE FUTURE OF CREDIT SCORING

The early years of the second millennium promise to be dynamical and exciting ones for the field of credit scoring. Risk managers are turning more and more to quantitative techniques to understand risks and manage their portfolios. The credit-scoring field is growing and new and better techniques are being brought to bear every year. Increasingly, lenders are bringing in-house the expertise to build and use models as they recognize the competitive advantage that may be gained from using first-rate models well. Lenders who recognize these advantages early and use scoring and modeling to their best advantage will see the biggest benefit in their bottom lines.

Chapter 2
GENERIC AND CUSTOMIZED SCORING MODELS: A COMPARISON

Gary G. Chandler
President
GGC Consulting, Inc.

INTRODUCTION AND OVERVIEW

Since generic[1] credit bureau scoring models were introduced in the mid-1980s, the growth in their usage and acceptance has been astonishing. Today more credit decisions are affected by generic than by customized scoring models, though many creditors use both. Customized credit scoring[2] models are developed for the use of a single creditor. Generic scoring models are sold in the marketplace for use by multiple creditors.[3] Typically, a customized model is based on data from a creditor's past lending experience. A generic model is based on data from the past lending experience of a number of creditors. The most popular generic scoring models,[4] developed by using credit bureau information, are marketed to creditors by the

---

[1] Use of the term "generic" in the credit industry to categorize scoring models does not conform to general usage. Generic scoring models area named, trade or service-marked, and advertised by name.

[2] Although use of the term "credit scoring" is often limited to the measurement of risk, this chapter uses a broader meaning that also covers marketing, collection, revenue, attrition, etc.

[3] Although there are exceptions to the definitions, concepts, discussions of issues, and conclusions presented in this chapter, the general approach remains intact.

[4] The most popular generic models are BEACON, Experian Bankruptcy Model, EMPIRICA, Bankruptcy Navigator, National Risk Model, and TransRisk New Account. See the next section and Table 2.1 for an expanded listing of generic models.

three major credit bureaus. The three major credit bureaus have introduced products that allow consumers to purchase their own individual scores on selected generic scoring models.

Creditors must decide whether to use customized scoring, generic scoring, or a combination of both.[5] The creditor will also have to choose among competing generic scoring models. Proper evaluation should consider, among other factors, the credit product and type of decisions, the creditor's capabilities, the environment, the target market, and the characteristics and costs of the models available. The primary purpose of this chapter is to provide a framework for these evaluations.

This chapter compares generic with customized credit scoring models in terms of feasibility, development, implementation, economic, and management issues. It presents the advantages and disadvantages of each approach and of integrating generic scoring within an overall evaluation system. The generic scoring models available are described in detail.

The first generic credit bureau scoring model was PreScore, developed by Fair, Isaac and Company, Inc., from credit bureau information in 1984-85 to evaluate new applicant credit risk in direct mail solicitations. In 1987, MDS[6] introduced the first mass-marketed generic credit bureau scoring models (Delphi for TransUnion, Delinquency Alert System for Equifax, and the Gold Report for TRW Information Services) to predict bankruptcy risk. These models resulted in the rapid acceptance of generic bureau scoring. Fair, Isaac soon introduced competing generic credit bureau risk models—BEACON (1989) for Equifax, EMPIRICA (1990) for TransUnion, and the TRW Fair, Isaac Model (1991). These models have been periodically revised and many new models have since been added.

Over the years credit scoring vendors have also marketed generic scoring models not developed in conjunction with the credit bureaus for sale to individual creditors.[7]

---

[5] This chapter does not deal with those creditors (mainly smaller ones) that do not use any form of credit scoring, relying entirely on judgmental evaluation.

[6] MDS (Management Decision Systems, Inc.) was founded in 1976 and sold in 1985 to CCN (a United Kingdom company), where it was renamed CCN–MDS Division. In 1996, Great Universal Stores, CCN's parent company, bought Experian (formerly TRW Information Services) and merged CCN–MDS Division into it. Depending on the date, different names will appear in the literature and brochures describing generic scoring models.

[7] Examples include Application Risk Models, formerly CreditTable, by Fair, Isaac and Fast Start Models by Experian.

DEFINITIONS AND REGULATIONS

There are two basic processes for credit evaluation (1) judgmental and (2) credit scoring.[8] In the judgmental process, the traditional method, credit analysts evaluate the information and make decisions based on their experience and judgment. This process of human judgment may also include rules and policy guidelines.

CREDIT SCORING EVALUATION AND REGULATION B

Credit scoring was originally described as the use of a numerical formula assigning points or values to key attributes of applicants to determine whether they were creditworthy. Regulation B,[9] which implements the Equal Credit Opportunity Act, divides credit evaluation processes into two distinct types (1) *empirically* derived, demonstrably and statistically sound, credit scoring systems (EDDSS) and (2) *judgmental* systems. Any system that does not meet the requirements of EDDSS is defined as a judgmental system. Systems that meet EDDSS requirements may consider (score) applicant age directly. Judgmental systems may not.[10] A system that does not score the age of the applicant can be considered a judgmental system under Regulation B regardless of how it was developed and implemented.

Over the years, the consumer credit industry has greatly expanded the use and meaning of credit scoring. Today, scoring models are used not only to predict creditworthiness, but also potential bankruptcy, revenue response, activation, usage, profitability, collectability, attrition, fraud, insurance loss, and small business credit risk. A working definition for the industry, and this chapter, would be that credit scoring is *the use of a numerical formula to assign points to specific items of information to predict an outcome.*[11]

CUSTOMIZED SCORING SYSTEMS

Customized scoring systems developed for an individual creditor are based on a sample of the creditor's past decisions. Often the creditor influences the actual scoring model by participating in sampling, characteristic selection, and implementation decisions. Such scoring models are proprietary,

---

[8] See Chandler, Gary G. and Coffman, John Y. (1979). "A Comparative Analysis of Empirical vs. Judgmental Credit Evaluations." *Journal of Retail Banking* 1 (2): 15-16.

[9] See Regulation B, 12 CFR §202.2(p).

[10] See Regulation B, 12 CFR §202.6(b)(2)(ii-iv).

[11] An even broader definition that could include systems that do not assign points would be: Credit scoring is *the use of an empirical evaluation of specific information to predict an outcome.*

available only to the individual creditor. Many of these systems meet the requirements of EDDSS.

GENERIC SCORING SYSTEMS

Generic scoring systems are typically based on a sample from the past experiences of several lenders. Generic systems are sold to creditors who believe they will find them useful. The systems are often available on a transaction as well as a purchase basis.

EDDSS generic credit scoring systems are described in Regulation B as "borrowed systems" and "pooled data scoring systems."[12] However, they must comply with Regulation B's definition of EDDSS only if they actually score the age of the applicant. If they intend to comply with Regulation B, individual creditors have their own validation and revalidation requirements.[13] Most generic scoring systems do not score applicant age.

GENERIC CREDIT BUREAU MODELS

The most dominant generic models are those available through the three major credit bureaus—they influence most credit decisions made by major creditors. While these actual scoring models are not available to creditors, the bureaus provide generic scores as part of their credit reports (on line) or as a stand-alone product (batch). Each bureau has its own models—the competition is intense.

Generic models were developed both by scoring vendors working with credit bureaus and by internal credit bureau development staffs. Though only information from a single credit bureau is used in model development, sample sizes typically range from the hundreds of thousands to over a million files. In general, the predictive powers of the generic bureau models are outstanding, comparable to those of customized models.

NON-CREDIT BUREAU GENERIC SCORING MODELS

Years before the credit bureaus developed models, vendors were marketing their own generic models, which had been created in response to creditors who wanted a systematic way to predict risk without a customized system.

Often data from several creditors were pooled in the development of generic scoring models. Some generic models were specified by the model developer based only on their own past experience. Both approaches yielded a scoring system that closely resembled customized models. The pre-

---

[12] See Regulation B, 12 CFR §202.2(p) (2) and (3).

[13] Regardless of legal requirements, the performance of a scoring system should be closely monitored for economic reasons.

dictive power was significant, though typically lower than customized scoring systems. Applicant age is not scored in most generic systems, since they may not always meet EDDSS requirments.

GENERIC SCORING MODELS IN THE MARKET

Over 70 generic credit scoring systems containing over 100 different scoring models or scorecards are listed alphabetically in Table 2.1, which also lists delivery firms, development firms, types of systems, brief descriptions and predicted outcomes, number of models, and prediction time periods. The content of Table 2-1 is illustrative of the models available. It will become, to some extent, obsolete before the printing of this book, since new systems appear, old systems are dropped, and revisions of current systems are marketed under the same or new names. See Table 2.2 for Web sites containing additional information and contacts on generic scoring models. Table 2.1 lists the following:

- *Scoring System Name.* The trade or service mark of the product.

- *Delivery Firm.* Provides either a service that delivers generic scores to the creditor or sells generic scoring models. Generic credit bureau model scores are generally available on-line and in batch mode from the credit bureaus, both priced per transaction (score).

- *Model Developer.* The vast majority of generic models have been developed by Fair, Isaac, Experian, Equifax, or TransUnion.

- *Type.* Systems are classified according to their intended usage, usually a broad outcome prediction. Systems of the same type developed by the same vendor will tend to produce similar forecasts, given similar credit bureau file content.

- *Description/Predicts.* Although different terms may be used in brochures marketing risk systems—"rank orders risk," "predicts risk," "predicts," or "measures" likelihood—they all describe the same effect. Most risk systems analyze outcomes as either "desirable" or "undesirable." While differences in the exact definitions can be important, they tend to overlap, so the models tend to be somewhat similar. For instance, bankruptcy models will also predict charge-offs and serious delinquencies. Risk models will predict bankruptcy as well as charge-offs and serious delinquencies.

The best evaluation of what a model predicts and how well it predicts different outcomes is to examine forecasts and validations of predictive power based on specified outcomes. Creditors can compare these results based on outcomes defined by their own objectives to determine model selection.

- *Number of Models/Prediction Period.* To increase accuracy, generic scoring systems often contain multiple scoring models. The selection of which model to use will often depend on the content of a given credit file and/or the product. For example, an applicant with numerous delinquencies may be scored with a different model from one with no delinquencies. In almost all cases, each applicant is scored on only one model, which is selected automatically by the bureau. Many creditors believe that more models are always better, but again, it is important to look at the forecasts and validations.

    The prediction period is the time appearing in marketing brochures or supplied by the firm's representative, usually the same as the outcome period used in model development. It is not necessary that the two periods be the same. In fact, scoring models are often validated on time periods both longer and shorter than the development times. Again, it is wise to examine forecasts and validations over different time periods.

GENERIC OR CUSTOMIZED[14]

Conceptually, a customized credit scoring system should be more accurate than a generic one. The customized system is tailor-made from the creditor's own past experience to fit the creditor's lending environment and objectives. However, there are situations in which the development and implementation of a customized scoring system are either not feasible or not the most appropriate alternative.

Three important issues in the decision are (1) feasibility, (2) development, and (3) implementation. The discussion will focus primarily on new applicant scoring models, but similar points could be made for other types of models.

---

[14] The focus will be on generic credit bureau scoring models, with only limited treatments given to non-credit bureau modes, because the issues are similar, the non-bureau models play a minor role, and the variation in their development and characteristics cannot be covered in a brief discussion.

TABLE 2.1 GENERIC SCORING MODELS

Scoring System Name	Delivery Firm	Model Developer	Type	Description/Predicts	Number of Models/ Prediction Period
AdvanceBK	Integrated Solutions Concepts, Inc.	Fair, Isaac ISC	Bankruptcy	Model design optimized for bankruptcy also includes non-bankrupt charge-off; using combination of transaction, issuer supplied account performance data and third party information.	Fourteen models; 12 months.
Application Risk Models	Fair, Isaac	Fair, Isaac	Application Risk (Origination)	Application Risk Models are based on a national pool of lending data and designed to give consumer lenders a cost-effective means to assess credit risk for a variety of portfolios, such as revolving, direct, indirect, and home equity line of credit loans. Empirically developed specifically for use in credit origination decisions.	Models for direct, indirect, revolving, and HELOC.
ASSIST® 2.0	TransUnion	Fair, Isaac	Insurance Risk	Rank orders applicants and policy-holders by risk in terms of likely relative loss ratio	Eleven models (five auto models, six property models); 12 months.
Authenticatio n Solutions Level One Score	Experian	Experian	Fraud/Verification	Verifies consumer information including name, Social Security number and telephone number.	One model; 12 months.

TABLE 2.1 GENERIC SCORING MODELS, *CONT'D*

Scoring Systems Name	Delivery Firm	Model Developer	Type	Description/Predicts	Number of Models/ Prediction Period
Authenticatio n Solutions Level Two Score	Experian	Experian	Fraud/Verification	Verifies the likelihood that the correct consumer supplied credit application information.	One model; 12 months.
Auto Risk Model	Experian	Experian	Industry-Specific Risk	Predicts the likelihood of seriously delinquent or derogatory credit behavior on an auto loan or lease over the next 24 months (prime and subprime).	Seven scorecards; 24 months.
Bankcard Response Model	Experian	Experian	Response	Predicts likelihood of a prospect's response to a bankcard direct mail solicitation.	Four scorecards; five months.
Bankruptcy Navigator	Equifax	Equifax	Bankruptcy Risk	Likelihood of consumer to file bankruptcy.	Multiple scorecards; 24 months.
Bankruptcy Watch	Experian	Experian	Bankruptcy	Likelihood of bankruptcy or serious delinquency within 12 months.	Six scorecards; 12 months.
BEACON®	Equifax, Fair Isaac (PreScore, ScoreNet)	Fair, Isaac	Risk	Predicts bankruptcies, charge-offs, repossessions, defaults & serious delinquencies A classic FICO® score designed to rank order consumers as to whether credit obligations will be paid as expected.	Ten models. Based on credit history (also two product-specific models for each of four products (auto, bankcard, installment and personal finance); 24 months.

TABLE 2.1 GENERIC SCORING MODELS, CONT'D

Scoring System Name	Delivery Firm	Model Developer	Type	Description/Predicts	Number of Models/ Prediction Period
CollectScore℠	Experian	Fair, Isaac	Collection	Rank order delinquent accounts according to likely repayment amount.	Two—General and tailored to lender; six months.
Credit Forecast.com	Equifax	Equifax and Economy.com	Econometric Credit Risk	Series of historical and forecasted attributes and bad rates under differing economic scenarios.	Multiple models.
Credit Union Risk Model	Experian	Experian	Industry-Specific Risk	Predicts the likelihood of seriously delinquent or derogatory credit behavior on a credit union account over the next 24 months (including revolving, installment, auto and mortgage accounts).	Six scorecards; 24 months.
Cross View	Experian	Experian	Risk	Predicts likelihood of 90 day + delinquency using combination of debit and credit data.	Two scorecards; 12 months.
DELPHI	TransUnion	Experian	Bankruptcy	Likelihood of bankruptcy within 12 months.	Nine models; 12 months.
Desktop Underwriter	Fannie Mae	Fannie Mae	Mortgage Risk Assessment	Used by mortgage lenders to determine whether loans meet Fannie Mae underwriting guidelines.	Statistical underwriting models and collateral assessment models.

TABLE 2.1 GENERIC SCORING MODELS, *CONT'D*

Scoring System Name	Delivery Firm	Model Developer	Type	Description/Predicts	Number of Models/ Prediction Period
Early Indicator	Freddie Mac	Team El Freddie Mac	Mortgage Risk Assessment	Collection–likelihood of a loan due for current month's payment being delinquent at month's end. Loss mitigation–probability of a mortgage due for two or more payments resulting in a loss to creditors.	Five–Collection: Subprime and conventional. Loss Mitigation: Subprime, FHA/VA, and conventional.
EMPIRICA®	TransUnion, Fair, Isaac (PreScore, ScoreNet)	Fair, Isaac	Risk	Predicts bankruptcies, charge-offs, repossessions, defaults and serious delinquencies. A classic FICO® score designed to rank order consumers as to whether credit obligations will be paid as expected.	Ten models. Based on credit history (also two product-specific models for each of four products (auto, bank-card, installment and personal finance); 24 months.
Enhanced Delinquency Alert System (EDAS)	Equifax	Experian	Bankruptcy/Risk	Likelihood of bankruptcy within 12 months. Also predicts serious delinquency.	Six scorecards; 12 months.
Equifax Emergent Score	Equifax	Equifax	Thin File Credit Risk	Predicts probability of consumer becoming 90 days past due.	Multiple scorecards; 24 months.
Equifax Income Predictor	Equifax	Equifax	Income Prediction	Predicts the gross annual income of a consumer.	Multiple models.

TABLE 2.1 GENERIC SCORING MODELS, CONT'D

Scoring System Name	Delivery Firm	Model Developer	Type	Description/Predicts	Number of Models/ Prediction Period
Equifax Mortgage Score	Equifax	Equifax	Mortgage Credit Risk	Predicts probability of 60 days or more mortgage delinquency.	Multiple models; 12 months.
Equifax Risk Score '98	Equifax	Equifax	General Credit Risk	Likelihood of consumer to become 90 days past due.	Multiple scorecards; 24 months.
Equifax Smart Score	Equifax	Equifax	Sub-Prime Credit Risk	Predicts probability of consumer becoming 90 days past due.	Multiple scorecards; 12 months.
Equifax Telco '98 Score	Equifax	Equifax	Telecommunications Credit Risk	Predicts serious delinquency on a telecommunications account.	Multiple models; 12 months.
Equifax Wireless 2.0 Score	Equifax	Equifax	Wireless Credit Risk	Predicts serious delinquency on a wireless account.	Multiple models; 6 months.
Experian Bankruptcy Model	Experian	Experian	Bankruptcy/Risk	Likelihood of bankruptcy within 12 months. Also predicts serious delinquency.	Six. Level of bureau information and type of primary credit; 12 months.
Experian/Fair, Isaac Attrition Score	Experian	Fair, Isaac	Attrition	Rank orders existing bankcard accounts base on the likelihood of balance reduction of 50 percent or more over the next 12 months.	Ten. Recent revolving usage; 12 months.

TABLE 2.1 GENERIC SCORING MODELS, *CONT'D*

Scoring System Name	Delivery Firm	Model Developer	Type	Description/Predicts	Number of Models/ Prediction Period
Experian/Fair, Isaac Insurance Score	ChoicePoint	Fair, Isaac	Insurance Risk	Rank orders applicants and policy-holders by risk in terms of likely relative loss ratio.	Eleven models (five auto models, six property models); 12 months.
Experian/Fair, Isaac Advanced Risk Model	Experian, Fair, Isaac (ScoreNet, Prescore)	Fair, Isaac	Risk	Rank orders consumers according to the likelihood of future default on credit obligations. This next generation FICO® score provides more refined assessment across the entire credit risk spectrum.	Eighteen models base on credit history; 24 months.
Experian/Fair, Isaac Risk Model	Experian, Fair, Isaac (PreScore, ScoreNet)	Fair, Isaac	Risk	Predicts bankruptcies, charge-offs, repossessions, defaults and serious delinquencies. A classic FICO® score designed to rank order consumers as to whether credit obligations will be paid as expected.	Ten models. Based on credit history (also two product-specific models for each of four products (auto, bank-card, installment and personal finance); 24 months.
Expert Models	Magnum Communications, Ltd and Cypress Software Systems	Scoring Solutions, Inc.	Risk	Expert based generic risk models.	Product specific models.
FAST START	Experian	Experian	Risk	Empirically derived generic risk models based on pooled data.	Industry and product specific models.

TABLE 2.1 GENERIC SCORING MODELS, *CONT'D*

Scoring System Name	Delivery Firm	Model Developer	Type	Description/Predicts	Number of Models/ Prediction Period
Fraud Detect Model	TransUnion	Advanced Software Applications	IdentifyFraud	Verification tool that evaluates applications for inconsistencies in information provided by consumer. Likelihood of using fraudulent information.	N/A. Uses a combination of statistical techniques; Point of sale prediction.
Fraud Shield Score	Experian	Experian	Fraud	A score that combines fraud and credit variables into a single score, giving the full perspective on fraud risk and potential first payment default.	One model; 12 months.
GEM℠	TransUnion	Scoring Solutions, Inc.	Risk	A risk model for the gas and electric industry that predicts the likelihood that a customer will become seriously delinquent or result in a loss.	Three. Split on credit profile (depth of file and serious delinquencies); 12 months.
HORIZON℠	TransUnion, Fair, Isaac (ScoreNet, PreScore)	Fair, Isaac	Bankruptcy	Rank orders consumers based on bankruptcy loss ratio (dollar losses from bankruptcy divided by net revenue from "good" accounts).	Eleven. Based on consumer profile; 18 months.
In the Market Model	Experian	Experian	Response	Identifies individuals likely to be "in the market" for an automotive lease or loan prior to mailing.	Two scorecards; 5 months.

TABLE 2.1 GENERIC SCORING MODELS, *CONT'D*

Scoring System Name	Delivery Firm	Model Developer	Type	Description/Predicts	Number of Models/ Prediction Period
InScore® 3.0	Equifax	Fair, Isaac	Insurance Risk	Rank orders applicants and policyholders by risk in terms of likely relative loss ratio.	Five models (three auto models, two property models); 12 months.
Loan Prospector	Freddie Mac	Freddie Mac	Mortgage Risk	Predicts mortgage default risk.	Multiple models: segmented on key risk characteristics and by conventional conforming, government, subprime, and jumbo.
National Risk Model	Experian	Experian	Risk	Predicts serious derogatory behavior during the next 24 months, including charge-off and bankruptcy.	Eight. Based on past credit profiles; 24 months.
Omni Sore	GE Capital Mortgage Insurance (GEMICO)	GEMICO	Mortgage Risk	Validated to be an effective delinquency and foreclosure predictor over the entire life of the loan.	Life of the loan.
Pinnacle℠	Equifax	Fair, Isaac	Risk	Rank orders consumers according to the likelihood of future default on credit obligations. This next generation FICO® score provides more refined assessment across the entire credit risk spectrum.	Eighteen models base on credit history; 24 months.

TABLE 2.1 GENERIC SCORING MODELS, *CONT'D*

Scoring System Name	Delivery Firm	Model Developer	Type	Description/Predicts	Number of Models/Prediction Period
PRECISION^SM	Equifax, Fair, Isaac (PreScore, ScoreNet)	Fair, Isaac	Risk	Rank orders consumers according to likelihood of future default on credit obligations. Next generation FICO® score provides more refined assessment across entire credit risk spectrum.	Eighteen models base on credit history; 24 months.
Property Loss Score (PLS)	ChoicePoint	Fair, Isaac	Insurance Risk	Rank orders applicants and policy-holders by risk in terms of likely relative loss ratio.	Six property models; 12 months.
Recovery Score–Bankcard	Experian	Experian	Recovery	Predicts high to low levels of collectability in 6 months.	One scorecard; 6 months.
Recovery Score–Retail	Experian	Experian	Recovery	Predicts high to low levels of collectability in 6 months.	One scorecard; 6 months.
Retail Risk Model	Experian	Experian	Industry-Specific Risk	Predicts the likelihood of seriously delinquent or derogatory credit behavior on a retail account over the next 24 months.	Six scorecards; 24 months.
Retention Evaluator®	Equifax, Fair, Isaac (ScoreNet)	Fair, Isaac	Attrition	Rank orders existing bankcard accounts base on the likelihood of a balance reduction of 50 percent or more over the next 12 months.	Ten. Recent revolving usage; 12 months.

TABLE 2.1 GENERIC SCORING MODELS, *CONT'D*

Scoring System Name	Delivery Firm	Model Developer	Type	Description/Predicts	Number of Models/ Prediction Period
Revenue Opportunity Indicator (ROI[SM])	Experian, Fair, Isaac (ScoreNet, PreScore)	Fair, Isaac	Revenue	Rank orders consumers based on relative amount of revenue likely to be generated on a revolving account over the next 12 months.	Four. Recent revolving credit usage; 12 months.
Revenue Evaluator®	Equifax, Fair, Isaac (ScoreNet)	Fair, Isaac	Revenue	Rank orders consumers based on relative amount of revenue likely to be generated on a revolving account over the next 12 months.	Multiple models; 12 months.
REWARD®	TransUnion, Fair, Isaac (ScoreNet)	Fair, Isaac	Collection	Rank orders three- to seven-cycle delinquent accounts according to likely repayment amount.	Six–three general and three tailored to lender; 6 months.
Risk Profiler	TransUnion	Fannie Mae	Mortgage Risk	Identifies seasoned mortgage loans with greatest risk of foreclosure.	Three
RPM® (Revenue Projection Model)	TransUnion, Fair, Isaac (ScoreNet)	Fair, Isaac	Revenue	Rank orders consumers based on relative amount of revenue likely to be generated on a revolving account over the next 12 months.	Four. Recent revolving credit usage; 12 months.
SENTRY®	TransUnion, Fair, Isaac (ScoreNet)	Fair, Isaac	Attrition	Rank orders consumer bankcard accounts on how likely consumer is to close or pay the balance down to zero during the three- to five-months following scoring.	Ten. Recent revolving usage; 3-5 months.

TABLE 2.1 GENERIC SCORING MODELS, *CONT'D*

Scoring System Name	Delivery Firm	Model Developer	Type	Description/Predicts	Number of Models/ Prediction Period
Small Business Risk New Account Score	Fair, Isaac/ D&B	Fair, Isaac	Trade Credit Risk	Rank orders risk of transactions involving business lending to other businesses based on data about the business from D&B and about the principal of the business from consumer reporting agencies.	Six models; 24 months.
Small Business Risk Portfolio Score	Fair, Isaac/ D&B	Fair, Isaac	Small Business Portfolio Risk	Rank orders small business credit customers based on data about the business from D&B and about the principal of the business from consumer reporting agencies.	Five models; 24 months.
Small Business Scoring Service^SM (SBSS^SM)	Fair, Isaac	Fair, Isaac	Small Business Application Risk (Origination)	Predictive model suite used by 90 percent of top small business credit grantors that rank-orders small business credit applications based on data about the business from the business bureaus and financial statements, and about the principal of the business from consumer reporting agencies.	Eleven models for commercial card, lines of credit, and leasing.
SPECTRUM®	TransUnion	Scoring Solutions, Inc.	Risk	A risk model for the wireless communications industry. Predicts likelihood of a customer becoming seriously delinquent or result in a loss.	Three. Split on credit profile (depth of file); 6 months.

TABLE 2.1 GENERIC SCORING MODELS, *CONT'D*

Scoring System Name	Delivery Firm	Model Developer	Type	Description/Predicts	Number of Models/ Prediction Period
STRATUM	TransUnion	TransUnion Modeling Services	Segmentation Tool	Assigns one of 21 clusters according to similar credit lifestyles (spending and payment behavior).	N/A
SureView	Experian	Experian	Industry-Specific Risk	Predicts the likelihood of seriously delinquent or derogatory credit behavior on a subprime bankcard account over the next 12 months.	Five scorecards; 12 months.
Telecommunications, Energy Cable Risk Model	Experian	Experian	Risk	Likelihood of becoming 90 or more days past due on a wireless (cellular(account.	Four scorecards; 12 months.
Tele-Risk	Experian	Experian	Industry-Specific Risk	Predicts the likelihood of seriously delinquent or derogatory credit behavior on a telecommunications account over the next 12 months.	Two scorecards; 12 months.
TELESCOPE[SM]	TransUnion	Scoring Solutions, Inc.	Risk	Risk model for the telecommunications industry. Predicts the likelihood that a customer will become seriously delinquent or result in a loss.	Five. Split on credit profile (depth of file and risk); 12 months.
TIE	TransUnion	TransUnion	Income	Analyzes behavioral characteristics for predicting income–includes debt to income.	Two

TABLE 2.1 GENERIC SCORING MODELS, *CONT'D*

Scorying System Name	Delivery Firm	Model Developer	Type	Description/Predicts	Number of Models/ Prediction Period
TransRecovery	TransUnion	TransUnion Modeling Services	Collections/Recovery	Predicts likelihood of collection ($50+) within 12 months on accounts in collection.	Three models; 12 months.
TransRisk Auto	TransUnion	TransUnion Modeling Services	Subprime Risk	Predicts delinquency on subprime auto borrowers within 12 months.	Three models; 12 months.
TransRisk Account Mgmt.	TransUnion	TransUnion Modeling Services	Risk	Predicts delinquency on existing accounts within 24 months.	Eight models; 12 months.
TransRisk New Account	TransUnion	TransUnion Modeling Services	Risk	Predicts delinquency on new accounts within 24 months.	Nine models; 24 months.
TransRisk Bankruptcy	TransUnion	TransUnion Modeling Services	Bankruptcy	Predicts bankruptcy within a 12-month period (incidence based).	Seven models; 12 months.
Visa Issuer Fraud Detection	Visa	Visa	Fraud	Predicts based on authorization patterns, merchant profiles and cardholder spending profiles (hybrid modeling technology). Automatically refreshed using recent world fraud trends.	Multiple models/Multiple time periods.
Vista® Account Management Risk Score Service	Experian	Fair, Isaac	Small Business Credit Risk	Rankorders small business credit customers base on likelihood of future bankruptcy, charge-off, defaults, and serious delinquencies.	Three models; 24 months.

TABLE 2.2 GENERIC SCORING MODELS WEB SITES

Web Site	Hints/Path
www.experian.com	*http://www.experian.com/products/bureau_scoring.html*

www.transunion.com	Business Solutions
	    Targeted solutions
	        Risk management
	            Related products
	Also see Solutions by industry

www.fanniemae.com	Single-Family
	    Tools and resources
	        On-line Tools

www.scoringsolutions.com	Products/Services
www.freddiemac.com	Single-Family Loan Prospector

www.fairisaac.com	Solutions
	    Product List
	        Scores and Predictive Models

www.fairisaac.com/scorenet	
www.fairisaac.com/liquidcredit	
www.equifax.com	ePORT LOGIN On-line access to EQUIFAX PRODUCTS Products

FEASIBILITY

Few credit situations are absolutely perfect for modeling. Therefore, trade-offs between what would be ideal and what can be done must be considered in deciding between customized and generic systems.

HISTORICAL LENDING EXPERIENCE

Since development of a scoring system requires the analysis of past decision, the creditor must have offered credit in the past. Therefore, no historical data *equals* no customized scoring system. Usually the question is, what data are available and how close are they to what is really needed? Ideally, the scoring model should be used for the same product, market area, and economic environment that generated the historical experience. Experience in bankcard loans, for instance, may not be relevant to a scoring system for auto loans.[15]

Generic credit bureau models are based on historical credit bureau files that contain a vast wealth of credit experience—in fact, they contain nearly all creditors' experiences. Although there are generic models for differ-

---

[15] In some instances, the appropriateness of different models and strategies can be tested.

ent types of credit, types of decisions, and in a few cases different geographic regions, these models are not based on a single creditor's experience.

DATA RETENTION

Information used to support past decisions must have been retained in a usable form in order to build a custom model. For example, the credit application and credit bureau report existing when a new applicant was evaluated would be relevant as a database for model development, but not a more recent credit report or updated application. Although Regulation B requires creditors to retain certain information for 25 months after notification of the action taken, it is often necessary for model development to retain information for longer periods of time.[16]

Since the early 1990s, credit bureaus have archived their entire file of reports on a monthly or quarterly basis.[17] These archived records are retained for long periods and are used to develop and validate generic scoring models.

KNOW OUTCOMES OF PAST DECISIONS

The outcomes of past decisions must be available in a quantifiable form. Account payment histories can be used to classify outcomes as good or bad loans. The level of detail of historical payment records must be examined, and data archiving and purging procedures and be important. For instance, when creditors purge charged-off accounts from the records, efforts must be made to recover the information on these accounts.

On one hand, credit bureaus have less detailed payment history than most creditors have internally. On the other hand, they have payment histories for more credit relationships. Classifying the outcomes can become more complex for the generic credit bureau models since payment behavior of many individual debtors varies from creditor to creditor.

AGE OF DECISION

The decisions must have aged enough to allow appropriate measurement and classification of the outcomes. For example, bankcard accounts approved three months previously are not old enough to be accurately classified as good or bad risk outcomes, whereas accounts approved two years

---

[16] See Regulation B, 12 CFR §202.2(b).

[17] In the mid-1980s, credit bureaus began annual archiving in order to develop the first generic credit bureau models and to create databases for the development of a few customized scoring models.

ago probably are.[18] At the other extreme, bankcard accounts approved 10 years ago are too old, since the relationships between their historical credit applications and credit bureau reports and their outcomes would not likely reflect current relationships. Model developers will specify a sample time frame in which decisions must have occurred if they are to be included in the development.

SAMPLE SIZE

The number of credit decisions made must have been large enough to allow an appropriate sample size. Credit scoring developers often ask for a sample of at least 4,500 applicants—1,500 goods, 1,500 bads, and 1,500 rejected applicants—to develop a customized new applicant scoring model. Smaller creditors or smaller product offerings will try to develop customized models with smaller samples, but developers do not like to work with samples that contain less than 400-500 bad accounts.

The least frequent outcome that must be predicted will often determine if a large enough sample can be obtained. Since bad should be the least frequent outcome, the number of available bad accounts would be the limiting factor.[19] In fact, sample availability may influence the sample time frame— a creditor with fewer accounts might sample decisions made from two to four years ago, while a larger creditor might only sample from two to three year ago.

The samples available for generic bureau scoring models are typically huge. Developers often use samples of tens to hundreds of thousands of files and in some cases may use over a million files. Some of the first generic credit bureau models focused on bankruptcy, since very few creditors had enough bankrupts (in those years) to develop customized bankruptcy prediction models.

ECONOMIC FACTORS

The cost and benefits of a customized model must be compared to those of a generic scoring model. Costs are included in developing, implementing, and managing the system. The cost of developing and implementing a customized system has been estimated to be from $40,000 to well over $100,000.

---

[18] The appropriate time will vary with the product and type of decision. Some types of behavioral scoring models are developed using short aging periods, because the time between the decision (collection effort) and the outcome (payment or no payment) is relatively brief (one- to three-months).

[19] If the number of bad accounts is sufficient, the number of good and declined accounts should be more than sufficient.

There is no direct cost to the creditor for the development of the generic scoring system. Generic credit bureau scores are purchased on a transaction basis. (Some non-credit bureau generic scoring systems can also be purchased on a transaction basis.) While the transaction-based pricing of the generic system can be less expensive at lower volumes, it can be more expensive at higher volumes.

MODEL DEVELOPMENT ISSUES

During the development of any credit-scoring model, decisions are made that will affect its performance and implementation. Many of the differences between generic and customized models are the result of the individual creditor's interaction with the model developer.[20] These interactions do not occur in the development of generic models.

OBJECTIVE OF THE MODEL

In development a customized scoring model, a creditor selects the objective of the model and the target population. Objectives may be general—reduction in credit losses from new accounts—or specific—reduction in bankruptcy filings by new accounts within a six-month window after approval.[21] The objective will influence decisions ranging from outcome definitions to implementation.

Generic credit bureau scoring models tend to have general objectives that are not modified for individual creditors. However, different generic models have different general objectives. Creditors may agree with the general objective or just feel it is close enough. Generic models try to be a lot of things to a lot of creditors. In general, their approach works.

TARGET POPULATION

Target population refers to the applicants who will be evaluated by the model. For a customized model, applicants who do not fit the target population can be eliminated from the development sample. For instance, if the scoring model will not be used on student loans (decisions will be made judgmentally), data on student loans can be eliminated from the development sample.

It is sometimes difficult for the credit bureau to identify the target population unless it is based on the credit bureau's files. For instance, if the creditor wanted to target low-income applicants, the credit bureau would

---

[20] Often model developers will provide guidance to the creditor and share their experiences, but decisions will vary from creditor to creditor according to the situation.

[21] The variation in objectives in behavioral scoring can be very wide, covering any measure of account performance.

have to use proxies such as zip codes to estimate income, or use an income-estimating model. A creditor might have an income question on the application that would accurately identify past applicants for a customized development sample. Thus, the individual creditor's objectives can influence the sample and the resulting scoring model.

In addition, generic models will only be developed for larger populations. If the creditor is targeting a relatively small group, a customized model may be more appropriate than a general targeted model.

DATA/SAMPLE DEVELOPMENT

Creditors may retain historical credit experience in either manual form, such as paper or microfiche, or automated from (computer files), or both. The development of any scoring system requires that the data be in computer-readable form. Coding data requires human interpretation and data entry, which is expensive and time-consuming. Automated data requires no entry, but may not contain the level of detail contained in the manual records. In addition, historical payment records are often on a computer systems separate from application information, thus requiring a match/merge process.

Credit bureau data are entirely computerized. The database is *huge,* with millions of records all containing detailed information about applicant credit inquiries, credit accounts and payment records. But they do not contain detailed demographic information.

DEPENDENT VARIABLE DEFINITIONS

The dependent variable is the outcome. The most traditional dependent variable for a new applicant model is whether payment performance is good or bad. In the development of customized models, creditors can specify the definitions to meet their objectives. For instance, one creditor might require that an account be 60 days or more past due before it is considered a bad account. Another might specify 90 days or more. Customized scoring can accommodate either. In addition, the payment history is based on the information on the creditor's own master file, which can accommodate complex definitions.

Definitions of generic credit bureau model dependent variables are based on the credit bureau files of individual debtors. For instance, a bad account might be anyone who has any 90 days past due or worse history with any account on the bureau file, with certain exceptions.

Since debtors often pay certain types of debt before other types, different creditors will be looking at the credit bureau dependent variable definitions from different points of view.

INDEPENDENT VARIABLE DEFINITIONS

Independent variables are the characteristics that determine the value of the credit score. In a customized model for new applicant scoring, the independent variables are typically taken from the application and the credit bureau report. When working with an outside model developer, the creditor often participates in decisions regarding which variables will be tested, the construction and structure of the variables, and which variables will be in the final model. This input can be important, because the creditor understands the quality of the data elements and their target market and must live with the ensuing adverse action reasons.[22]

Independent variables used in generic models are selected by the credit bureaus and their developers. Traditionally, only credit bureau data area available for analysis. Little or not input is provided by creditors. In fact, credit bureaus do not divulge the exact variable definitions or the associated point values to creditors or applicants. However, creditors must use the adverse action reasons provided by the bureaus.

MODEL DEVELOPMENT PROCEDURES

A creditor can select different scoring development techniques by choosing a development firm that uses those techniques or allows creditors to select from alternative techniques in creating a customized model.

A creditor has no input in selecting development techniques for generic credit bureau models. However, most generic and customized scoring models for the same type of application are developed using the same or similar techniques.

REJECTED APPLICANTS

There is payment history only for applicants who have been extended credit and have used it. Lack of information about the performance of the rejected population creates a statistical and practical problem. Model developers attempt to compensate for this with reject inferencing procedures.[23] The higher the rejection rate, the more important the problem and the less effective the compensation. Hence, creditors with higher approval rates have less significant rejected applicant problems.

Since the credit bureau database contains payment performances for nearly all potential credit applicants (except for new entries into the credit

---

[22] See "Adverse Action Reasons" on page 40 and Regulation B, 12 CFR §202.2(c) and 202.9(a)(1)-(2).

[23] For a thorough treatment of this topic, see Hand, David. (2001). "Reject Inference in Credit Operations," in Elizabeth Mays, ed., *Handbook of Credit Scoring*. Chicago: Glenlake Publishing, pp. 225-240.

market), the rejected applicant problem is nearly nonexistent in developing generic credit bureau scoring models.

DEVELOPMENT TIME

It can take from three to 12 months to develop a customized scoring model. Implementation adds more time, ranging from a month to years. Generic scoring systems already on the market are available for use on relatively short notice. Sometimes a creditor's need is so immediate that the general models are the only feasible alternative.[24]

IMPLEMENTATION ISSUES

A creditor must be able to successfully implement the scoring system. Implementation can be as important as the predictive accuracy of the system. If you cannot implement it, don't develop or buy it. Implementation issues include information interpretation and entry, computer automation, forecasts of performance, validation and monitoring, adverse action reasons, shared experience and advice, security, and management.

INFORMATION INTERPRETATION AND ENTRY

In order to implement most scoring systems, applicant information must be entered into a computer. The cost of data entry is a function of the number of applicants, the amount of information entered, and the amount of interpretation required.

Accurate and consistent interpretation of some information can be quite difficult, as with classification of employment information into occupational categories. While high standards of accuracy and consistency can be achieved for developing a sample, it is more difficult and expensive to achieve the same results in an ongoing production environment.

Customized scoring systems and some non-credit bureau generic scoring systems often require extensive data entry. Generic credit bureau models require minimum entry information (identification of the applicant), and are often a byproduct of obtaining a credit report on the applicant.

COMPUTER AUTOMATION

Nearly all credit-scoring systems use computers for implementation. Although customized implementations will differ, in general information is entered, edit checks are performed, exclusions and policy rules are implemented, scores[25] are calculated, additional information is requested as need-

---

[24] Some creditors will use a generic scoring model until a customized model can be developed and implemented.

[25] Multiple scores using multiple scoring models can be calculated.

ed, actions are recommended, and adverse action reasons determined. Software to implement the customized model can be developed internally or purchased. Sometimes implementation is performed by a third party.

Generic credit bureau models are implemented by the credit bureaus, which deliver scores and adverse action reasons to creditors. Of course, the creditor, as with customized models, must also be able to input the sources, take actions, and retain scores as needed in order to use the information.

FORECASTS OF PERFORMANCE

It is relatively simple to develop performance forecasts for customized scoring models. Typically, the developer calculates the scores for a sample of known outcome applicants from the creditor's files, which may be the development sample, a holdout or validation sample, a sample from a specified time frame or geographic region, or a sample for a product entirely different from that used in model development.

Forecasts of score performance for the generic credit bureau models are based on large samples of files applying standard outcome definitions. While the credit bureau can provide several different forecasts, creditors using the models do not have the flexibility that comes with using their own data and models.

However, a creditor can supply a credit bureau with a list of accounts, get historical generic credit bureau scores at approximately the time of decision, and produce customized performance reports for the generic bureau scores. In fact, credit bureaus often offer customized forecasts as a service.

VALIDATION/MONITORING

Although the Regulation B requirement to validate applies only to systems that score the age of an applicant, any creditor must know how its scoring system is performing in order to manage the system. The predictive power of the model will change as the relationships between variables and outcome change. It is important to monitor changes and react. In addition, proper monitoring of a scoring system provides a wealth of information about customers, marketing efforts, and the overall credit evaluation system.

In order to validate or monitor the performance of any scoring model, the actual score at the time of the credit decision must be retained. With a customized scoring model, retention is often a natural byproduct of the computerized system. This information may be easily matches with payment performance to determine outcomes. The scores, input information, and outcomes are available for analysis.

Using a generic credit bureau scoring model requires additional efforts to retain the scores and merge them with payment performance. Since the creditor does not automatically receive applicant-by-applicant characteristics from the bureau, detailed credit bureau data are not typically analyzed and compared with performance.

ADVERSE ACTION REASONS

Creditors must inform declined applicants either of the specific reasons why they received adverse action or of their right to receive specific reasons. Creditors would like the reasons to make sense to the applicants while being as inoffensive as possible. However, the reasons must comply with the regulatory intent that they be accurate, educational, and informative. The only controls after a scoring model is developed are the method of selecting the reasons and the exact language used to describe a variable.

In a customized scoring environment, creditors have complete control over both, within legal boundaries. Creditors using a generic credit bureau scoring model receive only factor codes that refer to specific language supplied by the credit bureaus. Without the ability to change the selection method and without knowledge of the exact definitions of the scored characteristics, creditors have very little control.

SHARE EXPERIENCE AND ADVICE

Since every customized scoring model is unique, creditors cannot discuss their experiences with others who are using the same scoring model. The many creditors using exactly the same generic bureau scoring models can and sometimes do share experiences in order to learn from each other. In addition, credit bureaus and model developers maintain staff to advise creditors on the use of the models.

SECURITY OF THE SCORING SYSTEM

The details of a scoring system must be secure from those who would manipulate the system. A customized scoring system is a security issue for the individual creditor. Software and implementation procedures must guard against manipulation.

The details of credit bureau generic models are not disclosed to anyone who does not need to know. Creditors using these scoring models do not know the details of the models. Even if these details were disclosed, it would be difficult to manipulate the scores since the content of the credit bureau files would have to be manipulated.

MANAGEMENT

The management of any credit scoring system is the critical element for successful implementation. Management must address each of the issues presented in this section during implementation and provide ongoing active management of both the scoring system and the overall evaluation system. Management of a generic credit bureau scoring system implementation should be somewhat less demanding than management of a customized scoring system, since several aspects of management have already been addressed by the model provider and are not really under the control of the creditor.

EVALUATING THE ISSUES

The final factor in choosing between a customized and a generic scoring system (or a combination of both) is the type of credit decisions being made and the generic models available, along with their strength and weaknesses and their inherent advantages and disadvantages.

TYPES OF DECISIONS AND MODELS AVAILABLE

There are many types of credit decisions, among them targeting a preapproved offer, approving "take one" applicants or young college student applicants, increasing or decreasing credit limits, amount of loan, and collection prioritization.

Some types of decisions are naturals for generic credit bureau models—for instance, prescreened, preapproved credit solicitations. All three credit bureaus offer a range of generic models for this purpose (see Table 2.1) that have outstanding predictive power. In this case, there is no credit application. Thus, the only information is the credit bureau information. Rarely would a creditor develop a customized model based on historical credit bureau reports from their own offers or other accounts.[26] In fact, a major goal of such a mailing would be to reach populations of creditworthy individuals who were not part of the creditor's previous experience. Generic credit bureau models have a natural advantage over other applications for which there is very limited application data, such as instant credit.

There would be problems, however, if a creditor attempts to use only generic credit bureau models for certain other credit decisions, such as take-ones or offer-to-apply targeted to young people, for whom credit

---

[26] Before credit bureau generic models were developed, a few large creditors did develop customized scoring models based on their own past offers.

bureau files contain very limited information. The credit bureaus have developed "thin file" generic models for cases where credit information is limited. However, the most predictive information for your people could be the credit application. In these circumstances, a customized model based on the lender's past experience with young people would be the most appropriate approach. In such cases, many creditors would use a customized model to provide overall risk evaluation in combination with a generic credit bureau model to eliminate applicants with bad credit.

PORTFOLIO VALUATION AND RATING AGENCIES

Today, generic credit bureau scoring models play a central role in the valuation of credit portfolios. They create a standard measurement for portfolio risk by which different portfolios can be compared that is usually simple, fast, accurate, and relatively inexpensive. Those who buy and sell portfolios, provide securitization, and rate portfolio quality all use these scores. Customized scoring models cannot compete for these types of decisions.

MORTGAGE EVALUATION

Barely nine year ago, the mortgage lending industry began a very rapid transition from judgmental mortgage evaluation to credit scoring.[27] While judgmental evaluation is still important, the pace of this transition has far exceeded that experienced by any other segment of the credit-granting industry. Both Fannie Mae and Freddie Mac have endorsed the use of existing generic credit bureau scoring models and have developed their own generic mortgage scoring models. Generic models are also being used by mortgage insurance companies and rating agencies.

CREDITOR'S STRENGTHS AND WEAKNESSES

Creditors should consider their own strengths and weaknesses when choosing between generic and customized models. In general, creditors with extensive experience in the use and management of scoring systems will select customized scoring models when feasible, to use either alone or in conjunction with generic models. Such creditors can derive maximum benefit from customized systems due to their input into development, their knowledge of how to integrate policy rules with the scoring models, their experience in implementing scoring systems, and their expertise in monitoring and management.

---

[27] Before this transition started, only a few large mortgage lenders had customized credit-scoring models. Judgmental evaluation processes dominated the industry.

Creditors with limited staff will often opt for generic scoring, as will those who are new to scoring, in order to gain experience before attempting to develop customized models.

INHERENT ADVANTAGES AND DISADVANTAGES

ADVANTAGES OF GENERIC SYSTEMS

Generic scoring systems have several natural advantages over customized systems. They are:

- Available to all creditors, even smaller ones or those with small-volume products. Development feasibility is not an issues.

- Not limited by the creditor's historical experience with population groups, credit products, and geographic areas.

- Available immediately, without development time or cost.

- Less reliant on the user's knowledge of and experience in using scoring.

- Easy to implement—often the scores are generated by others.

- Less expensive for small numbers of decisions.

- Detailed in their treatment of credit bureau information.

- Very economical in their use of credit bureau information.

- Better able to predict certain outcomes, such as bankruptcies.

- Supported by a network of advice.

- Secure, because they are protected by the credit bureau.

DISADVANTAGES OF GENERIC SYSTEMS

Generic scoring systems to have certain disadvantages when compared to customized systems. They are:

- Potentially less accurate because they are not based on the creditor's own experience, product, and customers.

- Available to competitors.

- More expensive for high-volume users paying on a transaction basis.

- Proprietary—details of the scoring system are often confidential.

- Harder to use in forecasting system and monitoring performance.

- Rigid in their definition of adverse action codes and selection procedures.

INTEGRATION OF GENERIC SCORING WITH OTHER SYSTEMS

OVERALL EVALUATION SYSTEM

The overall evaluation system, even for a single type of decision, will seldom consist of a generic scoring system alone. The components of an evaluation system may include one or more generic scoring systems, a customized scoring system with policy and exception rules, and even judgmental analysis.[28] The importance, the role, and the use of each component will vary with the creditor's strategy, the accuracy of the component, and the type of decision being made.

COORDINATION OF COMPONENTS

The design of the overall evaluation system must consider the impact of all its components and how they work together. Examining independently the forecasts of the performance of a generic model, a customized model, exclusion criteria, and policy criteria could be very misleading. While the use of each component might produce desirable results independently, the impact when combined into an overall evaluation system could be disastrous. For example, while independently each could be justifiable, combining high cutoffs (low risk) on the generic scoring model, high cutoffs (low risk) on the customized scoring model, broad exclusion criteria, and highly limiting policy criteria could result in far too few approvals.

SEQUENTIAL OR MATRIX STRATEGIES

In *sequential* implementation of an overall evaluation system, the components are processed in a sequence of steps. An applicant who fails a step does not proceed to the next. Such an approach is easy to implement and can minimize labor and information costs. However, it does not allow tradeoffs of the evaluations of the different components.

In a sequential approach, a new applicant might be evaluated by a scoring model based on the credit application only as the first step and a model based on credit bureau information as the second step. Applicants could be rejected by a score below the cutoff on the first model, thus eliminating the second step and the expense of a credit bureau report.[29] Because the second

---

[28] Some customized and some generic models include a generic score within their models.
[29] Conceptually, applicants with high scores could be approved at this point, but few creditors are willing to approve applicants without any examination of the credit bureau report.

model is likely to be more accurate, it is important not to set the first cut-off too high, eliminating potentially good customers in order to save on bureau reports and labor.

In *matrix* approach, the components of the overall evaluation system are used together, with tradeoffs between the forecasts of the individual components. For example, an individual might score low on one scoring model and very high on another for an overall forecast of satisfactory performance. The matrix approach is more accurate but requires more effort, with higher labor and information costs. It is more difficult to design and manage a matrix approach than sequential strategies. Selecting adverse action reasons can also be more difficult.

Many overall credit evaluation systems will be a hybrid in which some components are used in a sequential format and others are used in a matrix format. For example, exclusion and policy criteria might be applied in sequential format, followed by multiple scoring models applied in a matrix format.

ACCURACY OF THE COMPONENTS

Less accurate components may be adequate for a low volume of easy decisions. More accurate components are necessary for high-volume and difficult decisions. In the sequential example, the first step should only reject a few really high-risk applicants and the second step should make the bulk of the decisions, including the more difficult ones.

DATA RETENTION AND MONITORING RESULTS

In order to monitor the performance of the overall evaluation system and its components, the creditor must retain sufficient historical information. The exact specifications of the overall evaluation system and the data required typically include all exclusion and policy criteria, details of all scoring models, all scoring cutoffs, forecasted results, override specifications (if permitted), all data used in the evaluation and decision, all component evaluations, the system recommendation, the decision made, the implementation made, the date of decision and implementation, identification of each applicant, and the source of the applicant. It is very important that this information be archived without any modification. The creditor must match information with performance to produce reports that monitor how well the evaluation system is performing.

The monitoring reports produced over time will be used to modify the overall evaluation system by changing exclusions, policies criteria, cutoff scores, etc. Often larger creditors evaluate different strategies (for instance, a change of cutoff score by designing tests and tracking the results).

TYPES OF DECISIONS

The type of decision will often influence the role that generic models and other components play in the overall credit evaluation process.

- *Prescreened mailing.* Generic credit bureau scoring systems will almost always be used as the most important components of the system. Sometimes multiple generic scoring models are used in matrix format. For example, a credit could implement generic credit bureau models such as Revenue Evaluator and EMPIRICA (risk), using matrix strategies that considered the tradeoffs between revenue and risk.

  While the scoring model will evaluate tradeoffs between good and bad information, there are certain requirements that creditors themselves will often dictate. For instance, individuals with prior bankruptcies may be excluded, or minimum incomes may be required.

  Creditors will often use several different strategies (different scoring models, cutoffs, marketing strategies, exclusions, or policy criteria) and monitor the results. It is very important that the different strategies be well designed.[30] These results will help determine new strategies and design new tests.

- *New applicant evaluation.* To evaluate new applicants, creditors may use customized or generic scoring models (bureau and non-bureau), depending on the type of decision and the information available. If the credit application is limited (instant credit, for instance), it is more likely that generic credit bureau models will be used. If a complete application is supplied, it is more likely that a customized model will be used. Some will use both. In any case, the creditor will usually incorporate exclusions and policy criteria as components.

  Often, generic scores from the credit bureau are used as an additional checking initial credit limit assignments for revolving credit and for cross-selling other products, even though the applicant had previously been evaluated with a customized scoring model.

---

[30] If a strategy is strictly a designed test, it is important that the number of decisions be sufficient and that the items tested be limited so that the cause of the resulting behavior can be identified. The number of decisions for a given level of statistical significance is not a function of the size of the portfolio, size of the mailing, etc., as is often stated in the credit industry.

- *Managing existing accounts.* In managing existing accounts, the creditor (particularly the revolving creditor) is faced with a stream of decisions (e.g., credit limits, renewals, authorizations, cross-selling, collections, fraud potential, etc.). Many large creditors have developed customized behavioral scoring systems based on the payment histories of their own customers. While such models area accurate, they cannot incorporate information on how their customers are performing with other creditors. It is simply too expensive to get credit bureau reports even in an automated environment for the vast majority of ongoing decisions required. In these cases, generic credit bureau scoring models have a natural advantage and are typically used in addition to customized models.

  Most creditors acquire generic credit bureau scores on a periodic basis (monthly, quarterly, etc.) on their existing accounts as well as event-triggered times such as a request for a large increase in a credit limit. The more often generic scores are purchased, the greater the cost. Hence, the same score is used over and over until replaced. These scores are stored in computer databases so that they can be easily incorporated into the overall evaluation system. Although old scores are replaced with newer, more relevant, scores for decision purposes, the old scores must be archived, because monitoring reports of the scoring system's performance must be based on the scores used for the decision, not the new scores.

SUMMARY AND CONCLUSIONS

Creditors must decide whether to use customized or generic scoring systems or a combination of both. This chapter provides a framework for the evaluation of alternative by comparing generic with customized credit scoring models.

The six main conclusions of this chapter are that:

1. Generic scoring systems have taken a major role in credit evaluation. They can level the playing field between smaller and larger creditors. Generic credit bureau scoring systems allow the use of credit bureau information for managing existing accounts economically and efficiently. They provide a standard measurement that can be used to evaluate and price portfolios.

2. The overall credit environment will often determine whether to use customized or generic scoring systems or both. Since generic scor-

ing systems have generic definitions of outcomes, creditors should seek performance forecasts based on outcome definitions that match their own objectives. Many creditors will use both customized and generic systems in order to minimize risk.

3. Any component of an evaluation system, including scoring systems, policy and exception rules, and even judgmental analysis, must be designed and implemented to fit within the overall evaluation system. Coordination of the components is critical. Sequential evaluation is often more economical and easy, but a matrix approach can be more accurate.

4. It is critical that the overall evaluation system and its components be closely monitored in order to properly manage the system.

5. The purchase of generic credit bureau scores by consumers will continue to increase. Scores from additional scoring models will become available for purchase. Consumers will become more knowledgeable about credit, credit scoring, and credit risk versus interest rates and credit terms. To some extent, the ability of consumers to purchase scores will make the credit market more efficient and will help to level the playing field between consumers and creditors.

6. The role of generic scoring will continue to increase and new models and types of applications will emerge. Standardized risk measurements from generic models will have a major impact on credit-granting industries. Customized scoring will still have a place, however, though it will rarely be used without generic modeling.

Chapter 3
CREDIT BUREAU DATA: THE FOUNDATION FOR DECISION MAKING

Rhonda Sicilia
Assistant Vice President and Managing Consultant
Equifax

INTRODUCTION

Credit bureau data is the most reliable and solid foundation for making credit decisions ranging from target marketing and credit approval or declination to account management and recovery action. Credit bureau data improves the efficiency of both decision-making and operations.

Accurate and timely reporting of customer data by financial companies to credit reporting agencies is critical if lenders are to make timely and accurate credit decisions. Both lenders and consumers depend on this data source: Individual institutions gain and maintain a profitable customer base, and consumers reap the benefits of having a variety of financial products made available to them.

Use of credit data is pervasive in today's environment. From decisions on whether to grant credit to tenant checks to employment background checks, credit bureau data is a necessary element in our world. All these uses depend on innovation and gains in process efficiency in how we use the data. Whether credit data is used in a static mode (as it appears at one point in time), on a trended basis, or as the foundation for forecasts, its productivity and predictive strength are unparalleled in their importance in credit decision-making.

While continued innovation and search for new methods for using the data is critical, because this data source is highly regulated in its use, compliance with the many laws affecting it is paramount. The Federal Trade Commission (FTC), which regulates the credit reporting agencies, ensures that the credit reporting agencies adhere to the federal antitrust and consumer protection laws.

Changes to the laws and the ways credit bureau data may be used are continuous. There are three major laws that those who work in the credit area should be thoroughly familiar with (1) the Fair Credit Reporting Act (FCRA), (2) the Equal Credit Opportunity Act (ECOA), and (3) the Gramm-Leach-Bliley Act (GLB). It is highly advisable that everyone who works with credit keep abreast of changes in these three laws. At the slightest question, always contact your internal legal department for an opinion about the use of credit bureau data.

This chapter reviews the most utilized sources of data in the credit file—public records, inquiries, and tradelines. All three sources are used often in decision making, criteria determination, analytics, and modeling. The sections of the credit file that contain employment history and identity information will not be covered in this chapter. For information on everything the full credit report contains, please contact one of the three major credit bureaus (1) Equifax, (2) Experian, or (3) TransUnion.

CREDIT BUREAU DATA

Information in the credit bureau data, the credit file, is gathered from many different sources. Banks, consumer finance companies, credit unions, and collections agencies are some of the entities that periodically report to the credit bureaus. Data is also obtained from state and federal courts on judgments, liens, and bankruptcy filings; the credit bureaus use third parties to collect it.

Typically, individual financial companies and others report to the credit bureaus every month. The timing of updates from the courts can vary; depending on the size of the court, it may be collected daily, weekly, or monthly. No matter what the size of the court, bankruptcies are usually updated daily.

A credit file is created when an individual applies for or uses credit or a public record is reported to the credit bureau. Once a credit file is established for an individual, updates are posted on the consumer's credit-seeking behavior, payment and purchase behavior, and any changes to the public records.

PUBLIC RECORDS

The public records section of a credit file contains severe derogatory information on subjects like bankruptcy, judgment, garnishment, foreclosure, lien, and collection accounts:

- *Bankruptcy* information obtained from the federal courts covers all chapters of the bankruptcy code and details whether the court discharged (accepted) or dismissed (denied) the bankruptcy petition, and the amount of the bankruptcy.

- *Judgment, foreclosure,* and *lien* records from both state and federal courts list the amounts in dispute and whether a judgment or lien was satisfied or released (paid off).

- *Collection* items are posted in the public record section if they are collected by a third-party collections agency. Amounts collected by the original credit-granting firm may also be reported in the trade-line section of the file.

Items are kept in the public records section of the credit file for varying lengths of time depending on the event. Table 3.1 illustrates the different purge time frames for specific events.

TABLE 3-1 PURGE CYCLE FOR PUBLIC RECORDS

Type of Event	Purge (# of years)	From
Collections	7 years	Date of occurrence
Open (unsatisfied) tax liens	Indefinitely	Date filed
Paid (satisfied) tax liens	7 years	Date released
Judgments/garnishments	7 years	Date filed
Bankruptcy: Chapters 7 and 11 (open, discharged, and dismissed)	10 years	Date filed
Bankruptcy: Chapters 12 and 13 (open and dismissed)	10 years	Date filed
Bankruptcy: Chapters 12 and 13 (discharged)	7 years	Date filed

INQUIRIES

Whenever a consumer's current credit file is accessed, an inquiry notice must be posted to that credit file. The three types of inquiries that may be posted to a consumer's credit file are (1) consumer-initiated inquiries, (2) account review or account management inquiries, and (3) promotional inquiries. When consumers request their own credit bureau reports from a reporting agency, all three types of inquiries will be displayed.

Consumer-initiated inquiries, called hard inquiries, are posted to a credit file when the consumer applies for credit and the lender accesses the credit report. This type of credit file is commonly referred to as an "on-line" file. The consumer-initiated inquiry will only be posted at the agency or agencies from which the lender obtains a file, not at all three of the credit reporting agencies. For credit acceptance or decline decisions, only this first type of inquiry may be used.

The reporting agencies code each of the three types of inquiries separately. A lender can include or exclude any type of inquiry in custom credit scores or policy screens by creating a different variable to examine each specific type of inquiry. As with any analytical project, any type of variable should be included only after consideration of what a particular variable represents and how it could enhance the analysis at hand.

Account review (AR) or account management (AM) inquiries are posted to a credit file when an institution that already has a credit relationship with an individual, accesses that person's credit file for monitoring purposes. Many lenders obtain the credit files of all borrowers in their portfolio every month or every quarter. The credit files are typically run through statistical models that assess the risk of a lender's portfolio or receivables base. These monitoring programs are never executed one by one. This type of inquiry does not in any way affect an individual's ability to *obtain* credit. It is not used in any decision criterion or model.

A promotional (PRM) inquiry is posted to a credit file when the individual receives a firm offer of credit through direct marketing channels such as mail, typically in the form of a preapproved credit card. A person who receives a firm offer of credit through direct marketing channels has acceptable credit and fits the profile of the type of customer sought by the firm that sent the offer.

Firms that execute these promotional campaigns mail to large numbers of people but the law does not allow the firms to view the credit files themselves until the person elects to be a customer. Credit bureau files of people that meet the criteria of a given lender are sent to a third-party vendor, typically a direct mail company, that mails the offer directly to the customer. This type of inquiry is not used in making decisions about whether to grant credit and therefore does not affect a consumer's ability to obtain credit.

All consumer-initiated inquiries are kept on the credit file for 24 months. AR or AM and PRM inquiries are kept for 12 months.

xxxxxxx

TRADELINES

Tradelines are typically the largest section of any credit file. This section (see Figure 3-1) lists all the credit products the subject of the file possesses. This is the richest source of data in the entire file, providing multifaceted information that details the type of credit people use, how responsible they are about paying their debt on time, and how long they have had credit.

FIGURE 3-1 EXCERPT OF TRADELINE SECTION OF CREDIT FILE

FIRM/ID CODE	RPTD	OPND	H/C	TRM	BAL	P/D	CS	MR	ECOA	ACCT NUMBER
Bank ABC *123BB6789	10/02	04/04	850	200	500		R1	06	I	12345
										DLA 10/02
Bank DEF *122BB4321	10/02	10/01	3000	700	900		R1	12	J	21212
073 Line of credit										DLA 10/02
Finance1 *124FP6543	10/02	10/00	3600	36M	1200		I1	24	J	65432
										DLA 10/02

Figure 3-1 is a very simple example of a typical tradeline section in a credit file. The subject of the file has three current credit relationships—two with banks and one with a consumer finance company. This is evident by the naming convention used in the example, but further examination of a firm's ID code can also reveal the type of institution. This will be discussed further below under Industry Codes.

Figure 3-1 shows, from left to right:

- Firm name and ID code or reporting member number.

- Reported date (RPTD).

- Opened date (OPND).

- Maximum dollar amount the customer can use or has used on revolving tradelines (on installment tradelines, it is the original loan amount) (H/C).

- Monthly payment amount or the term of the existing loan (TRM), with term represented with an M for months or Y for years (the financial institution decides whether to report term or payment amount).

- Balance amount (BAL).

- Past due amount (PD) as of the report date.

- Current status of delinquency (CS) and what type of credit product the tradeline is—R-revolving, I-installment, or O-open. The number next to the letter is the current status of that account, starting with a 1 for current (see Table 3-2 for further information about current status).

- Months reviewed or reported (MR).

- Whether the account is individual, joint, etc. (ECOA = Equal Credit Opportunity Act).

- Account number (scrambled or truncated for security purposes).

- Date of last activity (DLA) in the last column, referring to either a payment or a purchase.

The DLA establishes the date for purging. Tradelines are purged after seven years from the date of last activity, with one exception: "Paid as agreed tradelines" (for example, a paid-off auto loan) are purged from the credit file 10 years from the date of last activity.

Tradeline data consists of the accounts receivable activities of financial institutions. On a periodic cycle (typically monthly), institutions report the activities of their customers to the credit reporting agencies: payment behavior, new account activity, collection behavior, recovery behavior, changes in credit line assignment, balance activity, and potential account closure. However, closer examination of the data in the tradeline section can give an analyst or modeler even more detailed information.

INDUSTRY CODES

Industry codes are two letters in the firm identification number. The code designates the specific industry to which the reporting firm belongs: BB for banks, for example, and FP for personal finance. The industry code is often used in classifying firm type in statistical models, such as credit risk or response models. For example, a highly predictive variable in both these types of models is number of bankcard tradelines that have a balance to high credit (HC) ratio of 75 percent or higher. In Figure 3-1, the first two are bankcard tradelines (1) the industry code is BB and (2) the account type (CS field) is revolving. Since the balance/HC ratio is well below 75 percent or higher, the value for this variable is zero.

In the vast majority of cases, firms use the same industry codes for reporting to all three reporting agencies, but in rare examples there can be differences. Examining industry codes can help analysts audit differences among scores at the bureaus when all other sources of data appear identical.

Moreover, institutions sometimes change their industry codes with the reporting agencies. If a bank were to acquire a finance company, for example, it is likely that the finance company's accounts would from then on be reported as BB (bank) accounts, even though the accounts had been reported with an industry code of FP. When both acquirer and acquired firms are large, meaning that large amounts of data are converted from one industry code to another, lenders should examine the variables in their score models to see if code change affects the predictive power of their models.

CURRENT STATUS

The current status field indicates both type of account and current delinquency status. The majority of the credit file is comprised of R (revolving) and I (installment) tradelines. There will be very few Os (open). The number in the CS field indicates the current delinquency status. Table 3-2 lists the different status values, which apply to all three types of tradelines.

TABLE 3-2 CURRENT STATUS VALUES

Current Status Value	Meaning
0	Too new to rate.
1	Current account, paid within 30 days of the due date.
2	Paid in more than 30 days from the due date but less than 60 days; not more than two cycles past due.
3	Paid in more than 60 days from the due date but less than 90 days; not more than three cycles past due.
4	Paid in more than 90 days from the due date but less than 120 days; not more than four cycles past due.
5	Paid in more than 120 days from the due date, not more than 5 or more cycles past due.
7	Making plans under debtor's plan or similar arrangement.
8	Repossession (should indicate whether this was voluntary or involuntary).
9	Bad debt (charge-off, collection account, bankruptcy).

Any rating of four or higher is considered a major derogatory item; ratings of two and three are considered minor derogatory items. Variables that evaluate major derogatory items such as the number of these on file are used in credit risk modeling because past credit behavior is indicative of future credit behavior. Other variables used in credit risk models examine the number of occurrences of late payments within a given time period. For instance, how often the consumer was 60 days past due in the past 12 months.

When auditing a score model or reviewing the credit file, it is important to check the date of the last report to the reporting agency because that is the field from which the time component of this variable is created. When a tradeline is not reported promptly to a credit-reporting agency, it can affect whether or not a delinquent tradeline is included in a time-sensitive variable.

ECOA Codes

ECOA codes indicate who has financial responsibility for the tradeline—whether an account is joint or individual. These codes, which are typically not used in score models, were created under the Equal Credit Opportunity Act to ensure that joint borrowers both receive recognition for the credit tradeline. Previously, the tradeline was reported only for the primary borrower. Table 3-3 defines the ECOA codes.

TABLE 3-3 ECOA CODES

Code	Meaning
I	Individual account.
J	Joint account; two or more people are equally responsible for payment.
A	Authorized use; though this is a shared account, one person is responsible for payment and the others are not.
U	Undesignated, indicating that the lender does not have enough information to give the account a more specific code.
S	Shared but otherwise undesignated, indicating that the lender knows that the subject and at least one other person share the account but does not have enough information to designate the account as either J or A.
C	Co-maker; the subject has cosigned for an installment loan and will be responsible for payment if the borrower should default.
M	Maker; the subject is responsible for payment of an installment loan but has a co-maker as assurance that the loan will be repaid.
B	The subject has financial responsibility for an account being used exclusively by another person, as when a parent opens an account for a child's use at college.
T	Terminated; the subject's relationship to this account has ended, although parties who once shared the account may continue to maintain it—used often after a divorce.

NARRATIVE CODES

Narrative codes are an important data source in the credit file. Figure 3-1 shows an example on the tradeline for Bank DEF, where the narrative code is a number and text: "073 Line of Credit." The purpose of narrative codes is to provide further information. In this case, Bank DEF is making it clear that this tradeline is a line of credit rather than a credit card. A remarkable breadth of information can be covered by narrative codes, ranging from clarification of the type of tradeline as in the example to performance on the tradeline to disposition—whether the tradeline was closed, transferred, or sold.

The reporting institution decides whether to supply narrative codes to the bureaus. There are hundreds of narrative codes, some used often, others rarely. Ten of the most common are (1) credit card, (2) account closed by consumer, (3) account closed by lender, (4) closed account, (5) account transferred or sold, (6) account discharged in bankruptcy, (7) account paid/zero balance, (8) conventional mortgage, (9) auto loan, and (10) charge.

A key element on this list is account discharged in bankruptcy. Bankruptcies are typically reported in the public records section of the credit file, but they may also be reported as a narrative code in a tradeline—as may be foreclosures, collection accounts, repossessions, and garnishments. It is critical that an analyst building a model or analyzing a credit file incorporate these narrative codes and tradelines.

COMMON USES OF CREDIT DATA

Credit data can be used in a variety of ways, but the most common are the three ways mentioned at the outset of this chapter (1) in a static mode (as it appears at one point in time), (2) on a trended basis, or (3) in a forecast.

STATIC CREDIT FILE DATA

Static credit file data, the most common mode, can be used for either the current or a previous time period. The reporting agencies archive credit file data for many years. In building an application risk model, a lender may require access to archived credit files at the time of application if the lender has not stored this data itself; the observation period is the application period.

Some lenders also access archived credit data at the point representing the end of the outcome period. As will be discussed in Chapter 4, one method of dealing with sample selection bias in scorecards is to incorporate data on rejected applications when the scorecard is built. Data on how rejected applications have performed on other tradelines during the score outcome period is used to infer how the applicant might have performed on the lender's own loan, had the applicant not been rejected.

TRENDED CREDIT FILE DATA

The value in trending credit file data is that it may be viewed over time. It might be, for instance, that an issuer wanted to find out if its customers were using its card more than competitors' cards.[1] An analyst would review how customers were using their bankcards over time. It might be that most of the issuer's customers were using the card in question more than cards of the competition. If a segment of its customers are using competitive credit cards more than this issuer's cards, further analytics could be undertaken to support a marketing offer to switch this group of customers back to preferring this issuer's cards.

FORECASTING

Using credit data in forecasts has strong appeal, both analytical and intuitive. Internal forecasters could do their own forecasts, or forecasts of credit and economic data might be bought from third-party firms or the reporting agencies. Forecasts can be used both strategically and tactically. Unlike static and trended credit file data, forecasts look to the future.

There are many ways to use forecasted data. For example, it could be incorporated into response models to support direct mail decisions. Direct mail has become an increasingly indispensable channel for acquiring new customers at a time when lenders are under escalating pressures to grow their portfolios. Within this focus of growth is the necessary requirement that growth be obtained responsibly and profitably.

Direct mail campaigns must be executed in the most efficient way possible. The average direct mail response rate for the financial services industry is currently about 1 percent. To be competitive, firms must achieve response rates to their direct mail campaigns that are higher than average in the sense of both acquiring new customers and acquiring them cost-effectively.

Finding target audiences that have a desirable credit risk profile and also a high likelihood of responding to the direct mail solicitation is central to planning a direct mail campaign. Refining the various methodologies for determining desirable targets has increased the efficiency of direct mail

---

[1] In this example, as in any other application, the credit-reporting agency would very carefully protect the identities of the competitors. The reporting agencies must be very cautious stewards of the data entrusted to them by the firms reporting to them.

campaigns. The first generation of targeting was based on subjective credit file criteria against which potential solicitation candidates would be evaluated. The second generation employed a more strategic application: using statistical modeling to predict response in conjunction with desirability criteria. The statistical models have inarguably allowed lenders to achieve much greater precision in targeting those customers more likely to respond to their offers.

Now we have the third generation of targeting—incorporating forecasted credit data into response models. This is intuitively appealing because it addresses the inherent time lag in executing a direct mail campaign. Incorporating forecast data into the campaign process addresses the disposition of prospects during the time period in which they receive and are likely to respond to the mailed offer.

The forecasted variables incorporated into strategic targeting are both credit and economics-based because including both credit and economic data gives a larger, more complete picture of each prospect's need and willingness to respond to the offer.

Forecasted credit data can also be used for operational analytics on questions like branch location. The foundation would lie in market analysis and institutional risk control. The objective would be to determine locations that fit a firm's client profile *and* stated risk level.

Similarly, forecasted credit data, economic data, and a firm's forecasted master file data can be used to create scenarios simulating what would happen to the firm's portfolio or accounts receivable during a period of recession. This has many enticing strategic and tactical applications, including "what if" analysis to compare options for mitigating the effects of a recession on a portfolio.

WHY REPORTING TO CREDIT BUREAUS IS IMPORTANT

To be truly valuable, credit performance data must be complete and timely so that credit decisions can be based on the most up-to-date information possible. Full reporting means that a financial services firm reports not only negative or delinquent information about its customers but also positive information, such as that a customer always pays on time. Certainly, consumers should get the full benefit of their responsible use of credit. Certainly, too, firms seeking to grant credit should have the benefit of knowing whether or not a given consumer pays bills promptly, or at least in an acceptable time. Different firms have different levels of tolerance for mild or even severe delinquencies on a person's credit file.

When there is full and timely reporting to the agencies, businesses benefit from a rich and accurate data source on which to base their analyses and decisions. Consumers benefit from the variety of credit products that businesses create and offer, tailored to their different risk profiles and needs.

Different products fit different consumer needs at different phases of their lives. It often used to be said that a bank would only loan money to someone who did not need a loan, and it would indeed be easy for an institution to take the risk position of lending only to individuals with stellar credit and ample financial resources. This, however, is not necessarily the way to greatest profitability. People throughout the entire credit spectrum need credit, whether in the form of installment loans or revolving credit cards.

The information in credit files allows firms to analyze different segments of the credit spectrum to determine those to whom it can profitably extend credit. Without credit data, decisions would be made much more inefficiently and much more subjectively. Credit bureau data is the foundation for sound credit decision-making.

Section Two

MODEL DEVELOPMENT AND VALIDATION

Chapter 4
SCORECARD DEVELOPMENT

Elizabeth Mays
Director of Retail Risk Modeling and Analytics
Bank One

In this chapter we describe how scorecards are developed. We discuss the statistical method most commonly used to build score models and show how the output of the model is used to calculate scorecard point weights. We cover important scorecard issues like the choice of the bad definition and the performance window, sample design, whether to build segmented scorecards, and what criteria must be met in deciding which characteristics to include in scorecards. Finally, we discuss why point weights may not reflect the true relationship between characteristics and the outcome variable and what can be done to make sure they do.

SCORECARD BASICS

A scorecard is a formula for assigning points to applicant characteristics in order to derive a numeric value that reflects how likely a borrower is, relative to other individuals, to experience a given event or perform a given action. For example, a scorecard may tell us if a particular applicant is more or less likely to default than another applicant, or if the response rate to a given mailing is expected to be higher or lower for one type of individual than for other potential applicants.

Table 4.1 illustrates a simple scorecard with only 3 characteristics (most scorecards have between 8 and 15). This scorecard is designed to predict the likelihood that a particular type of loan will go 60 days past due during the first 24 months of its life. Possible values for the characteristics (the attributes) are listed in Table 4.1 along with the point weight assigned to each.

TABLE 4.1. WEIGHTING ATTRIBUTES

Attribute	Attribute Intervals	Point Weight	Attribute Value for Borrower X	Points for Borrower X
Percent Revolving	30	35		
Utilization	31-50	25		
	51-70	10	56	10
	71+	0		
Debt-to-Income Ratio	1-20	74		
	20-40	30	29	30
	41+	0		
Number of Tradelines 30	0	50		
DPD in Last 12 Months	1	20	3	20
	2+	0		
SCORE				**60**

For the first attribute, percent utilization on revolving loans, the higher the percentage, the fewer points awarded. The point weights for the value of the applicants' other attributes are assigned similarly. The score is simply the sum of the point weights for the attributes.

An obvious question is: How do we determine which characteristics to include in the scorecard and how many points to assign for each? As we discuss in the rest of this chapter, most scorecards are built by estimating a regression model. Regression models examine how a particular variable (the outcome variable) is explained by another variable-or, more typically, by a whole set of other variables. The output from a regression model is a set of factors called regression coefficients. Each of these can be interpreted as the correlation between the outcome variable we are trying to predict and the explanatory variable or characteristic, holding constant all other influences on the outcome variable. Point weights for the scorecard are calculated using a simple mathematical transformation of the regression coefficients.

REGRESSION MODELS

The most common method for building credit scorecards today, at least in the United States, is logistic regression,[1] Though we will begin with a discussion of linear regression because that is something many people are familiar with from college statistics courses (logistic regression is in fact a special case of linear regression), let us define logistic regression here to set the context.

A logistic regression model is simply one where the explanatory variables times their coefficients are assumed to be linearly related not just to Y (as in linear regression) but also to the natural log of the odds that Y will happen. That is:

$$Ln(p/(1-p)) = B_0 + B_1*X_1 + \dots + B_n*X_n$$

where   p is the probability that Y will occur and
p/(1-p) is the odds that Y will occur.

Linear regression, the "parent" method, attempts to find a linear relationship between two variables, X and Y. Y-the one we are trying to predict-is referred to as the dependent variable because its predicted value depends on X. X is the explanatory variable because it explains why Y differs from one individual to another. The question we are trying to answer is this: If X changes, how much can Y be expected to change as a result? To determine this, we need a set of observations (the data sample) in which we can observe numerous pairs of X and Y.

Say we want to be able to predict loan loss severity for mortgages. Figure 4-1 plots a sample of 30 observations of the dependent variable—dollar loss as a percent of loan balance (loss severity)—against the loan's loan-to-value (LTV) ratio, the X variable. Clearly, there is a positive relationship between percent loss severity and LTV. That is, for larger LTVs, loss severity is greater.

Linear regression fits a line to this set of observations, the line that best explains the relationship between severity and LTV. The slope of the line defines the expected change in severity for a unit change in the LTV ratio. For example, if the slope is 0.5, a loan with a 90 percent LTV would be expected to have a loss severity that is 5 percent higher than a loan with an LTV of 80 (5 percent = 0.5 x 10, the amount of the change in LTV). We can thus write the equation for the line as:

---

[1] See Chapters 4 and 5 of Thomas, L. C., et al. (2002). *Credit Scoring and Its Applications.* Philadelphia, PA: Society for Industrial and Applied Mathematics for a discussion of other methods, both statistical and nonstatistical, used to build scorecards.

$$Y=B_0 + B_1*X$$

where B_1 is the slope of the line and

B_0 is the value of Y even if X is zero.

The two Bs are the regression coefficients.

FIGURE 4.1. PERCENT LOSS SEVERITY BY LTV RATIO

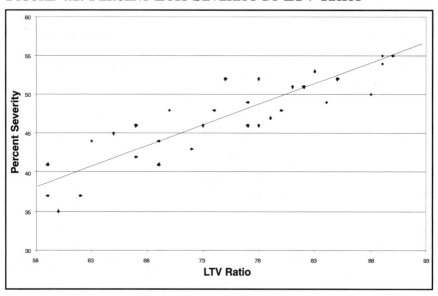

In most regression models, there are several explanatory variables, not just one as in the example. In those models the equation for Y becomes

$$Y=B_0 + B_1*X_1 + B_2*X_2 + \ldots + B_n*X_n.$$

LOGISTIC VERSUS LINEAR REGRESSION

In scoring applications typically we are not talking about a case where the dependent variable takes on a large range of values, as in the example above. Rather we are working with a *binary* variable, one that takes on only two values, such as whether a loan defaulted or not (or whether or not a consumer responded to a mailing). In those cases we typically code the dependent variable with a value of 1 for loans that have defaulted and 0 for those that have not. What the linear model would estimate in the case of a 0/1 variable is the *probability* that the loan will default or the consumer will respond. Although linear regression sometimes is used to estimate scoring models, logistic regression is generally preferred because it is designed specifically for the case where the dependent variable is binary.

A problem with linear regression is that it can produce predicted probabilities that are greater than 1 or less than 0, which does not make much sense. The logistic model prevents this by working with the *odds* of the event happening instead of the probability, and by taking the natural logarithm of the odds to prevent predicting negative probabilities (hence the name *log*istic).

In discussing linear regression, we said that the regression coefficient associated with each X represents the increase in Y that is expected for a unit increase in the explanatory variable. In logistic regression something similar is true except that the B tells you how much change in the log odds of Y to expect for a unit increase in X.[2] Logistic regression, because it is a multivariate statistical technique, is able to isolate the independent effect of each X on the odds of the event occurring, holding constant the effect of other variables that affect the likelihood of the event.

SCORECARD SCALING AND DERIVATION OF POINT WEIGHTS

Once the logistic regression model has been estimated, we can put in the X values for a given loan and calculate a score using the equation

$$SCORE = B_1X_1 + \ldots + B_nX_n.[3]$$

The resulting score, however, is on the hard-to-interpret natural log scale. A standard practice in the scoring world is to transform the score to

---

[2] Because it is difficult to comprehend the relationship between X and Y in log terms, we often "undo" the log relationship by raising the mathematical constant "e" to the B power (i.e., we calculate e^B for each variable). The result—the odds ratio for the variable—tells us by how many units the odds of, say, default are expected to increase for a unit of increase in the explanatory variable. For example, suppose we want to evaluate the odds of going bad (90 DPD) for a binary variable like an indicator identifying whether a mortgage was made for the borrower's primary home or a second (vacation) home. Suppose further that e^B equals 2.5. We would then expect the bad odds of second homes to be 2.5 times that of primary homes, all else being equal.

For continuous variables, the method is a little different. To evaluate how the odds change for a given change in the continuous variable, calculate e^{CB} where C is some number of units of change for the explanatory variable. Say the continuous variable here is debt-to-income ratio (DTI). Calculating e^{10B} where B is the regression coefficient associated with DTI, tells us by how many times the odds are expected to increase for each 10 point increase (e.g., from 30 to 40) in DTI.

[3] Note that we have not used the regression intercept, B_0, to calculate the score. In the next section we will see that we do need the intercept if we want to calculate the expected good/bad odds or the predicted probability that an account will go bad using the regression equation.

a linear scale where a given number of points will result in a doubling of the odds that the event will happen.

To do the transformation, we multiply the score by a factor equal to the number of points for which we want a doubling of the odds to occur, and then divide by ln(2).[4] Say we seek a score where the odds of going bad are expected to double each time the score increases 20 points. To obtain the scaled score, we would multiply the score that comes directly from the regression model by 20 and divide by the natural log of 2. That is, we would calculate

$$(B_1X_1+ \ldots +B_nX_n)*(20/\ln(2)).$$

We could also write that equation as

$$(20/\ln(2))*B_1*X_1+\ldots+(20/\ln(2))*B_n*X_n$$

to highlight the fact that we are multiplying each X by something to get the score—the "something" being the point weight for each characteristic. Thus, the point weight for each characteristic is nothing more than the product of its B and 20/ln(2).

In building scorecards it is typical (although not necessary) to separate the possible values for each characteristic into a number of discrete categories before including them in the regression model.[5] For example, percent revolving utilization could take on any value from 0 to 100 but might be divided into the four ranges listed under "Attribute Intervals" in Table 4.1. A separate 0/1 variable would be created for each range and all but one of the variables would be entered into the regression model.[6] In our example, the Bs that were determined from the regression are listed in the fourth

---

[4] See Scallan, Gerard. (1999). *Building Better Scorecards*. Autin, TX: Austin Logistics, p. 1013.

[5] For discussion of a study that compares the results of using *binned* variables to continuous variables in scorecards, see Ash, Dennis, and Dimitra Vlatsa. (2001). "Scorecard Modeling with Continuous vs. Classed Variables," in Elizabeth Mays, ed., *Handbook of Credit Scoring*. Chicago: Glenlake Publishing, pp. 71-85.

[6] One of the 0/1 variables would be excluded so that there would not be perfect collinearity between the explanatory variables, in which case the regression model cannot be solved. Perfect collinearity arises when explanatory variables in a set have an exact linear relationship among themselves, the most obvious case being $X_1+X_2=X_3$. Collinearity is a problem for a regression model because the regression coefficients measure the effect of each explanatory variable on the dependent variable assuming that all other explanatory variables *do not* affect the value of the explanatory variable in question. But the explanatory variables do affect each other's values if there is a linear relationship among them, because if X1=0 and X2=1, then X3 *must* equal 1. The solution is to eliminate one of the variables from the model; the point weight associated with that variable would then be 0.

column and the calculations for the point weights in the last column of Table 4.2.

One final step remains before the regression model is completely transformed into a score. Typically, a given number of base points is added to the score. All applicants receive this number of points in addition to the points associated with the values of their particular characteristics. The assignment of base points is done only for cosmetic reasons—to make sure the score distribution has a desirable range. For example, depending on how the characteristics in the score were constructed, the score (sum of attributes times point weights) might take on negative values, ranging from, say, -113 to 333. Assigning base points of 200 shifts the range, giving possible values from 87 to 533.

The number of base points is often set so that loans at a given score have a particular expected good/bad odds ratio. For example, if we decide we want a score of 500 to have an expected good/bad odds of 50 to 1, we would add the number of base points needed to make that occur. (How to calculate the expected good/bad odds is discussed next.)

TABLE 4.2 SCORECARD SCALING AND DERIVATION OF POINT WEIGHTS

Characteristic	Attribute Intervals	Point Weight	B	Point Weight Calculation
Percent Revolving	0-30	35	1.213	1.213*(20/0.69315)=35
Utilization	31-50	25	0.866	0.866*(20/0.69315)=25
	51-70	10	0.346	0.346*(20/0.69315)=10
	71+	0		0
Debt-to-Income	1-20	75	2.599	2.599*(20/0.69315)=75
Ratio	20-40	30	1.039	1.039*(20/0.69315)=30
	41+	0		0
Number of	0	50	1.733	1.733*(20/0.69315)=50
Tradelines 30	1	20	0.69	0.69*(20/0.69315)=20
DPD in Last	2+	0		0
12 Months				

CALCULATING EXPECTED GOOD/BAD ODDS AND PROBABILITY OF GOING BAD

After the scorecard has been implemented, we need to track how it performs. As is detailed in Chapters 6 and 13, one of the things we want to do is to compare the good/bad odds at a given score on actual data samples with what we expected the odds to be for that score when we built the model. The expected good/bad odds are derived when the scorecard is built and are used in the score cutoff analysis (see Chapter 12). Making sure the same odds ratio is being achieved at each score when the scorecard is used is important if the portfolio is to perform as expected.

Recall that the logistic regression model estimates the effect of the characteristics on the log of the odds that a certain event will occur. Because we usually define the event as a loan going bad, the log of the bad/good odds is linearly related to the sum of the characteristics times their regression coefficients:

$$\text{Log of bad/good odds} = (B_0 + B_1 * X_1 + \ldots + B_n * X_n).$$

To get the *odds* that the event will happen instead of the *log* of the odds, we simply undo the log operation by performing its inverse, which is to raise the mathematical constant, e, to the power of terms on each side of the equation. If we have estimated the log odds of being bad with our regression, the bad to good odds[7] is simply:

$$\text{Bad/good odds} = e^{(B_0 + B_1 * X_1 + \ldots + B_n * X_n)}.$$

It is traditional in the scoring world to do cutoff analysis and monitor scorecards using the good/bad rather than the bad/good odds. The good/bad odds is simply the reciprocal of the bad/good odds:[8]

$$\text{Good/bad odds} = 1/e^{(B_0 + B_1 * X_1 + \ldots + B_n * X_n)}.$$

Note that all these equations use the regression intercept, B_0, which was not used in calculating the score described in the last section. To estimate the expected odds or the bad rate at a given score, we must use the intercept. It gives us the starting point from which the explanatory variables in a regression model affect the outcome variable. The fact that the score is scaled to achieve a desired range or to make a given score have a particu-

---

[7] It is possible to estimate the log odds of being good with the regression model by simply changing a statement in the procedure, but it is more typical to estimate the log odds of being bad, then find the reciprocal (as described in the text) to generate the expected good/bad odds at a given score.

[8] If the development sample over- or under-samples certain segments of the population, it may have a different bad rate than the general population. As a result, we must weight the observations in the sample when we calculate the odds measures or the predicted probabilities so that they will accurately represent the total population. This must also be done if indeterminate accounts, discussed later in the chapter, are excluded from the development sample.

lar odds expectation makes the starting point irrelevant in the score calculation because the starting point is changed anyway by adding base points
when the score is scaled. As a result, the intercept is not used in generating
the score.

Besides generating the expected good/bad odds, sometimes we want to
predict bad rates—the probability that a set of loans or perhaps the entire
portfolio will go bad. (The terms "rate" and "probability" are used inter-
changeably throughout this book.) A bad probability of 4 percent for a loan
means that if we observe 100 loans with characteristics identical to it, four
are expected to go bad. The bad rate of this pool is expected to be 4 percent
and so is the probability that any individual loan in the pool will go bad. The
equation to generate the probability of going bad for a particular loan is:

$$\text{Probability} = 1/[1 + e^{-B_0 - (B_1 X_1 + \ldots + B_n X_n)}].$$

As we discuss later in the chapter, it is standard practice to validate the
score on a different sample from the one on which the scorecard was built.
Often this sample will be from a more recent period, one the lender may
feel better reflects the type of business it will be producing going forward.
Lenders may prefer to generate the expected good/bad odds from this sample rather than from the regression equation and may do so in the following way:

1. First, divide the validation sample into score ranges with the same
   number of points in each range (e.g., 200-219, 220-239, etc.) and
   calculate the ratio of the number of good loans to the number of
   bad loans in each range. The result is the actual good/bad odds for
   each score range for the validation sample.

2. Next, estimate a simple linear regression model on this set of
   points. (This can be done using the regression function that is part
   of most spreadsheet software.) The predictive variable for the
   regression is the mid-point of the score range and the dependent
   variable is the good/bad odds. The regression model coefficients
   can be used to produce a table showing the expected odds at each
   score.

Figure 4.2 shows an example of the actual odds in each score range (the
dots) and the regression line that represents the expected odds at each score.
Graphing the odds on a log scale produces a straight line for the score,
making it easier to see if the actual odds are in line with the expected odds.

FIGURE 4.2 ACTUAL AND EXPECTED ODDS BASED ON VALIDATION SAMPLE

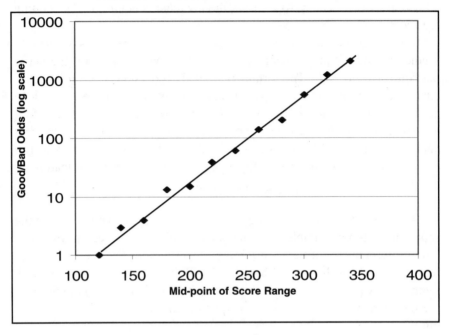

DETERMINING THE PERFORMANCE WINDOW

A number of important decisions must be made about the scorecard design before any work on it is begun, including what outcome period and bad definition to use.

The outcome period is the period of time over which we observe the loans in the sample to classify them as good or bad. Often, the choice of outcome period is limited by data constraints. Though lenders have come to understand in recent years that good quality data is a huge corporate asset, sometimes good-quality application and performance data have been retained only for loans booked in the recent past, say the last year or two. This of course limits the options for defining the outcome period.

In an era where mergers and acquisitions are common, another constraint is that there may be little data for at least part of the combined portfolio if historical loan performance data from the acquired company has not been converted to the acquirer's servicing system.

Some scorecard developers prefer to use a constant outcome period for all loans in the development sample even if a longer outcome period is available for some loans. For example, even though a lender may include in the sample loans booked from 1996 through 1999 period, it will often limit the outcome period to the first 18 months of the life of each loan. A loan that met the bad definition within the first 18 months would be considered a bad loan and one that did not would be considered a good loan even if it went bad at 20 months.

If a constant outcome period is used, the window should ideally be long enough to cover the period of the peak of default for the product in question.[9] Observing performance only over the first 12 months of life, for example, for a product whose default rates do not peak until, say, 3 to 4 years (typical for U.S. first mortgages), may produce a development sample that does not reflect the bad loans the scorecard is being designed to identify. Because early defaulters may have characteristics different from late defaulters, the resulting scorecard could misrepresent the importance of the characteristics exhibited by the late defaulters, who make up the largest portion of total defaulted loans.

Instead of using a constant outcome period for all loans, some scorecard developers prefer to use the longest outcome period available for each loan, using all performance information available for each loan even though some loans may be observed for several years and others perhaps only for one. Clearly, all else equal, the older loans have a higher likelihood of going bad because they have been observed for a longer period. This must be accounted for in the regression model by including a variable that represents how long the loan has been on the books. This variable would not become part of the final score. Its sole purpose is to control for the differing outcome periods of loans in the sample.[10] If this is not done, there is a risk of imputing incorrect effects to the predictors in the model.

In one case, a mortgage acquisition score was built with loans that had been on the books for varying amounts of time and staggered performance windows were used. Over time the lender had been accepting loans with

---

[9] In using older loans, there is the risk that they may be of a different type than the loans the lender expects to make going forward and therefore will not reflect future performance. An example would be a lender who previously made many balloon mortgages but no longer offers them. It might be wiser not to include these older loans in the development sample. Alternatively, it might be useful to include them but incorporate a control variable intended to capture the possible effect of product type on the outcome. We must weigh case by case the types of loans needed to obtain a larger sample and the desire to include loans that have hit their peak delinquency against the possibility that old business does not reflect future business.

[10] See Chapter 8, where the use of loan age control variables is discussed in the context of building a score-based loss-forecasting model, and Chapter 10, which recommends a control variable approach for reducing disparate impact on protected borrower classes.

higher and higher LTV ratios, which meant that recent loans had higher LTVs than the older loans. When time on books (loan age) was not included as an explanatory variable in the regression model, having a high LTV appeared to *lower* the risk of a loan being bad—contrary to what the lender knew to be true—because the high LTV loans with a shorter loan age had not had a chance to go bad. When loan age was included as a control variable, the effect of LTV on the outcome was reversed in the regression model and the true risk of the high-LTV loans became apparent.

Controlling for loan age is extremely important when staggered outcome periods are used. Failure to control for differences in the amount of time loan performance is observed can cause significant bias in regression models. (Scorecard bias is discussed at length later in the chapter.)

DETERMINING THE GOOD AND BAD DEFINITIONS

The choice of the bad definition depends on what the model is to be used for, the amount of bad loans available for the development sample when a particular bad definition is used, and what the business deems to be a bad event.

For response models and attrition models, whether or not the stated event took place is very clear. For credit models, determining which event we want to forecast is subjective. Does a lender consider a loan that goes 90 DPD an undesirable loan? Probably. Then what about a loan that reaches 60 DPD but then cures? That loan may be profitable to some but unprofitable and not worth the collection expense and added uncertainty to others. What about loans where the borrower declares bankruptcy but continues to make payments? These are all possible bad events, but lenders are likely to vary in what they consider a bad loan to be.

Because there are so many events a lender might consider "bad," lenders sometimes end up with a combination bad definition like 60 DPD or worse, 3 times 30 DPD, or borrower declared bankruptcy within the performance window. Sometimes combination bad definitions are necessary in order to generate a large enough sample of bad loans to build a model.

Although all the events mentioned are probably undesirable, it is important to make sure the different bad outcomes all relate to borrower characteristics in the same way. For example, a default model designed specifically to predict the event of default, without combining it with the event of bankruptcy, may better predict the likelihood of default because the predictor variables are likely to be related to bankruptcy and default in different ways.[11] Building separate default and bankruptcy scores could result in more powerful scores than if both outcomes were combined in a single score. This also gives the lender more flexibility in designing strategies for using scores.[12]

Some scorecard developers have three categories for their outcome variables (1) goods, (2) bads, and (3) indeterminates, but they drop the indeterminates from the development sample. Indeterminates are loans that perform worse than a good loan but better than a bad loan. For example, if goods are defined as loans that have been at most one cycle delinquent and bads as those that have been three cycles delinquent, undeterminates would be those that went a maximum of two cycles delinquent. Developers delete indeterminates from a sample with the hope that eliminating the gray loans will produce a scorecard that can better distinguish between goods and bads.

Although some score developers use this a standard practice, others find it not useful. Their reasoning is that all applicants need to be scored, not just those whose characteristics match borrowers whose loans are defined as good or bad. A well-known academic researcher calls dropping indeterminates from the development sample a practice that is "curious and difficult to justify."[13] In Chapter 9 we describe a study that found dropping indeterminates actually reduced score performance on a validation sample.

POPULATION SEGMENTATION

Segmentation divides the population into groups and builds a separate scorecard for each. Thomas and colleagues[14] identify three types of reasons for segmenting scorecards (1) strategic, (2) operational, and (3) statistical.

A lender may want to segment its scorecard strategically to target certain customer segments, such as borrowers who already have a loan with that lender. It wants a separate scorecard for this group because it wants to treat them differently.

An operational reason for segmenting would arise where different data are available for different customer segments. For example, different loan

---

[11] Even more extreme, default and bankruptcy may be related to entirely different predictors.

[12] For example, a lender might be willing to accept somewhat more bankruptcy risk if the delinquency or default risk is low.

[13] See Hand, David J. (1997). "Statistical Classification Methods in Consumer Credit Scoring: A Review." *Journal of the Royal Statistical Society,* 160 (Part 3): 525.

[14] See Thomas, L.C., J. Ho, and W.T. Scherer. (2002). "Time Will Tell: Behavioral Scoring and the Dynamics of Consumer Credit Assessment." *IMA Journal of Management Mathematics,* 12: 89-103.

applications may be used for applicants applying for credit in a bank branch, those phoning into a call center, or those applying through a Web site. This could mean that certain predictive characteristics are available for some applicant segments but not for others, necessitating segmented scorecards.

Finally, a statistical reason for segmentation arises when characteristics affect the outcome variable differently for some subpopulations of the general applicant population than for others. For example, the effect of a serious delinquency on a credit file may be more deleterious for an applicant who has only a small number of tradelines (say three or less) than one who has many tradelines.

One way to handle this is to build a single scorecard for all applicants but incorporate an *interactive effect* into the regression model. An interactive effect is present when the effect of a predictor on the outcome variable varies depending on the effect of a second predictor.[15] This is accounted for in a regression by creating a combination variable—an "interaction"—from the two predictors and using it in the regression along with the two predictors themselves. To continue with our example, in addition to including total tradelines and the number of serious delinquencies in the regression as predictors, a third (interactive) variable would be set equal to 1 if the number of accounts is three or fewer *and* there is at least one seriously delinquent account, and 0 otherwise. Adding this variable to the regression model accounts for the fact that the effect of a serious delinquency on a score varies with the total number of tradelines.

There may be many other variables in the score whose effects differ depending on the total number of accounts an applicant has. Rather than incorporating several interactive effects into a single scorecard, we might segment the applicant population into those with up to three accounts and those with more, building separate scorecards for each. Separate scorecards for these two populations are more straightforward and easier to understand then a single scorecard with several interactive variables.

Segmentation may or may not lead to a set of scorecards that is more predictive than a single scorecard, depending on the situation. The first consideration in deciding whether or not to segment is whether there is a strategic, operational, or statistical need to do so. If there is, the performance of the segment cards should be compared to that of a single card to see which would be most beneficial for the business.

---

[15] For a comprehensive discussion of interactive effects, see Jaccard, James. (2001). *Interactive Effects in Logistic Regression.* Thousand Oaks, CA: Sage Publications, Inc.

The performance of segmented cards should be significantly better than a single card before segmentation is adopted because there are draw-backs to using segmented scorecards. First, the incremental costs of using multiple scorecards can be significant—reviewing 10 sets of monitoring reports scorecards is considerably more time-consuming than reviewing a single set. Second, there may not be enough bad loans within each segment for reliable scorecard validation.[16] Finally, scorecard policies should be set taking into consideration the characteristics that comprise the score (see Chapter 12). Drafting and maintaining policies for 10 different scores within the same business can be both time-consuming and confusing. The gain from segmentation should be substantial before a developer opts for it.

SAMPLE DESIGN

Once the bad definition and the outcome period have been specified, the data set for scorecard development can be created. It is standard practice to create both a development sample and a validation sample. As the names imply, the development sample is used to build the scorecards while the validation sample is used to check the accuracy of the completed scorecard on a set of loans that had no influence on generation of the point weights. Ideally, the validation sample would be an *out-of-time* sample, a set of loans originated during a different time period than those in the development sample. The intent is to insure that the score is robust across different time periods.

If no such sample is available, the validation sample is a *hold-out* sample. A hold-out sample is formed by holding out a set of loans randomly selected from those that would otherwise be part of the development sample. That is, loans that were originated during the same time period as those in the development sample.

We want both development and validation samples to contain loans that are representative of the types of loans on which the scorecard will be used. Thus, certain types of loans should be excluded from both samples:

- *Product types that the lender does not intend to originate going forward.* Certain loan terms (e.g., interest-only loans) that may have been offered in the past but will no longer be offered would be an example.

- *Loans that were originated in a different way than those for which the scorecard will be used.* Those might include loans rewritten during a workout effort and loans purchased post-origination as part of a bulk loan package.

---

[16] At least a few hundred bad accounts are required to verify that a score is ranking risk well.

- *Loans that defaulted due to the death of the borrower or to fraud.*
  The borrower characteristics for these loans are unlikely to reflect
  their bad outcome and including them could distort the measured
  associations (point weights) between the scorecard characteristics
  and the loan outcome.[17]

A common question is: What is the minimum number of loans needed
in the samples? Typically, the number of bad loans is the limiting factor.
Although some scorecard developers will build a scorecard with as few as
300, the majority would be more comfortable with at least 1,000 bad loans
in the development sample, although a few thousand would be ideal. For
the validation sample, fewer loans are needed because no point weights are
being estimated. Here the absolute minimum would be about 300 bad
loans, but more is always preferred.

Sometimes there are not enough loans available to develop the scorecard on one sample and retain a separate sample for validation. There are
techniques designed to assist in building models in this case. They go by
names like *jackknifing* and *bootstrapping*. Their description is outside the
scope of this book, but they are described in Thomas et al. and Rud.[18]

CHOICE OF CHARACTERISTICS

Scorecard building is a combination of art and science: The science lies in
the statistical methods at the core of scorecard development. The art lies
in the many choices the scorecard developer must make throughout the
model building process. These choices have a major effect on the final
scorecard. Uninformed or incorrect decisions can result in an important
variable being excluded or an improper variable being included. Some of
the choices that must be made are how to treat data errors, missing values,
and *outliers* (extreme values of the characteristics); whether to use continuous or transformed variables or to make categorical (*binned*) variables
out of continuous variables; and whether to include variable interactions.[19]

---

[17] If these loans make up more than 2 or 3 percent of bad loans, their effect on expected
bad rates should be incorporated into the good-bad odds estimates at each score once the
scorecard is completed. Otherwise, the expected odds will be greater than the lender will
see in practice because fraud and defaults due to death are likely to continue in the future.
[18] See Thomas et al., op. cit., n. 14, pp.111-12 and Olivia Par Rud (2001), *Data Mining
Cookbook.* New York: John Wiley & Sons, Inc., pp. 134-46.
[19] We do not treat these technical topics, but for a detailed discussion of how to handle
missing data, see Allison, Paul, D. (2002). *Missing Data.* Thousand Oaks, CA: Sage
Publications.

Perhaps most important, the modeler must choose which characteristics to incorporate in the scorecard.

It is extremely important for the scorecard developer to have a good grasp of the business for which the scorecard is being built, and a firm command of the business's data. Otherwise, he can make mistakes in working with the data and interpreting the results of test runs.

If the scorecard is to be built by a third party, it is important to select a vendor who has experience with the particular product for which the scorecard is being built. An internal staff member with an excellent understanding of the data (and preferably a knowledge of statistical methods as well) should be assigned to work closely with the vendor to be on the alert for anything that does not make sense either in the data itself or in the outcome of the model.

As the project progresses the vendor should hold one or more sessions with a wide cross-section of experienced internal business managers to review the results. These reviews should discuss all the characteristics in the model and the magnitudes of their effects. Just as important, any characteristics business managers thought would be predictive but for which the expected relationship to the outcome variable was not found should be reviewed to seek possible explanations for the unexpected results.

There are few inviolable rules on how characteristics should be chosen for inclusion in scorecards. Here is a list of properties that we generally require of them. Characteristics should:

1. Not pose any legal, regulatory, or ethical concerns.

2. Help the score achieve its goal, whether that be to rank-order borrowers in terms of their likelihood of experiencing some bad event or to forecast the percentage of loans that will go bad within a given portfolio segment.

3. Be based on variables that are statistically significant in the regression model.

4. Make sound business sense in terms of the effect of the characteristic on the outcome variable.

First, a lender should leave out characteristics that are discriminatory to any protected class of borrowers. Congress enacted the Equal Credit Opportunity Act in 1975 with the intention of prohibiting discrimination in the granting of credit against members of certain classes. The Federal

Reserve Board's Regulation B (Reg B) sets out the rules for complying with the act. Reg B mentions some specific uses of characteristics to be avoided. For example, borrower age should only be included in empirically derived (nonjudgmental) scorecards if that characteristic does not penalize applicants over 62. A score should not assign fewer points to older than to younger borrowers. Lenders should have a lawyer as well as an expert in fair lending practices on the score development team to prevent including any problem characteristics in the scorecard.

Second, a characteristic should help the score achieve its goal. The traditional use of credit scores has been to rank applicants in terms of the likelihood of their loans having a bad outcome, rejecting those scoring below a lender-determined cutoff. Rank-ordering means that the scorecard should be able to say that applicant X has a higher or lower likelihood of experiencing the event in question than applicant Y.

Using measures like the KS statistic and the C statistic (see Chapter 6) makes it easier to evaluate whether adding a particular variable will be helpful in ranking borrowers by risk. If this is the only use for the scorecard, a variable whose addition does not enhance one of these measures may be omitted from the scorecard because it does not help separate borrowers into good and bad categories.

Today, however, scoring models are being used for other purposes, such as risk- based pricing and loss forecasting. For applications like these, it is extremely important to be able to correctly predict *how many* loans will go bad within certain portfolio segments. This is a different and more stringent requirement than merely ranking loans in terms of their risk of going bad. Even though a variable might not assist with ranking, it might still be included in the score if it enhances the model's ability to predict bad rates within particular portfolio segments.

We may, for example, believe it is important to price loans for new vehicles differently from loans for used vehicles, or mortgages for vacation homes differently from those for primary residences, because we have seen that the performance of the loan types differs over time. Even though the variables representing these characteristics may be statistically significant in our regression models, we may find they do not help risk- rank borrowers—they do not increase the usual separation and risk-ranking statistics.

This is especially true when such loans represent only a small portion of the development sample because there are not enough loans of the type to have much effect on the overall ranking of goods and bads. Nonetheless, we may include such a variable in our score model if it helps us hit the *pre-*

dicted level of the bad rate for the two groups (that is, loans on new versus used vehicles or mortgages on vacation homes versus primary homes). Evaluation of how well a particular characteristic helps in forecasting bad rates for portfolio segments is discussed in Chapter 6.[20]

The third property we want our characteristics to possess is statistical significance in the regression model. A variable is considered statistically significant if there is a high degree of confidence that there is a relationship between the characteristic and the outcome variable. For logistic regression models, the Chi-squared statistic and its associated probability (both are provided by all statistics packages that run regressions) permits us to evaluate this relationship. It is standard practice to require the probability to be less than .05 or .01 (the smaller the better) before a variable is said to be statistically significant.

Sometimes data limitations cause variables to be statistically insignificant. This often happens when there are too few loans with a particular characteristic to obtain a significant coefficient for that characteristic. Occasionally, if a variable has the expected relationship with the outcome variable but has a probability that does not meet our usual standard, we may still include it in the scorecard. This would be rare. However, it would probably only be done for variables for which there is a strong business or theoretical justification to include them in the score. Once sufficient data are obtained, the model can be re-estimated to see if the expected relationship is borne out. If the variable is still insignificant, it should be eliminated from any new versions of the scorecard.

Finally, a characteristic should make sense in terms of the direction of its effect on the outcome. Two examples that do not make sense would be finding that (1) the more equity a mortgage borrower has in a home the higher the bad rate or (2) increasing the DTI ratio for an auto loan customer lowers the bad rate. Such counter-intuitive effects probably point to a data problem within the development sample. We should not include a variable in a scorecard if we are unable to explain why it has the relationship it does with the outcome variable. That is why business knowledge is invaluable when building scorecards—the more discussions between the scorecard builders and experienced business managers, the better.

Besides making sure the characteristics make sense in terms of the overall direction of effect on the outcome, we generally require that the effects be monotonically increasing or decreasing—in other words, ever-

---

[20] See also Chapter 6 for a discussion of how to use plots of the odds to score relationships for various portfolio segments to help determine if a variable should be included in the model.

increasing values of the variable should result in ever-decreasing point weights (and vice versa). If they do not, the scorecard will often be called into question because borrowers with seemingly high risk values of a particular variable may get better scores than borrowers with lower risk values. If the developer is using binned (categorical) rather than continuous variables, bins may be combined until a monotonic relationship with the outcome variable is obtained.[21]

SOURCES OF BIAS IN POINT WEIGHTS

When any regression model is developed, a number of factors can lead to what statisticians refer to as *bias* in the regression coefficients. Bias means that if we could observe the true and exact effect of each predictor on the outcome, it would not be what the regression coefficients tell us it is. A predictor variable could have a greater or a smaller effect than the coefficient indicates. Even worse, the predictor could affect the outcome variable in the opposite direction from what the model indicates, or a variable that may not appear predictive could be excluded when it actually is predictive.

Since scorecard point weights are transformations of the regression coefficients, this bias would be present in the point weights as well, so that their values would not represent the true relationship between the predictor variable and the outcome variable.

Even if the scorecard builder does everything by the book, from properly handling the data to testing all available variables for predictiveness, there may still be bias. There is probably some bias in all regression models and scorecards. Our goal is to minimize the bias so that the scorecard will provide the most accurate predictions possible.

Some of the most significant sources of bias in building scorecards are:

- Bias from omitting important predictive variables from the score model.

- Bias due to errors in predictor variables.

- Sample selection bias.

Omitted-variables bias occurs when an important predictor is left out of the regression model. Because many of the variables we use to build scoring models are correlated with one another, excluding one or more variables that actually do affect the loan's outcome can have an effect on

---

[21] Occasionally we may let variables into the model even if their effect on the outcome variables is non-monotonic, but this is likely to be rare.

the coefficients of the predictors that *are* incorporated into the model. In leaving an important variable out, we may find that the coefficients for other variables are biased or some highly predictive variables may not appear predictive at all.

Why would we leave an important variable out? First, as happens all the time, we may not be able to get the data we need on certain variables. The data available on a particular variable may be so poor (numerous missing values or data errors) that we cannot enter it into the regression model. Or there may be no data at all for a variable that we wish we could observe (such as a mortgage borrower's likelihood of divorcing, which is probably correlated with default). Sometimes, we may know that variables are important but they cannot be used for operational reasons.

Often, too, we may not even recognize that a variable *is* important. Perhaps a set of borrowers within a geographic region defaulted because a local plant closed. We are unlikely to know this. Those defaults may, at least in part, be attributed to some other characteristic shared by the borrowers affected by the plant closing, and the coefficient of that other variable may be biased as a result.

What can we do about omitted-variables bias?

First, before model development starts modelers should always ask business experts to identify what they believe to be the most predictive variables. Then they should test all those thoroughly. No matter how scarce the data for a certain variable believed to impact borrower behavior, we should make every effort to obtain data and test the variable because including it could significantly affect the point weights of other variables in the model.

Second, we may occasionally include a variable in the regression model as a control variable to attempt to eliminate bias. A control variable is used as a predictor in the regression model but does not get implemented as a characteristic in the scorecard itself. Its purpose is to eliminate bias in other coefficients. For example, if we did indeed know that a set of borrowers defaulted because of a local plant closing, an earthquake, or another cataclysmic event, we could include control variables in the regression model to account for it and hopefully avoid the bias that might otherwise result.[22]

Changing economic conditions during the period over which we observe performance may have a big impact on borrower behavior and thus on loan performance. During the late 1990s and up through 2002, property

---

[22] The control variable would be an indicator equal to 1 for a loan to one of the borrowers affected by the plant closing and 0 for other loans.

values increased rapidly in many parts of the United States. This appears to have had a favorable effect on mortgage default rates, which otherwise could have been much greater.

The borrower's loan-to-value (LTV) ratio at origination is a common and important variable in most mortgage loan scorecards. Furthermore, a build-up in equity is likely to be more beneficial to high-LTV borrowers than to low-LTV borrowers because decreasing LTV from 95 percent to 85 percent lowers the likelihood of default more than decreasing it from 75 percent to 65 percent.[23] As a result, when property values are rising (which implies that LTVs are falling during the time we observe the performance of loans to classify them as good or bad), default rates of high-LTV loans decrease much more than default rates of low-LTV loans relative to what they would be if property values remained unchanged.

The effect of rapidly rising property values during the scorecard performance period would be to understate the deleterious effect that high LTVs have on loan performance. The opposite would be true in periods of falling property values.

Other economic factors, such as interest and unemployment rates, could affect borrower behavior as well. Economic variables might be included as control variables in scorecard models if they are believed to have a big impact on loan outcomes—this is not standard practice in scorecard building today but it is worth considering.[24]

The second source of possible bias in scorecard coefficients arises when one or more of the predictor variables is measured wrong. This can happen in a number of ways. Often, information collected from the applicant, such as monthly income or dollars of total assets, is used to develop scorecard characteristics like debt-to-income (DTI) ratio or the amount of assets in reserve. If the borrower does not give accurate information, or if the lender obtains different information from different borrowers, there is mismeasurement. Some lenders exclude self-reported items from score-

---

[23] See Chapter 8 for a chart showing how LTV ratios increase default rates at an increasing rate as we move from low to high LTVs.

[24] How to incorporate economic effects into logistic regression models where a set outcome period is used is not simple, because the influence of economic variables on loan performance varies over time. Perhaps a more promising method would be to use a different type of regression model called a *survival* model (also known as a *duration* or a *hazard* model) and include economic variables as time-varying covariates whose values can change over the loan's performance period. For an example of a scoring model built using this method, see Stepanova, Maria, and Lyn C. Thomas. (2001). "PHAB Scores: Proportional Hazards Analysis Behavior Scores." Paper presented at the Credit Scoring & Credit Control VII conference, University of Edinburgh, September 2001.

cards, believing that the variables can be so fraught with error that they are too unreliable.

The reliability of the data depends both on the method used to collect the information and on the type of documentation, if any, used to evaluate its veracity. These variables can be quite predictive, making scorecards more powerful when data is collected in a way that ensures reliability. (Credit bureau data is generally thought to be very accurate, but it too can be unreliable if lenders change the way they report data or fail to report to the credit bureaus promptly.)

Carefully cleaning the model development sample data may help avoid this type of bias. Data is cleaned by looking at distributions of variables and determining how to deal with outliers, data errors, and missing values. Say we are working with the variable DTI and see that although most values lie within the range of 10 to 50 percent, we have a few values above 80 or even 100 percent. Are these legitimate values? How should they be handled? Options include capping the variable and substituting the highest "legitimate" value for the outliers or handling them with whatever technique is chosen to deal with missing values.

Sample selection bias arises when a regression model is built using a subset of a population that is not entirely representative of the full population. In the scorecard context, lenders need to use application scorecards to make decisions about *all* applicants that come to them. Loan performance can only be observed for applicants whose loans have been *booked,* so it is only these applicants that can be classified as good or bad. What is missing is the population of applicants who were rejected. Bias in the model coefficients will occur to the extent that the relationship between the risk characteristics and the outcome variable would be different for these rejected applicants than it is for the booked population.

There can be different degrees of sample selection bias. At the extreme, certain values of some risk characteristics may not be represented at all within the booked population. For example, say a lender has carefully screened out applicants with two or more derogatory credit accounts on a credit report so that no booked account has more than a single derogatory credit. In this case that characteristic has been truncated and a scorecard based on the booked accounts would not properly evaluate the risk of an applicant with more than one derogatory account. Unless the lender continued to impose the same derogatory credit screen going forward, it would subject itself to additional risk by using this scorecard because it could not properly penalize applicants with two or more bad credits.

Sample selection bias can occur even when a characteristic has not been completely truncated but has been used in a scorecard or policy screen in the past. Perhaps credit policy does not reject applicants with two or more derogatory credit accounts outright, but penalizes them or requires them to pass additional policy criteria even if they score above cutoff. These applicants would need other very favorable characteristics to be accepted. If that is true, these borrowers would likely be better than typical applicants with numerous bad credits due to the compensating factors or they would not have been approved. As a result, the bad rate for such borrowers might be lower than that of the general population of applicants with the same number of derogatory credits and a scorecard developed on the booked accounts would not accurately assess the risk of the general population.[25]

Sample selection bias tends to be more pronounced when the acceptance rate is low. As the percentage of applicants booked decreases, it becomes less likely that the booked accounts will contain a representative sample of applicants with attributes that indicate high risk.

Much has been made about scorecard sample selection bias and several techniques have been used to attempt to eliminate it. These techniques are known as *reject inference* because they generally attempt to infer what the performance of the rejected applicants would have been, based on other available data, and then use that information in scorecard development.

Some lenders have actually made loans to borrowers they would typically reject in order to obtain the needed performance data on future rejects. However, the losses associated with lending to borrowers with high expected default rates make this a very expensive method of dealing with possible sample bias. It should only be used for lending products where the expected loss on default is relatively low.[26]

---

[25] If the other favorable characteristics required of borrowers in order to book them are also characteristics in the score, this bias would be minimized or eliminated. The regression model would presumably attribute the better performance to those characteristics and penalize the derogatory characteristic appropriately.

[26] To minimize the losses associated with this booking strategy, lenders often treat accepted score rejects differently from other accepted applicants. The amount of credit extended is usually held to the minimum, and often these accounts are flagged for an aggressive collection strategy. While the special treatment can mitigate losses on high-risk accounts, it can also introduce a bias in the very performance in which we are interested. Stipulation of a very low credit amount may result in only the worst of the group accepting the offer, while the same low credit amount plus an aggressive collection strategy may cause the booked accounts to perform better than they would with a higher credit amount and normal collection strategy. Yet even with these considerations this method of determining the performance of normally rejected applicants probably has fewer drawbacks than other methods.

Recently, it has become increasingly common to obtain data from the credit bureau on the rejected population to see how they performed on other accounts that came into existence after they were turned down by the lender building the scorecard.[27] In the most straightforward case, if a borrower was rejected for an auto loan by Lender One, only to have the loan funded for the same vehicle on the same day by Lender Two, Lender One might reasonably assume its experience with the borrower would have been the same as Lender Two's. In that case, Lender One would include this borrower in its development sample, coded as a good or bad depending on his performance with Lender Two.

This approach suffers from at least two drawbacks. First, unless the second loan was made immediately after the first loan and on the same terms, it may be unreasonable to assume the outcome of the first loan would have been the same as the outcome of the second. If the second loan were made a week later and collateralized by a different vehicle, the outcome could differ because the performance of auto loans is likely to depend at least in part on how the collateral holds up over time.[28] Or if the second loan were made at a rate 3 percent higher than the rate at which the first lender would have funded it, performance could be different due to the higher payment.

It is also true that even if the performance of the borrower on the second loan does reflect likely performance with the first lender, a portion of the population is still missing—those who did not receive loans from *any* lender—so this approach is unlikely to solve all our sample selection problems either. Nonetheless, thoughtful analysis of potential surrogate performance definitions based on credit bureau records can minimize, though not eliminate, the uncertainties associated with this method.

Instead of obtaining the actual performance on a set of what normally would be rejected loans or using a surrogate for that performance based on other credit accounts, other techniques for dealing with sample selection bias use statistical methods. Two such methods are the *augmentation* and the *extrapolation* methods.

With the augmentation method, only booked loans are included in the score development sample but each is weighted by the inverse of its probability of being accepted. This probability is derived by building a second

---

[27] Lenders contemplating this method should consult their credit bureau and internal counsel about potential legal issues regarding the purchase of such data.

[28] For example, a borrower may be less likely to continue to make payments on a loan for a vehicle that breaks down if he has little or no money to get it back into operating condition.

logistic regression model that includes both accepted and rejected loans, but instead of predicting which loans will be good or bad, it predicts whether an applicant will be approved or rejected. The reciprocal of the probability derived from this regression model is used as a weight in the credit-scoring model. In this way the booked loans with a high probability of rejection (which presumably are more like those of actual rejects) are given more weight when the credit-scoring model is built.

The extrapolation method actually uses the rejected loans as part of the development sample for the credit-scoring model. Typically a preliminary regression is estimated using only the booked loans (for which the outcome is known), the rejects are scored with that model, and the model is used to derive a good and bad probability for each. Finally, the regression is estimated again, this time using both booked accounts and rejected applicants. Rejects are duplicated and then weighted based on their estimated bad rate. If, for example, a rejected loan has a 40 percent probability of being bad, it is included as a bad loan with a weight of 0.4 and as a good loan with a weight of 0.6. The theory is that this second model that includes rejects and their inferred performance as part of the development sample should be free of sample selection bias.

There have been several academic studies on sample selection bias in recent years. Ross[29] concludes that score models suffer from only minimal selection bias if the models include variables that are used to approve or deny applications—that is, if the predictor variables included in the score-card are the same ones underwriters typically review when deciding whether to accept an application, sample selection bias should not be a big problem. Another academic study that included data on loans that normally would be rejected concluded, "The basic results suggest empirically that there is only modest scope for model improvement in considering the behavior of rejected applicants."[30] In sum, although there is a theoretical argument that the coefficients of a model estimated on booked loans alone may suffer from bias, there is little compelling evidence on how significant the bias is, or what is the best technique for dealing with it.

Which of the three bias issues described is the most serious or deserving of our attention is likely to vary case by case. The best we can do is to deal with those that can be dealt with and recognize that we may have to

[29] Ross, Stephen. (2000). "Mortgage Lending, Sample Selection and Default." *Real Estate Economics,* 28 (4): 581-621.

[30] Banasik, John, Jonathan Crook, and Lyn Thomas. (2001). "Sample Selection Bias in Credit Scoring Models." Paper presented at the Credit Risk Modeling and Decisioning Conference, May 2002, Federal Reserve Bank of Philadelphia.

live with some degree of scorecard bias. Even though the scorecard point weights may not capture the exact relationship between the predictor variables and the outcome variable, scorecards have proven themselves over and over again as reliable predictors. Even with some bias, we are almost always better off relying on a scorecard to evaluate applicants than making lending decisions on a purely subjective basis.

Chapter 5
VARIABLE ANALYSIS AND REDUCTION

Elizabeth Mays
Director of Retail Risk Modeling and Analytics
Bank One
Jean Yuan
Director of Prepayment Modeling
CitiMortgage's Mortgage Analytics

INTRODUCTION

In this chapter we discuss two important steps in scorecard development: variable analysis and variable reduction. Variable analysis investigates the relationship between the variables we want to test for predictive ability and the outcome variable we hope to predict. Variable reduction narrows a large number of variables that are candidates for inclusion in the scorecard to a smaller number that can be more easily analyzed with the multivariate statistical techniques used to build scorecards. Not only do we want a smaller number of variables, we want to retain only those that are most predictive of the outcome variable.

A typical scorecard contains eight to 15 predictive variables. Often, however, a scorecard developer must test dozens—even hundreds—of possible variables to determine which are most predictive. In this chapter, we discuss methods for determining if variables are promising candidates for the scorecard. First we describe three statistics commonly used to gauge the predictive ability of variables. Then we generate these statistics and compare them to each other using data from an actual scorecard development project. Finally, we demonstrate a technique for eliminating redundant variables to narrow the possible predictors down to a smaller set more easily managed in building the scorecard.

In the variable analysis section we discuss a hazard to be aware of when analyzing the predictive ability of a single variable based simply on its relationship to the outcome variable ("bivariate" analysis) rather than analyzing simultaneously the effect of all variables impacting the outcome (multivariate analysis): Sometimes a variable that does not appear predictive of the outcome based on bivariate analysis turns out nonetheless to be an important predictor in the scorecard. Any variable that business experts consider predictive should be thoroughly tested in the scorecard even if initial analysis indicates that the variable is not related to the outcome variable. Often, the relationship is masked by correlation with other variables, and the true predictive ability of the variable is only revealed when it is included in the regression model with other predictors.

Although the statistics discussed in this chapter are useful in building models, risk management staff may also find them valuable for portfolio analysis, because they provide measures of the association between risk characteristics and loan performance. In addition, if risk staff understand the calculation and meaning of the statistics, they can contribute more to discussions with developers when new score models are being built.

VARIABLE ANALYSIS

The three statistics that are commonly used to evaluate the relationship between candidate predictive variables and the outcome variable are (1) the chi-squared statistic, (2) the information value, and (3) the Spearman rank-order correlation statistic.

In Table 5.1 we list each of these statistics for 23 variables from a scorecard development project. Most such projects involve many more variables than this, but 23 is adequate for purposes of illustration. Table 5.1 also lists the ranking accorded each variable based on its association to the outcome variable. Note that the three statistics do not rank variables the same. For example, the information value ranks Variable 4, 4th while the chi-squared statistic ranks it 14th.

We have plotted these rankings in Figure 5.1 to illustrate how they differ for the three statistics. Note that while rankings for the chi-squared statistic and Spearman correlation are generally similar (with a couple of exceptions), the ranking based on information value often differs from both. Reasons for differences in rankings among the statistics are discussed throughout this section.

TABLE 5.1 EVALUATING PREDICTIVE VARIABLE ASSOCIATION WITH THE OUTCOME VARIABLE

Variable	Information Value	Rank by Information Value	Score Chi-Squared Statistic	Rank by Score Statistic	Spearman Correlation	Rank by Spearman Correlation	Cluster
Var1	1.742	1	4,421	3	-0.114	2	1
Var2	1.669	2	4,984	2	-0.112	3	1
Var3	1.022	3	1,436	8	0.085	5	9
Var4	0.982	4	219	13	-0.071	7	5
Log Var4	0.982	4	1,907	4	-0.071	7	5
Var5	0.681	6	1,884	6	0.074	6	4
Var6	0.665	7	1,640	7	0.070	9	4
Var7	0.545	8	5,999	1	0.157	1	4
Var8	0.499	9	540	10	-0.063	10	7
Var9	0.332	10	1,894	5	0.088	4	9
Var10	0.288	11	825	9	-0.058	11	6
Var11	0.254	12	134	16	0.036	14	2
Var12	0.247	13	441	12	0.043	13	3
Var13	0.182	14	482	11	-0.045	12	7
Var14	0.170	15	110	17	0.034	15	2
Var15	0.083	16	174	14	-0.027	16	3
Var16	0.081	17	144	15	-0.024	17	3
Var17	0.042	18	74	18	-0.017	18	7
Var18	0.042	19	61	19	-0.016	19	6
Var19	0.024	20	38	21	-0.012	21	6
Var20	0.020	21	41	20	-0.013	20	10
Var21	0.002	22	4	22	-0.004	22	3
Var22	0.001	23	3	23	-0.004	23	8
Var23	0.001	23	1	24	0.002	24	8

FIGURE 5.1. COMPARISON OF RANKING OF VARIABLES BY INFORMATION VALUE, CHI-SQUARE, AND SPEARMAN CORRELATION

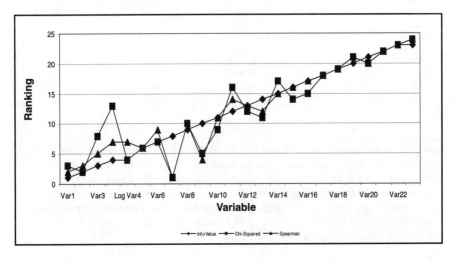

THE CHI-SQUARED STATISTIC

The chi-squared statistic tests for a linear association between a variable and the frequency with which loans have a bad outcome (go 90 days past due in this case) rather than a good outcome. In her *Data Mining Cookbook,* Rud recommends using the SAS PROC LOGISTIC procedure to generate chi-squared statistics for all possible predictive variables.[1] Rud recommends that variables with a p-value of greater than 0.5 be eliminated from further analysis. Thus, the variable set would be reduced by excluding such variables from the multivariate analysis that would follow. We show an excerpt from the SAS output from this method in Table 5.2 using the chi-squared statistics from Table 5.1. Since we have no variables with P values greater than 0.5 (Pr > ChiSq in Table 5.2), all variables would be retained under this criterion (setting a different criterion is always an option). We would be inclined to retain only variables with P values less than 0.3; in this particular data set we would still retain all 24 variables.

TABLE 5.2 CHI-SQUARED STATISTICS FROM THE SAS OUTPUT

Effect	DF	Score Chi-Square	Pr > ChiSq
Var1	1	4420.7097	<.0001
Var2	1	4984.2975	<.0001
Var3	1	1436.3827	<.0001
Var4	1	219.2783	<.0001
Log Var4	1	1906.8430	<.0001
Var5	1	1883.9817	<.0001
Var6	1	1640.1053	<.0001
Var7	1	5998.7338	<.0001
Var8	1	539.8235	<.0001
Var9	1	1893.6070	<.0001
Var10	1	824.6123	<.0001
Var11	1	133.8548	<.0001
Var12	1	441.1136	<.0001
Var13	1	482.1880	<.0001
Var14	1	110.4727	<.0001
Var15	1	173.8566	<.0001
Var16	1	143.6354	<.0001
Var17	1	73.8837	<.0001
Var18	1	61.4868	<.0001
Var19	1	37.8431	<.0001
Var20	1	41.0725	<.0001
Var21	1	3.9143	0.0479
Var22	1	3.0990	0.0783
Var23	1	1.3818	0.2398

[1] Rud, Olivia Par. (2001). *Data Mining Cookbook.* New York: John Wiley & Sons, p. 77. Choosing the options "selection = stepwise maxsep = 1" and "details" will produce chi-squared statistics for a set of predictive variables without actually having to run the logistic regression, but it is important to be careful if one or more of the predictive variables have missing values, because SAS regression procedures throw out such observations. Variables with many missing values should be run through the procedure by themselves. All other variables can be run through the procedure together.

Besides being an easy way to generate chi-squared statistics, the PROC LOGISTIC procedure produces chi-squared statistics that can be compared across variables for insight into which are most closely associated with the outcome variable.[2] Using this method, numerous logistic regressions are run, each using only a single predictive variable. The chi-squared statistic printed for each variable is the Score Chi-Square. It is a test that the regression parameter for the variable in question is different from zero.[3] This statistic lets us compare predictive variables and learn which are most closely associated with the outcome variable. Note that the value of the chi-squared statistic depends in part on the population bad rate, the number of loans in the sample experiencing the event. Thus, while we may compare the chi-squared statistic across variables for a given model and data set, we should not compare their values for different models or data sets.

Note that this chi-squared statistic is a test for a *linear* association between the candidate predictive variable and the log-odds of the outcome variable. If there is a nonlinear relationship, the chi-square may lead us to believe the variables are not associated when in fact they are—though not in a linear relationship. As an example, we have included a variable that we know has a nonlinear relationship to the outcome variable. Variable 4 has a Score Chi-Square of 219 in the logistic regression output.

A plot of the variable against the log of the odds of being bad within certain ranges showed a shape that indicated that a log transformation of Variable 4 would produce a linear relationship to the log odds of the outcome variable. After taking the log of Variable 4, the chi-square increases to 1,907. Thus the log of Variable 4 is likely to be highly predictive in our scorecard, yet the chi-squared statistic might lead us to underestimate its importance. Alternatively, the variable could be cut up into "bins" (a set of categorical variables) to capture this nonlinear effect.

SPEARMAN RANK-ORDER CORRELATION

The Spearman correlation statistic measures the correlation between the *rankings* of the predictive variable and the outcome variable. That is, instead of looking at the association between the actual values of the predictive and the binary outcome variables, in this calculation the rank assigned to each value of the predictive variable replaces the actual value.

---

[2] We are looking at the relationship between the log of the odds of being bad and the outcome variable because we will use logistic regression to build the scorecard. Logistic regression specifies a linear relationship between the predictive variables and the log of the odds of a bad outcome.

[3] In the econometrics literature this statistic is known as the Lagrange Multiplier Test.

The SAS Institute's Logistic Regression Modeling Course Notes recommend using this correlation statistic for bivariate analysis because it is less sensitive to outliers and nonlinear relationships between outcome and the input variables than some other statistics.[4] Though the Spearman correlation, unlike the chi-squared statistic, does not require that a variable have a *linear* relationship to the outcome variable in order to detect the relationship, the relationship must be *monotonic*—that is, increasing values of a variable must generally be associated with a higher incidence of being bad (or vice versa) in order for the Spearman correlation to be large.

Because it is looking only for a monotonic, not a linear, relationship, the Spearman correlation ranks Variable 3 as having the 5th strongest relationship to the outcome variable, while the chi-square ranks it 8th. If these two statistics give different indications of the strength of the variable, it is probably because the variable does have a monotonic relationship to the outcome, though one that is not linear, and a variable transformation may be in order. Also note that Variable 4 and the log of Variable 4 have the same Spearman correlation because a monotonic transformation (taking the log) does not change the ordering of the values, and that is what the Spearman correlation is concerned with.

An advantage of the Spearman correlation is that, unlike the chi-squared statistic and the information value, it shows the *direction* of the relationship of a predictive variable with the outcome variable. If the correlation is negative, it indicates that higher values of the predictive variable are associated with lower values of the outcome variable. We should always evaluate whether the effect of each variable on the outcome is consistent with our beliefs about how that variable *should* affect the outcome. Including the Spearman correlation in Table 5.1 permits us to do that without having to look at a cross-tabulation or log-odds plot for each variable.

INFORMATION VALUES

Information values for predictive variables range from 0 to about 3, with higher values indicating a stronger relationship with the outcome variable. The following formulae are used to calculate the information value where the *i* subscript refers to the ith grouping of values within a variable.

$$Info\_Value = \sum_i (\%G_i - \%B_i)WoE_i$$

---

[4] *Logistic Regression Modeling* Course Notes. (1999). Cary, NC: SAS Institute, p. 63.

where $$WoE = \ln(\# G_i / \# B_i) - \ln(\# G / \# B)$$

Table 5.3 shows how the information value is calculated for Variable 3.

TABLE 5.3 INFORMATION VALUE CALCULATIONS

1 Group	2 #Good	3 %Good	4 #Bad	5 %Bad	6 %G - %B	7 ln (#G/#B)	8 WoE	9 Info_Value
1	12,125	5.04%	31	1.3%	3.7%	6.0	1.35	0.050
2	12,112	5.03%	44	1.9%	3.2%	5.6	1.00	0.032
3	12,126	5.04%	30	1.3%	3.8%	6.0	1.38	0.052
4	12,118	5.03%	38	1.6%	3.4%	5.8	1.15	0.039
5	12,107	5.03%	49	2.1%	3.0%	5.5	0.89	0.026
6	12,091	5.02%	65	2.7%	2.3%	5.2	0.61	0.014
7	12,098	5.03%	59	2.5%	2.5%	5.3	0.71	0.018
8	12,084	5.02%	72	3.0%	2.0%	5.1	0.51	0.010
9	12,101	5.03%	55	2.3%	2.7%	5.4	0.78	0.021
10	12,044	5.00%	112	4.7%	0.3%	4.7	0.06	0.000
11	12,087	5.02%	69	2.9%	2.1%	5.2	0.55	0.012
12	12,085	5.02%	71	3.0%	2.0%	5.1	0.52	0.011
13	12,062	5.01%	94	4.0%	1.1%	4.9	0.24	0.003
14	12,105	5.03%	52	2.2%	2.8%	5.5	0.83	0.024
15	12,126	5.04%	30	1.3%	3.8%	6.0	1.38	0.052
16	12,125	5.04%	31	1.3%	3.7%	6.0	1.35	0.050
17	11,975	4.97%	181	7.6%	-2.6%	4.2	-0.43	0.011
18	11,959	4.97%	197	8.3%	-3.3%	4.1	-0.51	0.017
19	11,524	4.79%	632	26.6%	-21.8%	2.9	-1.71	0.374
20	11,691	4.86%	466	19.6%	-14.7%	3.2	-1.40	0.206
Total	**240,745**	**100%**	**2,378**	**100%**		**4.6**		**1.022**

Information values are calculated as follows:

- Rank the observations by the value of the predictive variable to be analyzed.

- Divide the observations into ranges with the same number of loans in each. Twenty ranges is typical.

- Take the log of the ratio of the number of goods to the number of bads for each group (column 7). This is the *log odds* for each group.

- From the log odds of each group, subtract the log odds of the population overall (4.6 in this case—see the bottom of column7). Each of these values is the *weight of evidence* (WoE—column 8) for each group. The more the log odds of a group differ from the log odds for all groups, the greater the absolute value of its WoE.

Finally, to get the information value for the characteristic:

- Calculate the percentages of good loans in each group (column 3) and bad loans in each group (column 5).

- Multiply the WoE for each by the difference between the good percentage and the bad percentage. This yields the attribute information value, which is always positive.

- Sum these values (column 9) to get the information value for the characteristic.

Generally, an information value of greater than 0.3 indicates that a variable has a large amount of "information" to help predict the outcome variable, although variables with information values as small as 0.01 should be retained for further testing and possible inclusion in the scorecard. An information value below 0.01 indicates that a variable has so little predictive ability, if any, that it should not be considered further unless there is a compelling business reason to do so.[5]

Let us examine Variable 7 to clarify how the information value deals with certain variables compared to the chi-squared statistic and the Spearman correlation statistic. The latter two statistics ranked Variable 7 (see Table 5.1) as having the strongest relationship to the outcome variable, but the information value ranks it 7th. Variable 7, a dichotomous (0/1) variable, indicates whether the loan was made under a particular loan program. Though the loans in this program represent less than 2 percent of the lender's portfolio, they have gone bad at a much higher rate than loans in any of the other programs.

Unlike the chi-squared statistic and the Spearman correlation, the information value gives little weight to variables like Variable 7, which provides information for only a small portion of the sample. Variable 7 has a value of 1 for only 2 percent of the portfolio and 0 otherwise, so even if the bad rate is very high when Variable 7 is 1 and low when it is 0, the information value will suggest that it is not a very promising variable for inclusion in the scorecard.

Our general experience has been that variables that have a high chi-square but do not vary widely over the sample typically do little to increase the rank-ordering ability of scorecards, but they usually are found to be sta-

---

[5] One problem is that information value measures all the information in a sample and cannot distinguish between real information and sample "noise." Sometimes a variable must be rebinned to eliminate sample noise in order to get a more accurate measurement of true information value.

tistically significant in the regression model. Further, they are likely to considerably enhance our ability to predict the bad rate for certain segments of the population, in this case for loans in this particular loan program. Though they generally do not increase statistics like the KS statistic, if the model is to be used not just for rank-ordering loans but to predict the rate of delinquency or default, such variables can be essential—especially where score models are being used to calculate risk-based pricing adjusters for various types of borrowers or portfolio segments and are also used to forecast portfolio losses at the loan level.

HOW THE STATISTICS COMPARE

In the preceding examples, each of the three statistics failed to identify something about the predictive variables that may be important to us.

Table 5.4 summarizes the discussion on how the three statistics we have used in the bivariate analysis compare. Each has its own strengths and weaknesses; we believe that bivariate analysis is most informative when these statistics are used in combination in a table like Table 5.1.

TABLE 5.4. HOW THE STATISTICS COMPARE

	What it Does	Pros	Cons
Score Chi-Squared Statistic	Tests for a linear relationship between input variable and log odds of the outcome variable.	Does not penalize variables whose values do not vary widely within the sample.	Does not show direction of relationship with outcome.
Information Value	Tests for any relationship between the input variable and the log odds of the outcome variable.	Penalizes variables whose values do not vary widely within the sample.	Does not show the direction of any relationship with the outcome variable.
Spearman Correlation	Tests for a monotonic relationship between the input and outcome variables.	Does not penalize variables whose values do not vary widely within the sample.	Shows the direction of any relationship with the outcome variable.

A WORD OF CAUTION

Although bivariate analysis can offer much insight into the predictive ability of variables and is an important first step in scorecard development, it should be done with caution. Evaluating the association between a possible predictor and the outcome variable without taking into account the influence of *other* variables can sometimes be misleading.

Consider the case of Variable 22, which represents a specific type of loan that the lender has long thought poses a high risk of default. The lender has adhered to policies designed to limit the risk of this type of lending, the major one being to limit LTV ratios to less than 80 percent to control losses in the event of default.

When Variable 22 is analyzed using the entire loan sample, as in Table 5.1, the Spearman correlation indicates that it has an inverse relationship to the outcome variable; that is, this type of loan is more often associated with a good outcome than other products. Recognizing that the good outcome may be the result not of the type of product but rather of the low LTVs, we restricted our sample to loans with LTVs below 80, and recalculated the statistics in Table 5.1. Not only does the information value increase from 0.001 to 0.002, but also the chi-squared statistic increases from 3 to 12. The most startling result, however, is that the Spearman correlation actually switches sign, from -0.004 on the full sample to 0.008 on the low-LTV sample. When we analyze the variable in a multivariate framework by putting it into the regression model with all other predictors (including LTV) to find the likelihood of a bad outcome, its relationship to the outcome variable is indeed positive.

Another potential problem with bivariate analysis arises when the development data set contains loans with differing outcome periods. In the section on determining the performance window in Chapter 4, we described a case where a lenders' LTV ratios were increasing over time, so that loans with high LTVs were observed for a shorter time than loans with lower LTVs. We recommended that a variable representing the length of time each loan has been on the books be incorporated into the model as a control. This same problem can exist for bivariate analysis, but unfortunately the fix is not so easy. If this is a problem, the only suggestion we can make would be to divide the data into two or more groups by age, then calculate the bivariate statistics on each set. (This, of course, assumes there is sufficient data to get meaningful results within each age category.)

In sum, bivariate analysis can lead us astray in certain cases if proper care is not taken. The best approach is always to further analyze *any* variable whose statistics run counter to expectations. On further analysis we often find that the relationship we expected between predictors and the outcome is borne out if we account for the influence of other variables that are correlated with the predictor.

VARIABLE REDUCTION

After we have analyzed all possible variables and eliminated those that appear to have no predictive ability (with exceptions as already noted), we can reduce the number of candidate variables further by eliminating those with largely redundant information. It is important to do this because including redundant variables in the multivariate analysis can:

- Destabilize the parameter estimates.

- Increase the risk of overfitting the model.

- Confound interpretation of the coefficients.

- Increase computation time.[6]

Variable redundancy occurs when two or more variables that are predictive of the outcome variable are so correlated with each other that one adds no predictive ability beyond that contained in the other. This happens often with credit bureau variables that have similar but not identical definitions.

The SAS procedure PROC VARCLUS for clustering variables can be used to tell if groups of variables among the total set of possible predictors are highly related. The clustering technique divides variables up into smaller clusters that are "as correlated as possible among themselves and as uncorrelated as possible with variables in other clusters."[7] Table 5.5 (page 102) is an excerpt from the PROC VARCLUS procedure.

It is possible to set the number of clusters to be formed by the procedure. For Table 5.5, we ran the procedure using 10 clusters. The number would be larger when there are more variables in the entire set of possible predictors.

The first column shows how well each individual variable correlates with the cluster of which it is a member. The second column shows how each variable correlates with the cluster with which it is most closely related. The third column, 1-R^2 Ratio, has 1 minus the R^2 of the variable's own cluster in the numerator and 1 minus the R^2 of the next closest cluster in the denominator. Thus, the higher a variable's R^2 is with its own cluster and the lower the R^2 is with the next closest cluster, the smaller the ratio will be, making the variable a more likely candidate for retention.

---

[6] *Logistic Regression Modeling,* Course Notes. (1999). Cary, NC: SAS Institute, p. 53.
[7] Ibid., p. 56.

TABLE 5.5 CLUSTER SUMMARY FOR 10 CLUSTERS

R-squared with

Cluster	Variable	Own Cluster	Next Closest	$1-R^2$ Ratio
Cluster 1	VAR1	0.8799	0.0511	0.1265
	VAR2	0.8799	0.0641	0.1283
Cluster 2	VAR12	0.8767	0.0684	0.1324
	VAR15	0.8767	0.0529	0.1302
Cluster 3	VAR13	0.3151	0.3005	0.9790
	VAR17	0.4184	0.0512	0.6130
	VAR16	0.2994	0.0940	0.7733
	VAR22	0.2809	0.0035	0.7217
Cluster 4	VAR8	0.4392	0.0284	0.5771
	VAR7	0.5364	0.0317	0.4788
	VAR6	0.5194	0.0391	0.5002
Cluster 5	VAR4	0.8493	0.1408	0.1754
	LOG VAR4	0.8493	0.0324	0.1558
Cluster 6	VAR19	0.3806	0.0132	0.6277
	VAR11	0.3852	0.1065	0.6881
	VAR20	0.3781	0.1635	0.7434
Cluster 7	VAR14	0.3860	0.0178	0.6251
	VAR18	0.3959	0.1764	0.7335
	VAR9	0.5012	0.1948	0.6195
Cluster 8	VAR23	0.5577	0.0179	0.4503
	VAR24	0.5577	0.0313	0.4566
Cluster 9	VAR3	0.5885	0.0867	0.4506
	VAR10	0.5885	0.0492	0.4328
Cluster 10	VAR21	1.0000	0.0588	0.0000

Once the clusters are specified, the idea is to select a single variable to represent that cluster. The clustering procedure looks only at the relationship among the possible predictive variables—not their relationship to the outcome variable—so the variable selected to represent the cluster should be as predictive of the outcome variable as possible. That is why variable analysis and variable reduction must go hand in hand. To choose which variables to retain, we need to see which variables are clustered together, then go back to Table 5.1 to see which appear to be most predictive of the outcome variable.

Cluster 7 contains three variables: 14, 18, and 9. Variable 9 is most highly correlated with its own cluster but is also most highly correlated with the next closest cluster. The "own cluster" correlation is so much higher, however, that the $1\text{-}R^2$ ratio is the lowest of the three variables, making Variable 9 the best candidate from the perspective of the VARCLUS analysis.

Fortunately, upon examining Table 5.1 we see that Variable 9 is also the most highly associated with the outcome variable according to all three measures. This makes it easy to decide to retain Variable 9 and eliminate the other two. When the decision is not so clear-cut, it is advisable to err on the side of leaving in too many variables rather than too few for the next step in building the scorecard.

SUMMARY

Bivariate analysis and variable clustering can create useful efficiencies in the scorecard building process by helping us pare an unwieldy number of variables down to a more manageable size. We have pointed out the advantages and disadvantages of three statistics commonly used for bivariate analysis. It is probably most beneficial to generate all three and compare the results. The comparison can sometimes provide insights into predictive variables that no single bivariate statistic can give.

Variable clustering can help developers eliminate redundant variables, further narrowing the field of possible predictors and streamlining the scorecard estimation step.

An important message of this chapter, however, should be that knowing the variables we are working with and the business for which we are building the scorecard should always take precedence over any "rules" of scorecard building. Any variable that experts in the business consider important in explaining the outcome variable should be retained for further analysis no matter what these statistics and procedures tell us. It may be that the data for a particular variable have been corrupted but can be fixed, or that the variable is predictive of the outcome when certain other conditions are true. If either is possible, the variables should be retained for detailed testing in the next stage of scorecard building.

Chapter 6
SCORECARD PERFORMANCE MEASURES

Elizabeth Mays
Director of Retail Risk Modeling and Analytics
Bank One

INTRODUCTION

The statistics described in this chapter may be used to evaluate scorecards either during scorecard development or in validation of existing scorecards.

Used during development, they indicate the scorecard's ability to perform the tasks it is intended to perform and permit comparisons of different model specifications, pointing up the strength of the scorecard when it contains one set of characteristics rather than another set.

These measures also serve as model validation tools and can augment or be incorporated into scorecard tracking reports.

When estimating the regression models that form the bases for scorecards, standard practice is to use one data set to develop the model and a different one to validate it. Model developers should calculate the measures described in this chapter for both samples. If the measures deteriorate considerably when generated on the validation sample, that suggests that the scorecard may not perform well if implemented.[1]

In what follows, we divide the performance measures into three groups (1) separation statistics, (2) ranking statistics, and (3) prediction-error statistics. The meaning of these terms will become clear as we discuss each.

SEPARATION STATISTICS

What we expect of a scorecard is that it will assign different scores to loans that have an undesirable outcome than to those that have a desirable outcome. For credit scorecards, we want to assign lower scores to loans that eventually go seriously delinquent or default than to loans that do not. Overall, bad loans should have lower scores than good loans.

Figure 6.1 shows the score frequency distribution for a group of bad loans (on the left) and group of good loans. Clearly, the distribution for the bad loans is centered over a lower scoring range than the good loans. The further apart these two distributions are, the more successful our scorecard has been in distinguishing bad loans from good. In fact, if a scorecard did a perfect job, there would be no overlap at all in the distributions—they would be side by side. Conversely, a scorecard doing a poor job would not be able to distinguish between the two groups of loans at all. At the extreme, the two distributions would lie on top of one another.

When people talk about how well a scorecard "separates," this is exactly what they are talking about—separating the distributions of good and bad loans. There are two popular statistics (1) the divergence statistic and (2) the KS statistic, that measure how well a scorecard separates good and bad distributions.[2]

---

[1] As discussed in Chapter 4, there are two types of validation samples (1) a holdout sample and (2) an out-of-time sample. Say we choose to use for building the model loans originated during 1999 and look at how they performed for 18 months to determine if a loan meets the bad definition. A holdout sample could be formed by holding out a set of loans from among the 1999 originations and not using them in scorecard development. We could then validate the scorecard on the loans that were held out to ascertain if the model holds up well on loans independent of the development sample. An out-of-time sample would be a set of loans originated in a period other than 1999. It could be before or after. An out-of-time validation sample is generally preferred because it is viewed as a higher hurdle for the scorecard to achieve good validation statistics on a sample originated in a different time period. If sufficient data is available, the score might be validated on both a holdout *and* an out-of-time sample.

[2] The KS statistic is named for two Russian statisticians, Kolmogorov and Smirnov.

FIGURE 6.1 FREQUENCY DISTRIBUTION OF GOODS AND BADS

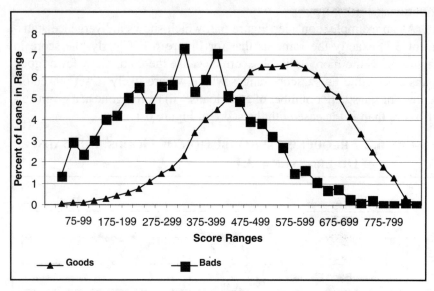

DIVERGENCE STATISTIC

The divergence statistic is very straightforward. It is simply the square of the difference of the mean of the goods and the mean of the bads, divided by the average variance of the score distributions.

The formula for the divergence statistic is:

$$D^2 = \text{(mean score of goods - mean score of bads)}^2 / \sigma^2$$

where $\sigma^2 = (\sigma^2_G + \sigma^2_B)/2.$

The square of the difference in the means is divided by the average variance. For distributions that are very spread out, there must be a large difference in their means before the distributions are said to be different.

The divergence statistic value is closely related to the information value statistic described in Chapter 5, where we discussed it as a statistic that could be used to evaluate the predictiveness of individual scorecard characteristics. To evaluate separation ability, either the information value or the divergence statistic may be calculated for any individual predictive variable or for the score itself. For a continuous predictive variable, divergence and information value are equal if the scores of the good loans and the bad loans are normally distributed and have equal variances.

Given its simplicity and ease of interpretation, divergence is probably a good statistic to report. One criticism can be made of it, however: It does not capture all the important information about the *shape* of the distributions.

As an example, consider Figure 6.2, which shows a divergence statistic of 3.1, exactly the same as that for Figure 6.1. Clearly, the score in Figure 6.2 is the more desirable score, because there are many fewer good loans among the lower score ranges where we are likely to set our cutoff score. Thus, a smaller number of good loans will be foregone at a given cutoff score than is the case with the score in Figure 6.1.

FIGURE 6.2 FREQUENCY DISTRIBUTION OF GOODS AND BADS: DIVERGENCE = 3.1

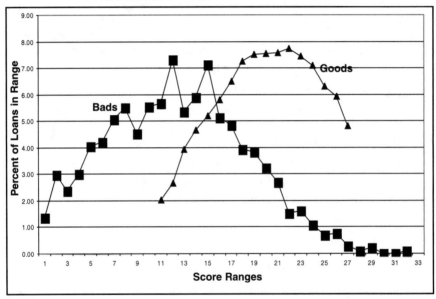

It is important to recognize that the statistics we use to evaluate scorecards are simply summary measures of some aspect of the difference between the good and the bad distributions. They do not—and cannot—tell us all we need to know about how well a scorecard is doing its job. If we rely on summary statistics alone there may be cases where we will be misled. To avoid this, in addition to calculating the statistics described here, we should also plot good and bad score frequency distributions and observe where the goods and the bads are found. It is a good practice always to generate plots of these distributions when reporting any scoring statistics.

THE KS STATISTIC

The KS statistic is also very easy to understand and to calculate. It is the maximum difference between the cumulative percent good distribution and the cumulative percent bad distribution. To see how to calculate the KS, look at Table 6.1, which is typical of the types of tables people produce when building or validating a scorecard. Loans are ranked from low to high by score, then separated into a number of score ranges. The first column lists the score range.

TABLE 6.1 EXAMPLE OF GOOD/BAD TABLE AND CALCULATION OF THE KS STATISTIC

1 Score Range	2 Interval Goods	3 Interval Bads	4 Good/ Bad Odds	5 Bad Rate	6 Cum Goods	7 Cum Bads	8 Cum Good%	9 Cum Bad%	10 Cum Total%	11 Separa- tion
0-20	5	5	1	50.0	5	5	0.0	0.9	0.02	0.9
21-40	10	5	2	33.3	15	10	0.0	1.8	0.05	1.8
41-60	9	4	2	30.8	24	14	0.1	2.6	0.08	2.5
61-80	37	18	2	32.7	61	32	0.1	5.8	0.19	5.7
81-100	24	7	3	22.6	85	39	0.2	7.1	0.26	6.9
101-120	51	19	3	27.1	136	58	0.3	10.6	0.40	10.3
121-140	53	15	4	22.1	189	73	0.4	13.3	0.55	12.9
141-160	90	19	5	17.4	279	92	0.6	16.8	0.77	16.2
161-180	118	16	7	11.9	397	108	0.8	19.7	1.05	18.9
181-200	210	30	7	12.5	607	138	1.3	25.2	1.55	23.9
201-220	268	23	12	7.9	875	161	1.8	29.4	2.16	27.5
221-240	371	31	12	7.7	1246	192	2.6	35.0	2.99	32.4
241-260	491	33	15	6.3	1737	225	3.7	41.1	4.08	37.4
261-280	654	25	26	3.7	2391	250	5.0	45.6	5.50	40.6
281-300	808	29	28	3.5	3199	279	6.7	50.9	7.24	44.2
301-320	1082	43	25	3.8	4281	322	9.0	58.8	9.58	49.7
321-340	1804	27	67	1.5	6085	349	12.8	63.7	13.39	50.9
341-360	2011	31	65	1.5	8096	380	17.0	69.3	17.64	52.3
361-380	2303	37	62	1.6	10399	417	21.9	76.1	22.52	54.2
381-400	2613	26	100	1.0	13012	443	27.4	80.8	28.01	53.4
401-420	3030	23	132	0.8	16042	466	33.8	85.0	34.36	51.3
421-440	3351	17	196	0.5	19393	483	40.8	88.1	41.37	47.3
441-460	3478	12	286	0.3	22871	495	48.2	90.3	48.64	42.2
461-480	3411	18	189	0.5	26282	513	55.3	93.6	55.78	38.3
481-500	3316	9	370	0.3	29598	522	62.3	95.3	62.70	32.9
501-520	3112	8	385	0.3	32710	530	68.9	96.7	69.19	27.8
521-540	3091	7	435	0.2	35801	537	75.4	98.0	75.64	22.6
541-560	2877	3	1000	0.1	38678	540	81.4	98.5	81.64	17.1
561-580	2617	4	667	0.2	41295	544	87.0	99.3	87.09	12.3
581-600	2120	2	1111	0.1	43415	546	91.4	99.6	91.51	8.2
601-620	1607	1	1667	0.1	45022	547	94.8	99.8	94.86	5.0
621-640	1112	0	NA	0.0	46134	547	97.1	99.8	97.17	2.7
641-660	663	0	NA	0.0	46797	547	98.5	99.8	98.55	1.3
661-680	414	0	NA	0.0	47211	547	99.4	99.8	99.42	0.4
681-700	189	0	NA	0.0	47400	547	99.8	99.8	99.81	0.0
701-720	91	1	91	1.1	47491	548	100.0	100.0	100.00	0.0

Columns two and three list the number of good loans and the number of bad loans in that range. The fourth column lists the good/bad odds. The good/bad odds is simply the number of good loans divided by the number of bad loans in that score range with the result multiplied by 100. Most scorecards are scaled so that a given number of score points should double the good/bad odds.[3] This column allows us to see if that is indeed true for the sample we are working with.

---

[3] See Chapter 4 for a discussion of scorecard scaling.

The fifth column lists the bad rate, the percentage of total loans in each score range that are bad. We can already tell that this scorecard is doing a very good job of ranking loans because those with low scores have a very high bad rate while those with high scores have very low bad rates.

Columns six through nine of the table are relevant to the calculation of the KS statistic. The columns labeled Cum Bads (cumulative bads) and Cum Goods are simply the total number of bads or goods in a given score range or lower. The Cum Good % and Cum Bad % columns are the *percentages* of goods or bads at that score or lower. We can see that 58.8 percent of the total loans that went bad score 320 or lower while only 9 percent of loans with a good outcome scored below 320 when they were originated.

The 11th column, Separation, is the one we are particularly interested in. This is the difference between the Cum Good % and Cum Bad % columns. It shows for each score level how much the percentage of bads at that level and below exceeds the percentage of goods at that level and below. The larger the cumulative bad percentage relative to the cumulative good, the higher this measure will be and the better our scorecard is at separating good from bad loans. To reinforce this idea, look at loans with scores of 320 and below. Since 58.8 percent of loans that went bad have scores at or below that level and only 9 percent of goods do, the separation is 49.7. The KS is the highest value of separation across the entire score range, which for our example is 54.2.

It may make the calculation of separation and the KS even more clear if we look at Figure 6.3, which plots the cumulative percentages of goods and bads. The bad distribution is the one on top. It rises more quickly than the good distribution because more of the bads are found among the lowest-scoring loans. The vertical distance between the two is the separation at each point. The maximum difference occurs at a score of about 380, where 76.1 percent of the bads lie below that score but only 21.9 percent of goods. The KS is 76.1 - 21.9 = 54.2.

One other thing it is especially important to look at besides maximum separation is what percentage of bads is found at the lower end of the score distribution, such as the bottom decile (10 percent) of total loans. This is important for setting policy cutoffs about which loans to accept and reject. From Table 6-1 we can see that somewhat less than 10 percent of total loans have scores below 320, though nearly 59 percent of bads are at or below 320. Thus, if we were to institute a policy that would only accept loans with scores above 320 we would eliminate a far larger percent of the bads than the goods.

FIGURE 6.3 CUMULATIVE PERCENT DISTRIBUTIONS FOR GOOD AND BAD LOANS

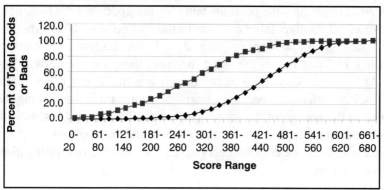

There are no hard and fast rules on what the expected value of the KS should be or how big it should be before we can be confident we have a good scorecard. The KS value we can expect to achieve will vary depending on the product we are building a scorecard for and on the data available. A relatively low KS does not necessarily mean someone has done a poor job of building the scorecard—it may be the best that can be obtained in that particular situation. For example, KSs for behavior scorecards where we have data on the borrower's payment pattern for that particular loan can be as much as 10 to 15 points higher than those on credit scorecards used to acquire new loans. Moreover, the KS on a portfolio concentrated on a very narrow range of credits (such as subprime loans) will almost always be lower, sometimes significantly, than the KSs for portfolios with a broader range of both high-quality and low-quality loans. Because the KS is probably the most widely discussed statistic in the scoring world (at least in the United States) an entire chapter, Chapter 7, is devoted to it.

While KSs can theoretically range from 0 to 100, in practice the range is generally from about 20 to about 70. If the KS is lower than 20, it would be reasonable to question whether the scorecard is worth using. Above 70, it is probably too good to be true and we should suspect problems with the way it is being calculated or with the scorecard itself.

The KS is based on a single point on the good and bad distributions—the point where the cumulative distributions are the most different. There may thus be cases where it would be a major mistake to blindly rely on the KS to tell you if you have a good scorecard without taking a careful look at the distributions of goods and bads to see how well the scorecard is ranking thems.

Table 6.2 duplicates the previous table for the goods but the bads have been rearranged. Unlike Table 6.1, where the bad/good odds and the bad rate start out high at low score ranges and get lower and lower (with minor exceptions), in Table 6.2, as the score increases there are few bads at low scores. At 71.1, the KS is even higher than it was in Table 6.1, but in this case the KS is misleading, because clearly the scorecard is not ranking the loans well in the bottom of the score distribution. That is why, just as with the divergence statistic, it is necessary to look at the distributions to get the whole story. This can be done by generating tables like 6.2 or creating plots of the distributions.

TABLE 6.2 GOOD/BAD TABLE WITH HIGH KS BUT WHERE SCORE IS NOT RANKING WELL

1 Score Range	2 Interval Goods	3 Interval Bads	4 Good/ Bad Odds	5 Bad Rate	6 Cum Goods	7 Cum Bads	8 Cum Good%	9 Cum Bad%	10 Cum Total%	11 Separation
0-20	5	1	5	50.0	5	1	0.0	0.2	0.02	0.2
21-40	10	1	10	33.3	15	2	0.0	0.4	0.05	0.4
41-60	9	2	5	30.8	24	4	0.1	0.7	0.08	0.6
61-80	37	4	9	32.7	61	8	0.1	1.5	0.19	1.4
81-100	24	7	3	22.6	85	15	0.2	2.7	0.26	2.5
101-120	51	1	51	27.1	136	16	0.3	2.9	0.40	2.6
121-140	53	0	NA	22.1	189	16	0.4	2.9	0.55	2.5
141-160	90	1	90	17.4	279	17	0.6	3.1	0.77	2.5
161-180	118	0	NA	11.9	397	17	0.8	3.1	1.05	2.3
181-200	210	1	210	12.5	607	18	1.3	3.3	1.55	2.0
201-220	268	0	NA	7.9	875	18	1.8	3.3	2.16	1.5
221-240	371	0	NA	7.7	1246	18	2.6	3.3	2.99	0.7
241-260	491	1	491	6.3	1737	19	3.7	3.5	4.08	-0.2
261-280	654	16	41	3.7	2391	35	5.0	6.4	5.50	1.4
281-300	808	3	269	3.5	3199	38	6.7	6.9	7.24	0.2
301-320	1082	2	541	3.8	4281	40	9.0	7.3	9.58	-1.7
321-340	1804	200	9	1.5	6085	240	12.8	43.8	13.39	31.0
341-360	2011	100	20	1.5	8096	340	17.0	62.0	17.64	45.0
361-380	2303	100	23	1.6	10399	440	21.9	80.3	22.52	58.4
381-400	2613	100	26	1.0	13012	540	27.4	98.5	28.01	71.1
401-420	3030	0	NA	0.8	16042	540	33.8	98.5	34.36	64.7
421-440	3351	0	NA	0.5	19393	540	40.8	98.5	41.37	57.7
441-460	3478	8	435	0.3	22871	548	48.2	100.0	48.64	51.8
461-480	3411	0	NA	0.5	26282	548	55.3	100.0	55.78	44.7
481-500	3316	0	NA	0.3	29598	548	62.3	100.0	62.70	37.7
501-520	3112	0	NA	0.3	32710	548	68.9	100.0	69.19	31.1
521-540	3091	0	NA	0.2	35801	548	75.4	100.0	75.64	24.6
541-560	2877	0	NA	0.1	38678	548	81.4	100.0	81.64	18.6
561-580	2617	0	NA	0.2	41295	548	87.0	100.0	87.09	13.0
581-600	2120	0	NA	0.1	43415	548	91.4	100.0	91.51	8.6
601-620	1607	0	NA	0.1	45022	548	94.8	100.0	94.86	5.2
621-640	1112	0	NA	0.0	46134	548	97.1	100.0	97.17	2.9
641-660	663	0	NA	0.0	46797	548	98.5	100.0	98.55	1.5
661-680	414	0	NA	0.0	47211	548	99.4	100.0	99.42	0.6
681-700	189	0	NA	0.0	47400	548	99.8	100.0	99.81	0.2
701-720	91	0	NA	1.1	47491	548	100.0	100.0	100.00	0.0

Figure 6.4 charts the cumulative percentage distributions for good and bad loans using the data from Table 6.2. It makes it very clear why this scorecard is undesirable even though the KS is very high.

FIGURE 6.4 GOOD AND BAD LOANS

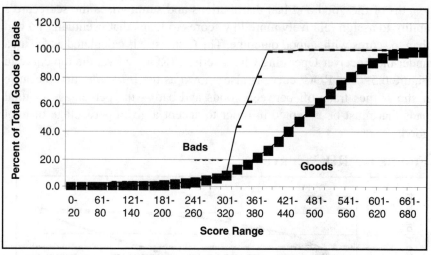

To set a score cutoff at the point where we would have to give up only 10 percent of the good loans, as we saw earlier we would need to set it at 320. In this case, however, a 320 cutoff would actually eliminate a slightly higher percentage of goods than of bads. Even though the KS is high, then, this scorecard cannot distinguish good from bad loans in the bottom of the score distribution—which is precisely where we want it to perform best.

One final point should be made about the KS statistic. After a new scorecard is implemented and a cutoff score set, the lender may observe a decline in the KS when the score is validated compared to its value in the model-building and validation samples. This happens when the lender has adhered to the new cutoff and booked fewer low-scoring loans than in the past. The KS is thus calculated on a narrower distribution of scored loans. That is, the newly-booked population is truncated compared to the lender's booked population before the new scorecard was implemented. The KS is sensitive to population truncation and can fall from one sample to the next even though the ranking ability of the score may not have declined (see Chapter 7 for more discussion of this).

RANKING STATISTICS—THE C STATISTIC

One of the possible drawbacks to the separation statistics that we have already noted is that they are based on only a single point on the good and bad distributions. The divergence statistic evaluates the difference in the distribution means, while the KS is based on the point of maximum separation between the cumulative percentage distributions.

The C statistic, on the other hand, uses information about the entire lengths of the good and bad distributions and summarizes the scorecard's ability to assign relatively more low scores to loans that eventually go bad than to scores with a good outcome. The C statistic is calculated as the area under the Receiver Operating Characteristic (ROC) curve, the top curve in Figure 6.5.[4] The ROC[5] curve is also known as the *trade-off* curve because it shows thes trade-off between goods and bads—the percentage of total bads that must be accepted in order to accept a given percentage of total goods.

FIGURE 6.5 ROC CURVE

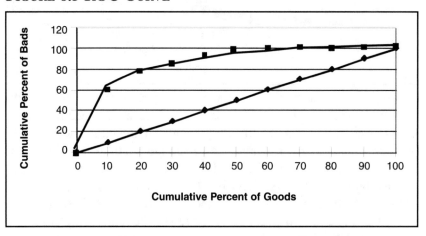

For this particular case, at the score below which 10 percent of the goods are found, we find 60 percent of the bads. We would like this curve to rise as quickly as possible because it means that more bad loans are assigned low scores relative to good loans. The faster it rises, the greater the area under it and the larger the C statistic.

The C statistic theoretically can range from 0.5 to 1 but in practice it usually ranges from 0.6 to 0.9 for credit scorecards.[6] Computer algorithms may be used to calculate the statistic, but fortunately the SAS System® generates it by default every time a logistic regression is run. Thus in building

---

[4] The 45° line on the graph shows a ROC curve for a score with no ranking ability. The point below which 20 percent of bads are found is the same score below which 20 percent of goods are found.

[5] That ROC curve's name reflects its origin, which was in estimating classification errors in transmitting and receiving messages.

[6] A completely random model (represented by the 45 degree line) would have a C statistic of 0.5.

a scorecard the C statistic is automatically available to the modeler using SAS. If we wish to generate the C statistic to validate a model by comparing it to the C statistic at development, we can simply regress the score on the bad outcome variable with PROC LOGISTIC and the C statistic accompanies the regression output.

Although the C statistic is calculated using data points along the entire good and bad distributions, it can still suffer from the same problem as the KS and divergence statistics. A score that does a relatively poor job of forcing bad loans into the bottom of the score distribution can have the same C statistic as one that does a better job. Its trade-off curve may get a slow start at capturing bads in the bottom decile of the distribution, but catch up with and surpass the other score in the second decile. We may not be as interested in what happens in the second decile, however, because the cutoff is likely to be set lower. Thus, the recommendation is the same as before. Calculate the C statistic, but also plot the trade-off curves for the two scores (or two samples if you are comparing development and validation statistics for a single score).

PREDICTION ERROR STATISTICS

Whenever a scorecard is developed, the modeler should produce a table showing the expected good/bad odds and the bad rate at each score range. Chapter 4 discussed how the expected good/bad odds can be calculated from the regression coefficients or calculated based on a validation sample at the time of scorecard development. One of the most important considerations when tracking scorecard performance after implementation is monitoring the good/bad odds or bad rates within score ranges. In Chapter 13 we describe a Good/Bad Separation Report that lists the percentages of goods and of bads in each score range for a recent sample and compares it to the percentages for the development sample.[7]

CHECKING PERFORMANCE

Two things can happen after a scorecard is implemented that affect its performance—and possibly portfolio performance as well.

First, the score can continue to rank risk well, with the relative odds between the score ranges staying the same, but the relationship can shift so that a given score now has a higher or lower odds than it did during score-

---

[7] In that report we actually list the *cumulative* percentages of goods and of bads at each score range. Whether we list the cumulative percentages or the marginal percentages and report the good/bad odds or the bad rates is immaterial. All that matters is that we compare the same thing for both the validation and the development sample.

card development. Graphing the expected to the actual good/bad odds for the validation sample tells us immediately if the loans are performing as predicted by the score. To produce a graph like Figure 6.6, we would rank the validation sample by score and separate it into a number of equal-sized score ranges like the 20-point ranges used here, then calculate the good/bad odds within each group and plot the odds against the midpoint of each range. We would also plot a separate line showing the expected good/bad odds that emerged during scorecard development. It is crucial to use the same outcome period for the validation sample as for the development sample. Otherwise, it is not appropriate to compare the lines for the two samples.

FIGURE 6.6 ACTUAL AND EXPECTED GOOD/BAD ODDS

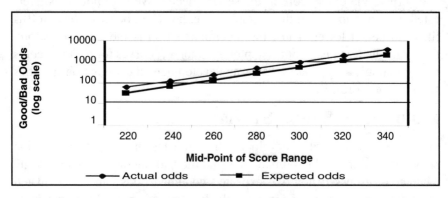

In Figure 6.6 the slope of the actual odds line is the same as the expected odds line but the line has shifted up so that at each score there are more goods per bad. The score is ranking risk as well as it ever did and the separation and ranking statistics are likely to be very similar to those calculated at the time of development, though the odds are now higher (bad rates lower). While having more goods than expected in a given score range is a good thing from the lender's perspective, it probably means that the cutoff score is not set optimally.

The line can shift as a result of changes in factors that are not score characteristics, such as changes in lending policies or in economic conditions. When this happens, it is important to try to understand the cause and determine if it is likely to continue into the future. If so, changes in the cutoff score and other policies may be warranted.

The second thing that can happen once a scorecard is in use is that its ability to rank risk can diminish—this implies the slope of the line has flattened. In the example in Figure 6.7, the odds at low scores increased and the odds at high scores decreased. The score is no longer discriminating between goods and bads as well as it was, and the separation and ranking statistics would decline. Such rotations of the line can occur when the effect of scorecard characteristics on the outcome event changes.

FIGURE 6.7 ACTUAL AND EXPECTED GOOD/BAD ODDS

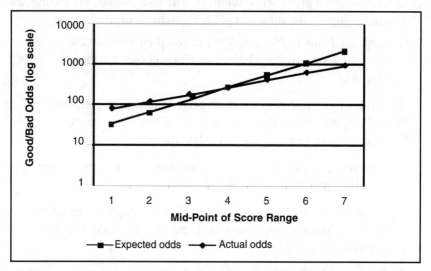

Thus, it is important that we identify both changes in the slope of the line and shifts in the line. Either can undermine the scorecard's ability to predict the number of bad loans the lender will sustain at each point on the score distribution.

GOODNESS OF FIT

In addition to generating charts like these figures, we can calculate a statistic that summarizes the scorecard's ability to predict the number of bad loans in each score range. This statistic could be generated on both development and validation samples to verify that the number of bad loans in a given score range in the validation sample is close to the amount of bads the model predicted for that range.[8]

The Hosmer-Lemeshow (H-L) statistic is a goodness-of-fit statistic for logistic regression models.[9] For credit scoring models, it measures how

---

[8] The scorecard will probably never perfectly predict the number of bads in every score segment, not even during development. Think of the logistic regression model as fitting a line through the set of points like those on the figures in this section; some of the points will always fall somewhere above or below the line.

[9] This statistic can be generated in SAS by using the LACKFIT option on the logistic regression statement.

well the model's prediction of the number of bad loans by score range matches the actual number of bad loans in each range. Unlike the separation and ranking statistics, it is testing not the score's ability to assign lower scores to bad loans but rather the model's ability to predict the actual number of bads within a given score segment. The H-L statistic is calculated as follows in testing a validation sample for goodness of fit:

1. Rank the loans in the sample by score, then separate the sample into equal-size groups (10 is a common choice for the number of groups).

2. For each group, calculate the expected number of bad loans by multiplying the number of loans by the expected bad rate (see Chapter 4 for more about this calculation).

3. Subtract the expected number of bad loans for the group from the actual number, and square the difference.

4. Divide the answer obtained in step 3 by the expected number of bad loans in the group times the expected good rate (that is, one minus the bad rate).

5. The sum of the 10 values generated is the H-L statistic.

The formula for the statistic, where SUM indicates summing across all 10 groups, is:

SUM [(actual # of bads - expected # of bads)^2]/(expected # bads * good rate).

Because the difference between the actual and the expected number of bad loans is in the numerator, the larger the difference between these two numbers the larger the value of the H-L statistic. Thus, we prefer that the H-L statistic, unlike the other statistics discussed in the chapter, be as *small* as possible. There is no typical range for the H-L statistic that says whether the model is adept at predicting the number of bads because the statistic varies for different samples depending on the expected bad rate.

We may use the statistic in several ways. First, obviously, we can compare the H-L generated at development to the H-L generated at validation to determine if the score can still predict the likely number of bad loans in each score range.

Second, when building scorecards we can use the H-L to compare the power of different specifications of the score model (the power of the model when it contains one set of characteristics rather than a different set). In fact, we can use all the statistics described in this chapter in that way.

In addition to using the H-L statistic to evaluate the usefulness of different variables—especially those that are statistically significant in the regression model but that do not increase the separation or ranking statistics relative to what they would be if the variables were not in the model—we should also produce odds/score charts like those in this chapter to further shed light on whether the variables are useful in predicting the number of bad loans within score intervals.

We used the example of property type within a mortgage default model in Chapter 4. Because loans on vacation homes make up a very small portion of the development sample, a binary variable indicating whether a particular loan is for this property type may not increase the ranking and separation statistics. To investigate whether the variable helps predict the number of bad loans within score ranges, separate sets of odds/score charts for loans on vacation and on primary homes could be generated, one set showing results with the property type variable in the model and one without it. If the model with the property type variable in the regression better predicts the number of bad loans for vacation homes, that variable should probably be included in the final model.

One criticism sometimes made of the H-L statistic is that it is sensitive to the number of score ranges used in its calculation. If we create so many intervals that there are few bad loans in each, it will be very difficult for the model to get the prediction correct and the H-L statistic will indicate the model performs poorly. If we use too few intervals (say, five) it will be too easy for the model to get the prediction right and the H-L statistic will indicate that the score is always predictive no matter which sample is tested. When you first start using this statistic, you may want to experiment with different numbers of score ranges and look carefully at what is being predicted in each interval to get a good sense for when the H-L is reliable.

SUMMARY

In this chapter we discussed four statistics that may be used to evaluate how well a score does its job. These statistics are used to evaluate three things (1) the scorecard's ability to separate the good and bad loan distributions (divergence and KS), (2) its ability to rank loans in terms of their risk of being bad all along the score distribution (the C statistic), and (3) its ability to accurately predict the number of bad loans in a given score interval (the H-L statistic).

Although these statistics will often agree, there are times when, for example, one statistic will decline from development to validation but the others will not, or may even increase slightly. Generally, it should be pos-sible to determine why the statistics disagree through careful analysis of plots showing the good and bad score distributions. Analysis of odds/score plots for different data samples is very useful in determining whether a score continues to be predictive of the actual number of bad loans (the bad rate). These plots may also be used to evaluate whether a particular variable is helpful in predicting the bad rate within given score ranges and whether the variable should therefore be retained in the score model.

Chapter 7
UNDERSTANDING THE KS STATISTIC

Elizabeth Mays
Director of Retail Risk Modeling and Analytics
Bank One

INTRODUCTION

It seems no conversation on credit scoring is complete without mention of the KS statistic.[1] Even senior executives of financial services companies are familiar with it and in fact try to impress each other by claiming their scoring model has a bigger KS than the next guy's. Yet two questions often arise in discussions of how to use KS statistics in analyzing the performance of scorecards. People want to know:

1. If the KS from a validation is lower than the KS from a scorecard development sample, does that mean the scorecard has deteriorated and a new one should be built?

2. Why are KSs for subprime portfolios, which are often in the 20s or 30s, so much lower than for prime portfolios, which can go as high as the 50s or even low 60s?

The answers to these two questions are related. To understand the answers, we first need to discuss how the KS statistic is calculated and talk a little about score distributions. After doing that, we will then address the two questions.

---

[1] The KS statistic is named for two Russian statisticians, Kolmogorov and Smirnov.

CALCULATING THE KS STATISTIC

Because calculation of the KS statistic was described in detail in Chapter 6, it is only summarized here.

The KS statistic measures how different two distributions are. In the scoring world we are typically concerned with how well a score distinguishes loans that eventually go bad[2] from those that turn out to be good, so we use the KS to measure how different the score distributions of bads and goods are. The more often a scoring model assigns a low score to loans that do indeed go bad and a high score to loans that have a good outcome, the more different the distributions will be and the higher the KS. Though theoretically the KS can range from 0 to 100, the KSs of credit scorecards generally range from a low of about 20 to a maximum of about 70.

Figure 7.1 shows the score frequency distribution of loans booked between 1995 and 1999 for an actual loan portfolio.[3] The scores range from 0 to the low 800s with a high concentration in the low 500s. Figure 7.2 shows the same set of loans divided into goods and bads. The bads are loans that have gone 60 days past due two or more times at any point up to August 2001 and the goods are all other loans. The bad distribution lies to the left of the good distribution, indicating that lower scores were assigned at origination to loans that eventually went bad while relatively higher scores were assigned to loans that had a good outcome. This is also clear in Figure 7.3, which plots the percentage of loans in each score range that have a bad outcome. Clearly, low-score ranges have a much higher bad rate than high-score ranges.

To calculate a KS statistic, we use the good and bad distributions. First, we generate cumulative frequency distributions for the goods and the bads by simply adding up the loans at or below each score range. In Figure 7.4, the cumulative bad distribution lies on top of the cumulative good distribution because the set of bads contains more low-scoring loans. As a result, a larger percentage of all bads than of all goods is accounted for at each point as you move from left to right on the figure. The larger the vertical difference between these two cumulative distributions, the more bads are identified among the lower-scoring loans relative to the good loans.

---

[2] The definition of bad may be charge-off, seriously delinquent, or whatever else the analyst wants to evaluate.

[3] A frequency distribution is a chart showing the percentage of all loans that fall into each score range.

FIGURE 7.1 SCORE FREQUENCY DISTRIBUTION

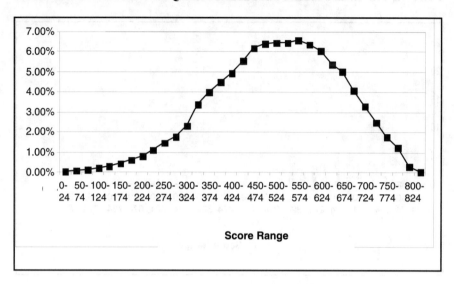

FIGURE 7.2 SCORE FREQUENCY DISTRIBUTION OF GOODS AND BADS

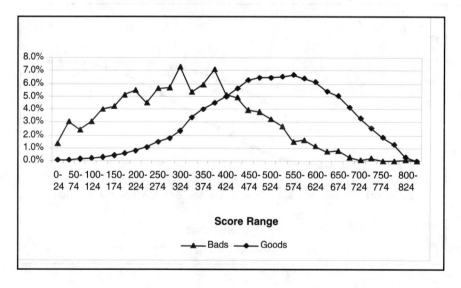

FIGURE 7.3 BAD RATE BY SCORE RANGE

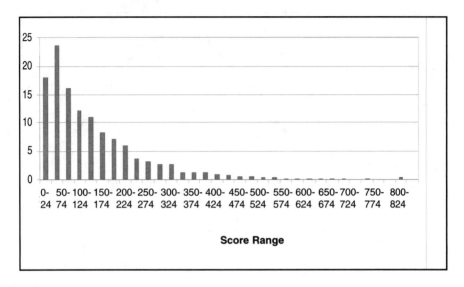

FIGURE 7.4 CUMULATIVE SCORE FREQUENCY DISTRIBUTION OF GOODS AND BADS

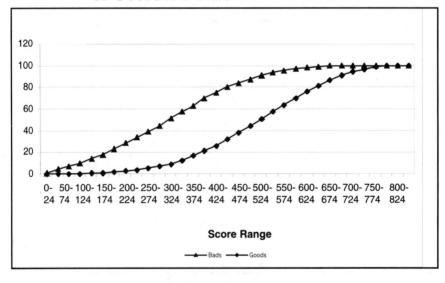

The KS is equal to the maximum vertical difference observed between the two curves. In Figure 7.4 this point occurs at a score of about 375, below which 75 percent of bads are accounted for but only 26 percent of goods. The KS is therefore 49 (75-26).

To summarize, the KS is nothing more than the largest difference observed between the cumulative bad percentage distribution and the cumulative good percentage distribution. A large KS means that many bads are found among low-scoring loans and relatively more goods are found among high-scoring loans.

DETERIORATION IN KS

To return to the first question posed at the beginning of this chapter—if the KS from a validation performed some time after the score was implemented is lower than the KS was on the development sample, does that mean the scorecard has deteriorated in its ability to rank applicant risk? The answer is not necessarily.

A lender that undertakes to build a scorecard uses a set of booked loans (and perhaps rejected applications if reject inference is used) along with data on their performance (outcome) and on loan and borrower characteristics to find the score that best separates the goods from the bads. This data sample is referred to as the *development* data set.

Once the scorecard is built, the risk manager performs an analysis to determine where to set the score cutoff—the score below which applications generally are not accepted unless a compelling case can be made, based on additional information, that the applicant is credit-worthy. Once a lender sees the ability of the score to segregate loans of poor credit quality at the bottom of the score distribution, it often sets the cutoff score at a level that cuts out a number of applications it would have accepted in the past.

If the lender adheres strictly to the cutoff and books few or no loans below it, the score distribution of the ensuing portfolio can be quite different from that of the set of loans used to build the scorecard, because relative to the development sample the score distribution of newly booked loans is truncated at the low end of the score distribution. A scorecard is typically not validated until enough time has passed to see how loans approved by the new score are performing. At that point the KS generated on the validation sample could be considerably lower than the KS of the development sample because there are far fewer low-scoring bad loans. Applicants rejected by the cutoff have been eliminated from this sample. Because that means the difference in the bad rates among the remaining score ranges is not as large as it was in the original distribution, the KS declines.[4]

This is easily illustrated using the score distribution from Figure 7.1. Say this set of loans is used to develop a new score. As we saw from Figure 7.4, the bad rate in this set is much higher among low-scoring loans than high-scoring loans. Suppose the lender determines that it cannot profitably make loans with bad rates as high as those associated with scores at or below 300 and thereafter accepts only applications with scores above this threshold.

Figure 7.5 shows the score distribution after loans with scores below 300 are eliminated.[5] The distributions of good and bad loans are much closer (see Figure 7.6) than they were when all scores were included. Figure 7.7 shows that the cumulative distribution of bad loans still lies on top of the cumulative distribution of goods, but they are closer than they were when scores 300 and below were included. When we calculate the KS for this new distribution we find that it has fallen to 36, a full 13 points lower than it was for the distribution in Figure 7.1.

FIGURE 7.5 SCORE FREQUENCY DISTRIBUTION ABOVE 300

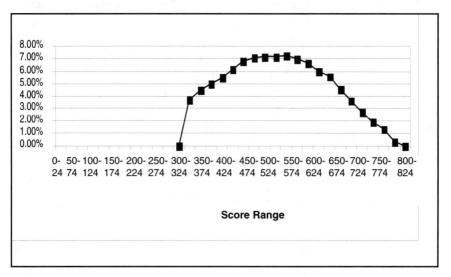

---

[4] This is true not just of the KS statistic but also of the other separation and ranking statistics like divergence and the C statistic as well.

[5] Thirteen percent of the loans in the original distribution have scores of 300 or below.

FIGURE 7.6 SCORE FREQUENCY DISTRIBUTION ABOVE 300

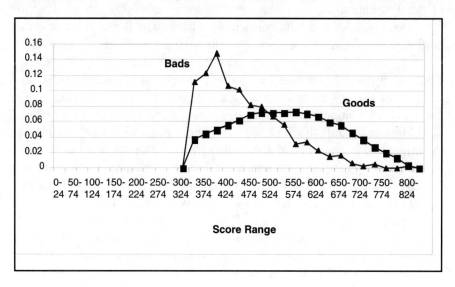

FIGURE 7.7 CUMULATIVE PERCENT OF GOODS AND BADS BY SCORE RANGE ABOVE 300

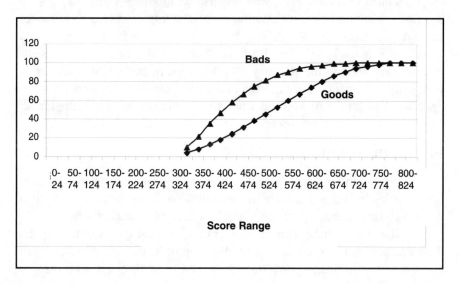

This example illustrates that if we eliminate the lowest scoring portion of the distribution and calculate the KS on the remaining intermediate to high scores, the KS can fall considerably. That is why if a lender cuts off a portion of the original score distribution through more stringent policies than those in place before the scorecard was implemented, the KS on the scorecard is likely to be lower than the KS for the development sample. It is somewhat ironic that if the scorecard is doing a good job of risk-ranking applicants and eliminating bad loans, its power may appear to have deteriorated.

How can we tell whether a deterioration in KS is a result of truncating the original distribution or of some other reason? This turns out to be simple. Even though the post-implementation score distribution is truncated on the low end, it is still possible to compare the expected to the actual odds of the validation for score ranges where the two samples overlap.

Figure 7.8 shows an example. The expected odds would be calculated using the method described in Chapter 4. The model developer would have generated an expected odds/score table when the scorecard was developed that the lender should have kept on hand. The actual odds line is generated by calculating the odds within each score range for the validation sample, then fitting a regression line through the points. Some refer to this line as the *fitted odds* because a regression line is fitted to the set of points.

Our assumption here is that after scorecard implementation the lender booked no loans below the 300 cutoff. A validation sample truncated at a score of 300 is likely to have a KS lower than that of the development sample, but even though the KS may fall, the slope of the actual odds line is very similar to that of the expected odds, indicating that the score continues to rank risk as well as it did when first implemented. Thus, the lender may be reassured that the scorecard continues to rank risk well.

KSs for Subprime Loans

The analysis in the last section also answers the second question about why KS statistics for subprime loans are usually lower, often much lower, than those for prime loans. Although portfolio quality for lenders who concentrate on the prime market is much higher than the quality of subprime portfolios, prime lenders often have a small subset of loans with relatively high bad rates. In the prime portfolio shown in Figure 7.3, the score ranges below 200 have bad rates of 5 percent or more. Because loans with scores below 200 make up less than 3 percent of the total portfolio, however, they are not likely to have much impact on portfolio return given the very low bad rates among higher-scoring loans.

FIGURE 7.8 EXPECTED VERSUS ACTUAL GOOD/BAD ODDS

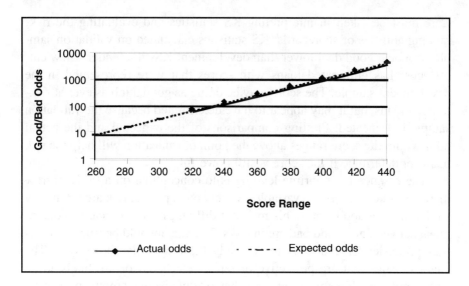

Subprime lenders accept borrowers with blemished credit, so, recognizing that their loss rates will be higher, they price up for the additional risk. Their portfolios tend to look very much like the set of loans scoring 300 and below in Figure 7.3—their portfolios are concentrated on the loan segment with high bad rates and they do not have the wider range of credit risks typical of a prime lender.

Recall that the KS for the portfolio illustrated in Figure 7.1 (for a prime lender) was 49. If we calculate the KS for the set of loans scoring less than or equal to 300 (representative of a subprime lender), the KS is only 27— lower than the KS of 36 for loans scoring above 300 and much less than the 49 calculated on the entire distribution. The concentration of the subprime lender on a fairly narrow market segment means that the scorecard is less able to rank borrowers within that segment.

Score characteristic attributes are typically very similar for subprime borrowers. For example, many subprime borrowers have major derogatory items on their credit reports. As a result, data differences between good and bad loans are not as large as those in prime portfolios. For example, most subprime borrowers have negative credit histories and high debt relative to income. The similarities in their characteristics make it more difficult for the scorecard to predict which of these very similar borrowers will have a good versus a bad outcome.

SUMMARY

Care must be taken in interpreting KS statistics and evaluating the risk-ranking abilities of scorecards. KS statistics calculated on validation samples can be a good deal lower than development KSs if a lender's new cut-off score has eliminated loans with scores that were represented in the development sample. The score may be doing as good a job as ever at risk-ranking loans, but it may appear to have deteriorated because the validation sample is truncated. Plotting comparisons of the expected and the actual odds within the score ranges above the point of truncation will help the risk manager determine if the score is still powerful.

The essence of subprime lending is to concentrate on a fairly narrow market segment where the variables we rely on to predict risk are often very similar among applicants. This makes it difficult for a scorecard to distinguish between good and bad credit risks. The same would be true for an A-plus prime lender concentrating on only the lowest risk borrowers: The characteristics that are predictive of repayment behavior are likely to be very similar within this group, so that distinguishing among borrowers becomes difficult.

The KS will typically be highest when the portfolio evaluated contains a wide range of credits and smaller as the range of credit quality narrows. A low KS does not necessarily mean that a score is performing suboptimally. It may be the highest that can be achieved for the borrower segment on which a given lender has chosen to concentrate.

Chapter 8
SCORE BASED LOSS FORECASTING MODELS

Elizabeth Mays
Director of Retail Risk Modeling and Analytics
Bank One

INTRODUCTION

Credit scores can play other useful roles at lending institutions beyond supporting loan approval decisions and account management decisions after loan origination. Increasingly they are being used as the basis for portfolio loss forecasts.

Often score-based forecasts are superior to those produced by traditional loss forecasting models. In this chapter we discuss how the shortcomings of traditional loss models can be overcome by calculating loss estimates using score-based models. How score-based models can remedy these shortcomings and potentially generate more accurate forecasts is illustrated by a description of a loan-level loss-forecasting model for first lien mortgage loans.

The score-based model we discuss is based on data available for each loan at the time of origination. It is used to derive an estimate of each loan's lifetime default probability as well as the likely amount of the loss if there is a default. The model projects the expected lifetime loss in dollars. The expected loss amount and the anticipated timing of the loss can be used as input into models to generate prices for loan pools or to calculate risk-based interest rates for individual loans. The loss estimates can also be used to forecast portfolio losses at each future point in the life of the portfolio to evaluate the adequacy of loan loss reserves.[1]

TRADITIONAL VERSUS LOAN-LEVEL SCORE-BASED LOSS MODELS

Traditionally, most lenders have relied on net flow models to predict portfolio losses. These models forecast delinquency rates and losses by predicting the rate at which outstanding balances will flow from one delinquency bucket to another in future periods. Net flow rates are also used to estimate the percentage of delinquent balances for which losses will be taken in future periods (and from what delinquency bucket they will flow, which depends on the institution's accounting practices).

These models typically assume that the flow rate for each bucket going forward is equal to the average flow rate observed over the recent past. Net flow models, however, ignore three important effects that influence the level and timing of losses.

The first important effect ignored is change in the credit quality of the loans in the portfolio. Because they use historical flow rates that are estimated as aggregates for the whole portfolio, net flow models implicitly assume that the credit quality of the portfolio does not change over time. But for a portfolio where credit parameters have been tightened, losses will decline as older, poorer-quality, loans either prepay, default, or pay off at term and new, better-quality, loans take their place. Net flow loss models, being very slow to capture this effect, tend to overestimate losses.

The second important effect ignored is how the likelihood of delinquency and loss varies with the age of loans. Typically for consumer loans delinquency and default ramp up over the first one to three years of the loan life (the timing varies by product), peak, then tail off. The likelihood of loss is much higher in the middle of loan life than at the beginning or end.

The age distribution of a portfolio can change very quickly, especially when a portfolio is either growing or contracting. Average age could be lengthened considerably if a lender acquires a large seasoned loan portfolio. Alternatively, average portfolio age would be shortened considerably for mortgages by a refinancing wave in which seasoned loans are replaced

---

[1] As we noted, the model generates the forecast using loan characteristics available at the time of account origination. After loans have been on the books a year or so, it is likely that a superior forecast can be generated using behavior rather than origination scores, because behavior scores are largely based on borrower payment patterns.

by new loans. Again, because net flow rates are historical averages, they would be slow to adjust to this portfolio shift.

The third problem, which applies to secured loans like mortgages or auto loans, is changing loss severities. Net flow models look only at net dollars flowing into a given bucket; they do not separate out the effects of loss incidence and loss severity. Thus, these models would fail to capture the effect of a portfolio segment with unusually high severity hitting the peak of its loss-timing curve.

Finally, all these effects could occur simultaneously. Even if high-credit-quality loans were segmented from low-quality loans, and loans of varying ages were separated out and net flow rates calculated for each, it is unlikely that enough segments could be created to capture all the effects. What is needed is a loan-level forecasting model that takes into consideration all the factors that affect the level and timing of losses and generates a unique loss estimate for each loan.[2]

In what follows we describe how to use custom credit scores along with severity estimates to derive expected loss at the loan level, which can then be aggregated to predict losses for a portfolio segment or the entire portfolio. This is illustrated by first lien mortgages, for which the loss includes not just the loss of principal and interest but also expenses related to foreclosure and disposition of the collateral, net of any mortgage insurance proceeds paid to the lender.

FORECASTING MORTGAGE LOSSES

Expected lifetime loss can be calculated for every loan in a mortgage portfolio. The expected loss for high-quality loans will be very low compared to poor-quality loans, but it is not zero because every loan carries some potential for default. The expected loss is equal to each loan's lifetime probability of loss times the loss expected in the event of default. That is:

Expected Lifetime Loss =
Lifetime Loss Probability x Expected Loss in the Event of Default

When we multiply the loss amount by the default probability to get expected lifetime loss, we are essentially weighting the loss expected on default by the likelihood that the loan *will* default. If the loan defaults, the loss taken is equal to the sum of the lost principal and interest plus associ-

---

[2] It is of course true that no loss model can always generate a perfectly accurate forecast. For one thing, changes in economic conditions can change the outcome of a loan; this is extremely difficult if not impossible to forecast.

ated expenses less the value of the collateral. Given that there is only a small chance of loss, however, the *expected* loss is much smaller than the loss in the event of default.

The full expected lifetime loss for each loan can be used as input in setting risk-based pricing adjusters for loans with particular characteristics or in pricing models used to value loan packages. The expected loss can also be distributed over the life of the loan to produce predicted losses for any interval of time desired. We discuss the derivation of the loss probability and the loss expected on default in the next two sections. At the end of the chapter we describe how to combine the loss probability and loss amount estimates to generate a loss forecast for the whole portfolio.

DERIVATION OF THE LOSS PROBABILITY

There are two ways to derive the loss probability, depending on whether a lender has available quantitative staff to do statistical work. In-house modelers can generate the loss probability using the logistic regression technique described in Chapter 4. If staff with statistical expertise are not availalbe, lenders can generate it by observing the long-term performance of loans in various score ranges and assuming those loss rates will hold into the future, as is explained later in the section.

The loss probability model is built on a set of predictive variables that are known at the time of loan application and on loan performance over a fairly long period. Logistic regression is specifically designed to estimate the probability that an event (such as a loan defaulting) will occur given a set of variables that influence the likelihood of the event. Thus, if we have enough loans that have gone to loss, we can regress our predictive variables on the dependent variable that indicates whether or not the loan has defaulted.[3] To apply the model we would use the regression coefficients to calculate the expected default rate (see Chapter 4).

---

[3] If too few loans in the data set have actually experienced a loss to build a regression model, another outcome measure can be used, such as whether a loan has gone 90 days past due. In that case, we would have to estimate an additional probability, which is the probability that a loan that has gone 90 DPD will go to loss. The product of the two probabilities is the probability of loss. The simplest approach to estimating this second probability is to use a constant equal to the percent of 90 DPD loans that have been observed to go to loss over some historical period.

FIGURE 8.1 PERCENT OF TOTAL LOSSES GENERATED IN EACH YEAR FOR PRIME FIRST MORTGAGES

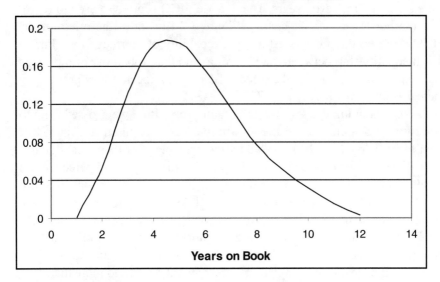

It is important to have seasoned loans in your data set if you want to estimate lifetime default probabilities for a long-lived asset like a mortgage. Unlike most other consumer loan products, the default rate on prime first-lien mortgages does not peak until about the third to fifth year of life.[4] Figure 8.1 shows a typical loss timing curve for first-lien mortgages. The curve shows the loans that default at each age as a percentage of all loans that eventually default. The curve tailing off to zero after the 12-year point indicates that few if any losses occur after a portfolio is that old.

The ideal data set would have performance information on loans up to 12 years old. However, if that span of performance data is not available, a lender can estimate lifetime loss by using loans at least as old as the point at which the default rate peaks, occurs, then gross up the resulting probability from the regression model to an expected lifetime loss probability.

It is well known that mortgage defaults are influenced by such standard underwriting variables as borrower's credit history (willingness to repay the loan), DTI (ability to repay the loan), the LTV ratio (the borrower's equity stake in the transaction), and other application and transaction-specific variables.

---

[4] First lien subprime mortgages, on the other hand, often reach their peak of default earlier, around the two-year point.

The numbers reported in this chapter are based on a default model for mortgage loans estimated using a set of booked loans, the oldest of which were seasoned for seven years. The generic FICO score was used to represent the borrowers' credit history. Figure 8.2 illustrates the effect of the FICO score on the model's estimated probability of mortgage loss, Figure 8.3 the relationship between the LTV ratio and the probability of mortgage loss. Note that the rate of the effect of LTV on expected loss probability increases faster the higher the LTV.

After obtaining the seven-year default probability, we grossed it up to a lifetime probability using the loss-timing curve pictured in Figure 8.1. That factor is equal to 100 divided by the percentage of loans that defaulted within seven years. The loss-timing curve indicates that 85 percent of all losses occur by year seven, producing a gross-up factor equal to 1.176 (100/85). If a lender does not have internal data for such a long period, a curve for the same loan type may be borrowed from a published source.[5]

Figure 8.4 shows the frequency distribution of expected lifetime default probabilities for a pool of prime first-lien mortgages originated in 2000. The default probabilities range from less than .02 percent to more than 10.0 percent. Note that the distribution is not symmetric but is skewed to the right, indicating a number of loans with default probabilities much higher than the portfolio average. That is due to extremely high default probabilities among high-LTV loans. Figure 8.3 shows that the default probabilities get very high beyond about a 90 LTV. This is reflected in the distribution of default rates in Figure 8.4.

FIGURE 8.2 DEFAULT PROBABILITY BY FICO SCORE

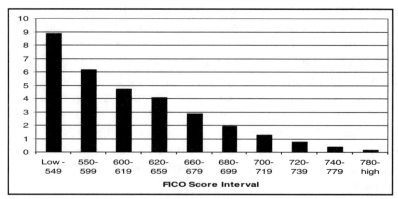

---

[5] See, for example, Sachs, Goldman. May 1993. *A User's Guide to Mortgage Default Calculations and the New PSA Standard Default Curve.* New York: Goldman Sachs. Goldman Sachs has several examples of mortgage default timing curves.

FIGURE 8.3 DEFAULT PROBABILITY BY LTV RANGE

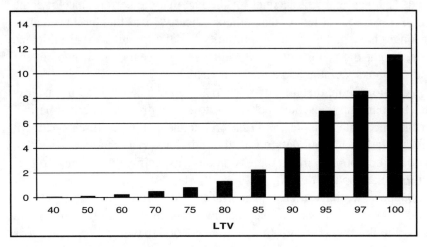

FIGURE 8.4 DISTRIBUTION OF DEFAULT PROBABILITY

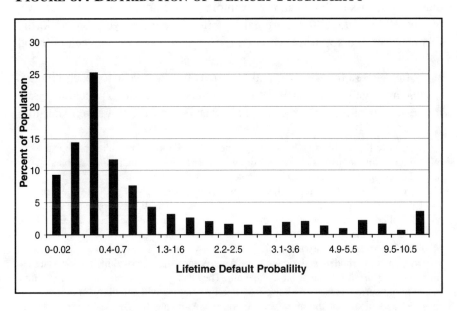

A few words need to be said about how loans of varying ages are treated in the regression model. If the data set available were to include loans aged from say, one year up through seven, we could use the data to get a seven-year default probability. To do so, we would combine all the loans and as one of the explanatory variables in the regression model we would include a variable indicating the amount of time since the loan was originated. This variable will account for the fact that the performance of some loans is observed for longer than others.[6] Clearly, loans that have been alive for longer have had a greater opportunity to default than short-lived loans. Then, to get the probability of default in seven years, we would set the time-on-books variable equal to seven years.[7]

A custom score that already ranks risk well can be used to forecast loss rates by mapping the score to observed loss rates from a historical period. Performance data on a portfolio of scored loans that are well seasoned will still be needed, but not data on all the individual risk characteristics that could be incorporated into a regression model specifically designed to predict the likelihood of default.

Suppose we have a custom mortgage score that ranges from 400 to 1,000. Table 8.1 shows the marginal loss rate by vintage (columns) and year on book (rows) for a given score range—600 to 649. The marginal loss rate for a given year is the percentage of that score range in the portfolio that went to loss in that year. For example, the column headed 1995 shows, for the 1995 vintage, the marginal loss rate in the first year on book, the second year, and so on for loans with origination scores between 600 and 649.

After generating the marginal loss rates for each year for each vintage, we can average the loss rates over the vintages to get an expected loss rate for each year of a loan's life (second to last column). For a seven-year loss

---

[6] If we believe the relationship between age and the likelihood of default is nonlinear, we might include in the regression a series of dummy variables (0/1 indicator variables) instead of using age as a continuous variable.

[7] Many of the loans whose default behavior we wish to observe will not last the entire performance period because they were paid off early. Some loans that pay off early would have defaulted had they not prepaid; these are said to be *censored* because we prematurely stop observing whether they default. Prepayments make the default rate of the original portfolio lower than it otherwise would have been. A special class of regression models known as survival models is designed to deal with censoring. Survival models estimate the time to the occurrence of an event like default. They can generate a probability of default in any future period or the cumulative likelihood that a loan will default on or before a specified period, such as the seven years used in our example. Survival models have been used in scoring only in the last few years. They may provide applications for acquisition scores, collections scores, and most definitely pricing and loss models where estimates of the likelihood of default and prepayment in each future month are needed to project future cash flows. Because they are relatively new and their explanation is somewhat complex, we leave their discussion to other books. For a detailed discussion of survival models see Hosmer, David, and Stanley Lemeschow. (1999). *Applied Survival Analysis.* NewYork: John Wiley and Sons.

rate (as in the regression model example), we simply cumulate the average marginal rates over the years. The cumulative average rate is shown in the last column. The expected loss rate on the portfolio at the seven-year point for loans with scores in the range of 600-649 is 1.93 percent. (The seven-year loss rate may be grossed up to a lifetime loss rate, as described earlier.)

TABLE 8.1 MARGINAL YEARLY LOSS RATES BY VINTAGE FOR SCORES 600-649

	1994	1995	1996	1997	1998	1999	2000	Ave. Yearly Loss Rate	Cum. Ave. Loss Rate
One year loss %	0.1	0.1	0.2	0.3	0.1	0.2	0.1	0.16	0.16
Two year loss %	0.2	0.3	0.2	0.7	0.2	0.3		0.32	0.48
Three year loss %	0.6	0.5	0.4	0.6	0.5			0.52	1.00
Four year loss %	0.3	0.3	0.3	0.3				0.30	1.30
Five year loss %	0.3	0.2	0.2					0.23	1.53
Six year loss %	0.3	0.1						0.20	1.73
Seven year loss %	0.2							0.20	1.93

When mapping scores into loss rates, it is important to look at the loss data carefully and scrutinize anything unexpected. For example, in Table 8.1, the second and third-year loss rates for the 1997 vintage are a good deal higher than for other vintages at the same point. If the performance of a particular vintage or subset of loans appears out of line with the performance of most other loans in the portfolio, we must analyze possible causes. The lender may have deviated from standard underwriting policies in that year in order to generate more volume. Or the prevailing economic environment may have affected that vintage negatively.

If the cause can be identified and if it is believed to be a one-time event, it might be wise to simply ignore that vintage in calculating cumulative loss rates. If whatever caused the unusual performance may recur, it should be included in the calculation—and perhaps even weighted more heavily, depending on the likelihood of recurrence.

To complete the loss rate forecast, a table like Table 8.1 would be generated for the other score ranges. If the score is ranking risk well, the lifetime loss rates will be increasing monotonically with score. If not, it may be necessary to smooth the score versus loss rate curve.

Of the two methods discussed for generating a loss probability forecast, the second is clearly the easiest. We gain at least three things, however, with the regression approach:

1. We can see exactly how each of the individual risk characteristics affects the loss probability.

2. A regression model designed specifically to predict the likelihood of loss is likely to be more predictive of loss than a custom score that may have been designed to predict delinquency, or perhaps delinquency and bankruptcy.

3. Finally, with the regression model we can incorporate variables not used in the custom score that may affect loan outcome. With an internal loss forecasting model, we are not bound by the constraints we might face when deciding which variables to include in a custom score. We can include anything that is predictive in forecasting the loss rate, such as economic variables like regional unemployment rates or variables collected in the loan origination system that for some reason are not available to the scoring system and therefore not usable in the custom score. The loss model could also take into account complicated interactions among variables that would be confusing to business operators if used in a custom score but that could increase the accuracy of the loss rate forecast.[8]

DERIVATION OF ESTIMATED LOSS ON DEFAULT

To estimate loss on default we must include all cash flows that are lost when a borrower defaults. For mortgages, this includes (1) unrecovered principal, (2) lost interest payments, and (3) expense incurred during foreclosure and while the lender owns the real estate before selling it (REO expenses).[9] If the debt is covered by mortgage insurance (MI), any proceeds the lender receives from the insurance company are added back in.

$$
\begin{aligned}
\text{Loss} = \quad &\text{Unrecovered principal} \\
&+\text{Lost interest} \\
&+\text{Foreclosure and REO expenses} \\
&-\text{MI payments}
\end{aligned}
$$

---

[8] See the section on segmentation in Chapter 4 for more discussion of variable interactions.
[9] Here we are discussing the loss should the lender foreclose on the property, take it into its inventory, and sell it. Although this happens in first lien mortgage defaults, there are cases in which the lender, not finding it worthwhile to take the property, simply charges off the outstanding balance or the property is purchased by a third party. The method described here can be adjusted to handle such cases.

Unrecovered principal is the difference between the outstanding loan balance at default and the amount for which the property foreclosed on is sold. There are two ways to forecast what this amount will be. The first is by estimating a regression model using the actual net credit losses (NCL) reported on the general ledger for loans that defaulted in the past. Unlike the loss probability, which has a yes/no (0/1) outcome, this variable is continuous and could be predicted with linear regression. For mortgages, important explanatory variables include loan-specific information like LTV ratio, property type, and loan type. That is the approach we have taken here.

An alternative is to build a model to forecast the value of the property itself at future points in time.[10] If we can forecast what the value of the property will be when the borrower defaults, we can subtract that value from the expected loan balance at the time of default (loan balance can be estimated at each future point using a mortgage amortization equation).[11]

The second component, lost interest—the sum of the interest payments lost during the delinquency, foreclosure, and REO periods—is calculated using the coupon on the loan and the loan balance at the time the borrower stops paying on the loan. We assume the REO period lasts seven months for all loans (based on a historical average) but the foreclosure period varies by state (again based on historical data).

The third component of loss is foreclosure and REO expenses: repairs to the property, advances of taxes and insurance, homeowners' association fees, payments for utilities, and the like. If these expenses are treated as a constant proportion of the original loan amount, their value in the future may be assumed to be equal to their historical values. Alternatively, a submodel can be built to predict expenses if contributing factors can be identified.

The fourth component, MI cash inflows (which as income to the lender offset the loss), are calculated according to the insurance contract arrangements. The claim amount for MI is equal to the stated coverage percentage times the sum of:

---

[10] The value of a property at a future point in time is likely to depend in part on how property values evolve in the region. If this is incorporated into the model, some method will be needed to forecast future property values, perhaps by using a simple trend, using a published regional forecast, or incorporating a process for generating numerous possible outcomes for property values, such as a Monte Carlo process.

[11] One complicating factor is that the balance in future months may not evolve as the amortization schedule describes because borrowers may miss payments; subprime loans especially are often extended when the borrower falls behind. If this is the case, an ad hoc adjustment can be made to the expected balances based on the relationship between the expected and the observed balance at various points in time for loans that eventually default.

- The unpaid principal balance due on the date of default.

- The accumulated unpaid interest due on the loan computed at the coupon rate through the date when the claim is filed.

- Foreclosure and REO expenses.

MI is typically used only on loans with LTVs above 80 percent—the higher the LTV, the greater the coverage rate.

FIGURE 8.5 PERCENT SEVERITY BEFORE AND AFTER MI BY LTV

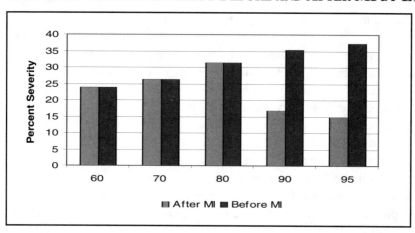

Once we have combined these four sets of cash flows, we can generate a loss estimate for each loan. Figure 8.5 shows average loss as a percentage of the original loan amount (loss severity) both before and after accounting for MI payments to the lender. Clearly, LTV has a strong positive effect on severity before M. MI payments lessen the loss substantially.[12]

Figure 8.6 shows the distribution of loss severity for a pool of mortgages. Forecasted severity can range from less than 4 percent of the original balance to more than 60 percent, depending on the loan.

---

[12] This does not imply that the expected default cost is lower for high-LTV than for low-LTV loans. The loss probability for high- LTV loans is very large. When this probability is multiplied by severity after MI, default cost continues to increase monotonically with LTV but not by as much as it would were there no MI coverage.

FIGURE 8.6 DISTRIBUTION OF % SEVERITY

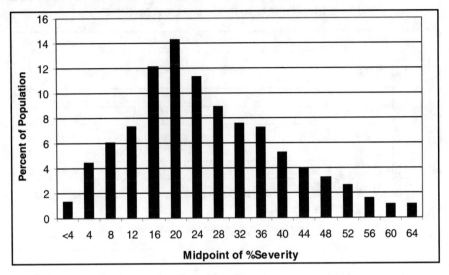

BRINGING IT ALL TOGETHER: THE LOSS FORECAST

Figure 8.7 shows the distribution of forecasted lifetime losses for a pool of mortgages that originated in 2000. The values are the expected loss as a percentage of the original balance, in basis points (bps) and range from less than five to more than 400. Many loans have very low expected default cost, below five bps, but for a good number the expected default cost is over 100 bps, and for about 2 percent of the portfolio it is over 400 bps. This wide range in expected losses suggests that there is significant room for pricing risk even within the prime mortgage market.

As an example of calculating expected loss for a specific loan, consider a $100,000 loan with an 85 percent LTV ratio, 12 percent mortgage insurance (MI) coverage, and a FICO score of 720. The FICO score suggests that this loan has a fairly good credit profile. Its LTV may be a bit higher than average in the prime mortgage industry but the MI coverage lowers the loss to the lender considerably. LTV affects the expected default cost in two ways (1) high LTVs lead to higher probabilities of loss (borrowers with more equity have less incentive to default) and (2) high LTVs increase loss severity if there is default because there is less cushion to protect the lender from loss.

FIGURE 8.7 DISTRIBUTION OF FORECASTED LIFETIME LOSS AS PERCENT OF ORIGINAL LOAN AMOUNT

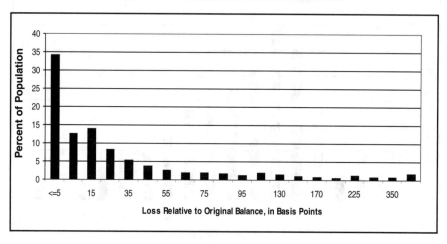

The model estimates the lifetime loss probability of this loan to be 1 percent, and the likely loss on default as 27 percent of the original balance, or $27,000. The expected loss is calculated as follows:

Expected lifetime loss = 0.01 x 0.27 x 100,000 = $270

Although total lifetime loss is useful to know in buying or selling loans, in many loss-forecasting exercises we want to know the expected losses over specific periods. To generate those estimates, we need to make some assumptions about when losses will take place.

Fortunately, we have at hand the loss-timing curve shown in Figure 8.1. Recall that this curve shows the percentage of total lifetime losses that are expected to occur in each future period of a mortgage portfolio's life. Thus, we can find expected losses for any period in a loan's life by multiplying the expected lifetime loss dollars by the percentages that underlie the curve. For example, say we want to know what losses to expect in the fourth year of the life of that $100,000, 85 percent LTV mortgage. The loss-time-curve indicates that 18 percent of total losses for a portfolio would occur in the fourth year. Our forecast for the loan in that period is 18 percent of $270, or $48.60. The forecast for the entire portfolio would be obtained by summing the forecasts for all the individual loans.

SUMMARY

These, then, are the steps in obtaining a loss forecast using loan data available at origination:

1. Build a loss probability model for the longest performance period for which data are available, either by estimating a regression model using data on all available risk characteristics or by mapping historical loss rates to a pre-existing custom score.

2. If that period does not cover the entire period over which losses are expected, gross up the probability to a lifetime probability using a loss curve (which may be built from internal data or obtained from a published source).

3. Build a loss model that includes all possible cash inflows and outflows that would be experienced if the loan defaults.

4. For each loan, multiply the loss given the default estimate produced by the lifetime loss probability. This is the expected lifetime loss for a loan with those particular characteristics. Each loan in the portfolio would have a unique loss estimate.

5. To forecast losses over the next quarter, year, or two years, use the loss-timing curve to distribute the lifetime losses over each interval of interest (see step 2).

A loan-level loss-forecasting model like the one we have outlined overcomes three shortcomings of traditional models:

1. By estimating a loss rate or probability for each loan based on its unique characteristics, the model can easily pick up any changes in credit quality that occur when new loans are added to the portfolio or old ones roll off.

2. The effect of loan age on losses is incorporated, so that loans have a lower expectation of loss early and late in their lives and higher expected losses in the middle years.

3. Loss rates and amounts are forecast separately to pick up the effect of any changes in variables that affect dollar losses, such as increases in the LTV ratios of loans in the portfolio.

Chapter 9
IMPACT OF INDETERMINATE PERFORMANCE EXCLUSIONS ON CREDIT SCORE MODEL DEVELOPMENT

Mark Beardsell
Director of Home Equity Modeling, Consumer Asset Division
Citigroup

INTRODUCTION

It is common practice when building scorecards to define an *indeterminate* class of loans and exclude them from the model development sample. For example, suppose accounts never greater than 29 days past due are considered good, accounts 30-59 days past due are indeterminate, and accounts 60 days or more past due are bad. Indeterminate performance exclusions are applied if the accounts 30-59 days past due are omitted from model development.

An alternative approach is to classify all performance outcomes as either good or bad and to build the model using the entire population. For instance, the set of good accounts could be redefined to include the indeterminate accounts, so that accounts never more than 59 days past due are good. Accounts ever 60 days past due are bad. Table 9.1 summarizes these performance definitions with and without indeterminates defined.

While some credit score model developers consider it beneficial to exclude indeterminate performance, others think it detrimental to scorecard development. The most popular argument supporting indeterminate exclusions is that modeling only the obviously good and the obviously bad accounts has superior predictive ability. Sharper distinctions between accounts exhibiting more extreme performance differences is thought to allow better model prediction. But a fundamental argument against excluding indeterminate accounts is that, as a general statistical rule, discarding sample information that is available lowers model predictive ability.

TABLE 9.1 PERFORMANCE DEFINITIONS: AN EXAMPLE

Case	Good	Indeterminate	Bad
Indeterminate performance defined	<= 29 days past due	>= 30 days past due and <= 59 days past due	>= 60 days past due
Indertminate performance not defined	<= 59 dayps past due	NA	>= 60 days past due

The positive or negative impact of excluding indeterminate performance boils down to how much statistical information is available in the indeterminate accounts. Proponents of excluding indeterminates presume the information content of these accounts is a net liability in the model estimation process; opponents of excluding them presume their information content is a net asset. The empirical tests of this chapter quantify how excluding indeterminates affects credit score model performance, with a view to providing empirical guidance to the credit scoring industry on the use of indeterminate exclusions.

EMPIRICAL TESTS

This chapter tests for the benefits of excluding indeterminate accounts from scorecards by constructing behavior score models using data from a large national mortgage portfolio.[1] Three pairs of models corresponding to account populations 0 days past due (0 cycle), 1-29 days past due (1 cycle), and 30-59 days past due (2 cycles) are estimated.[2] Within each pair, one model excludes indeterminate accounts during development. The other

---

[1] The most fundamental distinction in credit scoring applications is between models designed to approve or decline loan applications and models designed to manage existing accounts. Behavior scores are intended to predict existing account performance over a relatively short horizon, usually six months from the date of scoring; they are commonly used to prioritize collections of delinquent accounts, screen customers for cross-sell efforts, manage credit lines, and authorize higher account limits.

[2] Dividing the portfolio at the time of scoring into mutually exclusive segments based on delinquency status (0 days past due, 1-29 days past due, 30-59 days past due, etc.) is a standard behavior scoring approach. The goal of segmenting is to achieve better risk differentiation within the portfolio than would occur if accounts were pooled without regard to delinquency status.

model is developed treating indeterminate performance good or bad. Validation samples also include indeterminate accounts as good when the performance of each pair of models is evaluated.[3]

Including indeterminate accounts in the validation sample ensures that the performance of a model is tested on a sample that represents the account population to be scored in practice. While it is valid in building models to consider excluding indeterminate accounts from the estimation process, it is not valid to exclude them from model validation. Certainly, excluding indeterminate accounts from live scoring is not possible because how an account will perform is not known at the time of scoring. Therefore, these accounts should also be included in validation.

Classifying indeterminate accounts as good during validation ensures that the validation bad account definition (60+ days past due) and the validation good account definition (<=59 days past due) are the same whether or not indeterminate accounts have been excluded from model development. The validation bad account definition will also be identical to the development bad account definition. This clearly relates differences in model validation performance to the effect of excluding indeterminate accounts from development.

The empirical results also provide evidence that conclusions about the modeling impact of indeterminate performance exclusions are robust. Segmenting the account population by delinquency status is a convenient way to check whether the effects of modeling remain stable as the percentage of the development sample defined to be indeterminate increases.[4]

FRAMEWORK FOR THE BEHAVIOR SCORE MODEL

The analytical framework for developing behavior scores used in this chapter is a standard approach in the credit scoring industry. A single observation point is used. It marks the boundary between the end of a 12-month historical period and the beginning of a 6-month performance period, and defines the time at which development scores are calculated. The observation point also defines the time at which accounts are segmented into distinct populations by delinquency status. The historical period provides pre-

---

[3] A validation sample is a set of accounts not used in model development but used to test the model's predictive ability after it is developed. A 30 percent validation sample means the model is developed on 70 percent of available data and tested on the remaining 30 percent. Models developed on 0-cycle, 1-cycle, and 2-cycle accounts are validated on matching samples.
[4] The size of the indeterminate category is largest for the two-cycle population, next largest for the 1-cycle population, and smallest for the 0-cycle population. The reason for this is explained fully in footnote 13.

dictive data for model development. Account payment performance during the performance period is used to classify accounts into good, bad, or indeterminate outcomes. The goal is that the model provide the best estimate of the likelihood that an account will display bad performance. Figure 9.1 diagrams the observation, historical, and performance periods.

FIGURE 9.1 MODEL DEVELOPMENT FRAMEWORK

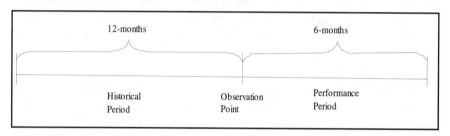

Table 9.2 summarizes key dates and segments used in building models. Account due dates in May 2001 are the observation points for all loans. Account delinquency status on the due date in May 2001 is used to group accounts into segments for modeling. Observations during the performance period of June 2001 through November 2001 and the historical period from April 2000 to May 2001 also occur on account due dates, so that modeled performance outcomes and measured predictive characteristics reflect the contractual obligations of each account.[5]

TABLE 9.2 DEVELOPMENT PERIODS AND MODEL SEGMENTS

Period	Dates
The observation point	May-01
The performance period	June-01 to Nov-01 (6 months)
The historical period	June-00 to May-01 (12 months)

Model Segments	Deliquency Status
0 cycle	0 days past due
1 cycle	1-29 days past due
2 cycle	30-59 days past due

---

[5] Due date models can be contrasted with month-end models, where account information recorded at the end of each calendar month is used in the scoring model. A weakness of month-end models is that accounts can become contractually delinquent, cure before month end, and never be recorded as delinquent. This blindness of month-end models to intramonth contractual delinquency events makes them inferior to due date scoring models.

In virtually every model development effort, definitions of good, bad, and indeterminate performance are driven primarily by account delinquency and write-off behavior during the performance period. While additional criteria may be included in the specific definitions used, an account is generally considered bad if it is ever 3+ cycles (>=60 days past due) delinquent.[6] An account is generally considered good if it is never more than 1 cycle past due. An account is considered indeterminate if, among other things, it is ever 2 cycles (30-59 days past due) delinquent during the performance period.

Observation exclusions are accounts dropped from the development sample because of account conditions that exist at the observation point. The primary purpose is to remove accounts from development that will not be scored in production. Typical examples are very new accounts (less than three months on book), closed accounts, and accounts in foreclosure (for mortgage credit scoring). *Performance* exclusions eliminate accounts from the development sample based on account conditions prevailing during the performance period; the most notable example is indeterminate performance exclusions.[7]

The predictive account characteristics used in this chapter are typical of those found in most behavior score models. Historical account delinquency, nonsufficient funds (NSF), extension, payment, and balance-related activity of the scored account are the most important kinds of information commonly found in behavior scores.[8] Historical data from each of these categories is considered for inclusion in the models discussed below.[9] Refreshed credit bureau characteristics or a refreshed generic credit score are also often incorporated into behavior scorecards to reflect changes in borrowers' overall credit standing.

---

[6] The actual performance definitions used for the models are proprietary.

[7] Again, specific criteria used to define observation and performance exclusions are proprietary.

[8] Nonsufficient funds (NSF) are returned (bounced) checks. Extensions, a loan servicing practice used commonly in the consumer finance industry, allow debtors to make up missed payments by tacking them on to the end of the loan term—the original loan term is "extended." They are used to make delinquent loans current.

[9] Many potential characteristics, several only slight variations from one another, are generated using these core sources of behavioral credit information. The development effort below considers six characteristics based on delinquency status at the due date, five based on NSF and extension information, and five based on payment and balance information.

MODEL WEIGHTS AND EXPLANATORY VARIABLES

Logistic regression is used to estimate model weights. When developing a credit scorecard a decision must be made about how to enter explanatory variables (historical account characteristics) in the model. The options are to enter all variables as indicator variables (classed variables), enter all as continuous variables, or enter some as indicator and some as continuous variables.[10] The choice made in this paper is to enter all explanatory variables as indicator variables.[11]

CORRELATION ANALYSIS AND CLASSING

Simple pair-wise correlation analysis is performed on the predictive characteristics considered for inclusion to identify groups of variables that contain essentially the same information for predicting account performance. For example, the *number of times* an account was delinquent in the last 12 months captures essentially the same predictive information as the *percentage* of the last 12 months an account was delinquent. Highly correlated characteristics are not allowed to enter model specifications simultaneously.

Defining classes for each characteristic in the final models is an iterative process:

- Initial classes for each characteristic are chosen.

- A logistic regression is estimated.

- Model weights are inspected for intuitive interpretation, directional impact, and statistical significance.

- Classes are then refined before the next estimation round.

Final models incorporate classes intuitively correct in sign and statistically significant at the 5 percent level.

---

[10] An indicator variable is defined as 1 if the variable falls in a certain range and 0 otherwise. For each characteristic, a set of mutually exclusive and exhaustive indicator variables is defined. During estimation one of the indicator variables for each characteristic is excluded to avoid the problem of perfect co-linearity—a standard regression modeling technique when indicator variables are used. Defining indicator variables is also referred to as *classing* in the vernacular of scorecard development.

[11] The choice to enter explanatory variables continuously, in classes, or a mixture of the two has been found to affect model performance only slightly. *See* Elizabeth Mays. (2001). *Handbook of Credit Scoring*. Chicago: Glenlake Publishing, Chapter 4 "Scorecard Modeling with Continuous versus Classed Variables," pp. 71-104.

EMPIRICAL RESULTS

Table 9.3 summarizes modeling results. KS and divergence statistics are used to quantify the model's predictive ability (these standard industry measures of model performance are discussed in detail in Chapter 6). For proprietary reasons, all reported KS and divergence statistics discussed below are scaled arbitrarily by a constant to mask actual levels. Model comparisons remain valid after scaling because the relative magnitudes of the reported statistics are the same as those of the actual results.[12] The percentage of indeterminate accounts in each segment is reported in Table 9.3.[13] Discussion of empirical results is limited to reported KS statistics; divergence is reported to demonstrate the consistency of results regardless of the statistic used to judge model performance.

Two fundamental conclusions are supported in Table 9.3. First, models developed without defining indeterminate performance (all accounts are classified as good or bad) are most predictive. Second, development sample KSs are spurious (overstated) for models developed with indeterminate accounts excluded. Validation KSs for these models will also be spurious if indeterminate accounts are not included during validation.

In the lower half of Table 9.3 labeled May 01 Validation Sample, within each delinquency segment validation KS is highest for the model in which indeterminate performance was not defined. For models developed without an indeterminate class (left-hand column within each segment), validation KSs of 46.56 (0-cycle), 38.30 (1-cycle), and 24.46 (2-cycle) are reported. For models developed excluding indeterminate accounts (right-hand column within each segment), validation KSs of 46.54 (0-cycle), 37.70 (1-cycle) and 21.60 (2-cycle) are reported. Model validation KS statistics are calculated on identical sets of accounts within each segment. KS differences measure how excluding indeterminate accounts in development affects model performance.[14]

---

[12] The proprietary estimated model weights, variables, and attributes included in each model are not divulged.

[13] In Table 9-3 the percentage of indeterminate accounts rises sharply from 7.7 percent for the 0-cycle segment to 19.4 percent for the 1-cycle segment and 44.7 percent for the 2-cycle segment. The indeterminate rate is lowest among the May 01 0-cycle population because relatively few current accounts satisfy the indeterminate criteria of two cycles past due between June and November. The indeterminate rate is higher for the one-cycle population because a two-cycle delinquency event between June and November is more common for these accounts. The indeterminate rate is highest for the two-cycle accounts because a two-cycle delinquency event is common for this segment in the next six months.

[14] It is important to understand that in the lower half of Table 9-3 indeterminate accounts are included as good accounts in all validation samples.

This is an important result: Model performance can be harmed when indeterminate accounts are excluded from development. Further, when the number of indeterminates excluded becomes large (e.g., 44.7 percent for two-cycle population), the negative impact is nontrivial (KS of 24.96 compared to 21.6).[15]

To see that development sample KSs are overstated when models are developed excluding indeterminate accounts, compare the statistics in the upper half of Table 9.3 to those in the lower half. For models developed excluding indeterminate accounts (right-hand column), reported development KSs (upper half) are 50.38 (0-cycle), 47.84 (1-cycle), and 31.30 (2-cycle). Validation KSs for these models (lower half) drop precipitously to 46.54 (0-cycle), 37.70 (1-cycle), and 21.60 (2-cycle) when indeterminate accounts are included as good accounts in validation samples. For models developed without indeterminate accounts defined (left-hand column), only modest declines in KS are observed between development (upper half) and validation (lower half) for the 0-cycle model (49.03 versus 46.56) and 1-cycle model (40.87 versus 38.30). An increase in KS (23.28 versus 24.46) between development and validation occurs for the 2-cycle model.

This reveals that development KS statistics are inflated for models developed excluding indeterminate accounts, and the sole cause of the inflation is the absence of the indeterminate accounts. Validation KS statistics will be similarly inflated if indeterminate accounts are excluded from the validation samples.

CONCLUSION

When model predictive ability is correctly measured (indeterminate accounts are included in validation samples as good accounts), excluding indeterminate accounts in model development negatively affects model performance. This is important to know for credit score modeling. The most common argument in favor of indeterminate performance exclusions—that sharper distinctions between the predictive attributes of accounts exhibiting more extreme performance differences allows better model prediction—is not supported by the results discussed in this chapter.

---

[15] On the other hand, this result demonstrates that the ranking ability of behavior score models is robust. Validation KS is only 12 percent lower (decline from 24.46 to 21.60) when almost half (44.7 percent) of the two-cycle data is discarded during development.

TABLE 9.3 MASKED MODEL SUMMARY STATISTICS: DEVELOPMENT AND VALIDATION SAMPLES

(6-month performance period: June 2001-November 2001)

	Population Segment					
	0Cycle		1Cycle		2Cycle	
	Indeterminate Treatment For Development		Indeterminate Treatment For Development		Indeterminate Treatment For Development	
May 01 Development Sample	NotDefined (Included as Good)	Defined and Excluded	NotDefined (Included as Good)	Defined and Excluded	NotDefined (Included as Good)	Defined and Excluded
Percent Indeterminate	0.0%	7.7%	0.0%	19.4%	0.0%	44.7%
Divergence	1.36	1.51	0.96	1.38	0.30	0.69
K-S	49.03	50.38	40.87	47.84	23.28	31.30
	Indeterminate Treatment For Validation		Indeterminate Treatment For Validation		Indeterminate Treatment For Validation	
May 01 Validation Sample	NotDefined (Included as Good)	NotDefined (Included as Good)	NotDefined (Included as Good)	NotDefined (Included as Good)	NotDefined (Included as Good)	NotDefined (Included as Good)
Percent Indeterminate	0.0%	0.0%	0.0%	0.0%	0.0%	0.0%
Divergence	1.22	1.24	0.81	0.82	0.32	0.26
K-S	46.56	46.54	38.30	37.70	24.46	21.60

Another concern with excluding indeterminate accounts from model development is the potential for overstating both development and validation performance statistics. Once indeterminate accounts are excluded from development it is unlikely that these accounts will be included in model validation. Including them would put the analyst in the awkward position of reporting substantial performance declines between development and validation.

The likelihood of overstated model performance is a real concern for risk managers. If model development excludes indeterminate accounts, risk managers should request a model validation on a sample that includes them. Otherwise, the risk manager will be unpleasantly surprised when actual model performance is not nearly as good as advertised.[16]

---

[16] For a similar viewpoint and conclusions about the use of indeterminate exclusions in scorecard development, see *Building Better Scorecards.* (1999). Austin, TX: Austin Logistics, p. 315.

Chapter 10
CREDIT SCORING AND THE FAIR LENDING ISSUE OF DISPARATE IMPACT

Michael LaCour-Little
Vice President, Risk Management Division
Wells Fargo Home Mortgage
Elaine Fortowsky
Director, Fair Lending Modeling
Wells Fargo Home Mortgage

OVERVIEW

Disparate impact arises when a lender applies policies and practices to all groups of applicants uniformly but there is nonetheless an adverse effect on a protected class of individuals. In this chapter we analyze the problem of disparate impact in credit scoring and evaluate three approaches to identifying and correcting it. The adverse effect can appear in the form of either lower application acceptance rates or less favorable loan terms.[1] We show that the usual approach of attempting to control disparate impact by eliminating variables from scorecards may have unintended and undesirable consequences, and we present a superior alternative.

Allegations of discrimination in financial services have increased over the past decade, particularly in home mortgage lending. In the mortgage market, the charges arise from two uncontested empirical observations (1) the volume of home mortgage loans per mortgagable dwelling unit in pre-

---

[1] For an example see Collins, M. Cary, Keith Harvey, and Peter Nigro. (2002). "The Influence of Bureau Scores, Customized Scores and Judgmental Review on the Bank Underwriting Decision Making Process." *Journal of Real Estate Research,* 24(2):129-52, which argues that certain scoring approaches may have a disparate impact on low-income borrowers.

dominantly white areas is two to three times the rate in minority neighborhoods and (2) the rejection rate for minority mortgage loan applicants is roughly twice that of white applicants[2] (for competing views on the controversy over discrimination in mortgage lending, see Ladd[3] and LaCour-Little).[4] More recently, the auto finance industry has been subject to a series of class action lawsuits alleging discriminatory pricing and disparate impact on minority groups. These charges arise from the pricing practices of auto dealers and captive finance companies, which allegedly result in African-Americans paying more for auto credit than similarly situated white borrowers (see U.S. Department of Justice[5] for facts and issues in a representative case).

Institutional lenders, especially those affiliated with depository institutions, are highly regulated. Regulatory agencies conduct periodic examinations to ensure that credit scoring, if used, is statistically sound and consistently applied to produce fair outcomes for all loan applicants. The major regulatory agencies coordinate these procedures through the Federal Financial Institutions Examination Council (FFIEC), which has published a detailed description of the procedures, which sometimes include estimation of regression equations.[6] The examinations are intended to ensure compliance with fair lending laws, especially the Equal Credit Opportunity Act (ECOA).

ECOA, enacted in 1974, is the primary statute under which legal proceedings alleging discrimination in financial services are brought. Originally designed to protect women from differential treatment, the law was amended in 1976 to include race and other protected categories. ECOA regulates all types of credit, not just mortgage lending, and prohibits discrimination based on race or color, religion, national origin, sex, marital status, age, receipt of public assistance, or good faith exercise of rights under the Consumer Credit Protection Act.

---

[2] Fix, Michael, and Raymond Struyk. (1993). *Clear and Convincing Evidence.* Washington, D.C.: Urban Institute.
[3] Ladd, Helen F. (1998). "Evidence on Discrimination in Mortgage Lending." *Journal of Economic Perspectives,* 12(2):41-62.
[4] LaCour-Little, Michael. (1999). "Discrimination in Mortgage Lending: A Critical Review of the Literature." *Journal of Real Estate Literature,* 7(1):15-52.
[5] U.S. Department of Justice (2000), Amicus Curiae Brief filed in Support of Plaintiffs' Opposition to Defendant's Motion for Summary Judgement, United States District Court, No. 3-98-0223, Nissan Motor Acceptance Corporation, Defendant.
[6] Federal Financial Institutions Examination Council. January 1999. "Interagency Fair Lending Examination Procedures." Washington, DC: FFIEC.

The discrimination prohibited by law may be most simply defined as differential treatment of otherwise similarly situated individuals on the basis of a protected characteristic. The general legal theory under which discrimination is unlawful is the equal protection provision of the Fourteenth Amendment. Courts have held that classifications based on race or gender are suspect and may be sustained only where a compelling interest can be shown.[7] Racial discrimination by government agencies themselves, either in intent or effect, has been alleged in criminal prosecution, capital sentencing, jury selection, and awarding of government entitlements, as well as many other areas.

Disparate *treatment* is considered intentional if the discriminating party took into account, overtly or covertly, the prohibited characteristic of the victim of discrimination. Claims of disparate *impact,* on the other hand, do not require a showing of intentional discrimination. Moreover, a showing of *business necessity* may rebut claims of disparate impact. Business necessity means that the factor used to discriminate, typically a positive correlate of the prohibited factor, serves a valid business purpose and is not merely a pretext for overt discrimination.

In the lending context, discrimination may consist of either (1) refusing to grant a loan or (2) varying the terms of the loan. Discrimination is generally categorized into three types (1) overt discrimination, (2) disparate treatment, and (3) disparate, or adverse, impact. Overt discrimination occurs when a lender openly discriminates based on a prohibited factor. Disparate treatment occurs when lenders treat applicants differently based on a prohibited factor. Adverse impact occurs when a business practice is applied uniformly but has a greater effect on a protected class.

Much of the law on discrimination in lending evolved out of the employment area,[8] where there is a solid base of case law. Lending discrimination actions, on the other hand, are rarely adjudicated. Complaints are often resolved by consent decree, in which the lender admits no wrongdoing but commits to revise its policies and practices, occasionally compensating victims of the allegedly discriminatory actions. Statistical evidence intended to show a pattern or practice of discriminatory behavior is common, particularly in class action cases.

---

[7] Kaye, David H., and Mikel Aichin, eds. (1986). *Statistical Methods in Discrimination Litigation.* New York: Marcel Dekker, Inc.
[8] Siskin, Bernard R. (1995). "Comparing the Role of Statistics in Lending and Employment Cases," in Anthony Yezer, ed., *Fair Lending Analysis.* Washington, D.C.: American Bankers Association.

Sandler and Biran[9] have criticized the use of statistics in legal proceedings based on complaints of discrimination (mainly employment discrimination cases). Courts have allowed statistical analysis to be offered as evidence if (1) the model is reasonably well specified, (2) statistics are based on a "proper pool" of applicants, (3) statistics show "substantial" discriminatory effect, and (4) the analysis can isolate the effects of a particular criterion used in the decision-making process.

The first criterion requires that the set of independent variables in any regression be reasonably comprehensive, with little likelihood of substantial omitted variable bias.[10] The second requires that the data sample be of adequate size. The third requires that the measure of discriminatory effect must be large, for example, the coefficient on the race variable must be of significant magnitude relative to other variables and have a significant t-statistic. The fourth requires that differential denial rates be attributable to a specific variable, not a combination of many factors.

The limited case law makes definitive statements about lending discrimination cases difficult, although analogies to employment law offer some guidance. If we assume that overt discrimination is rare, the distinction between disparate treatment and disparate impact is essential. Disparate treatment constitutes intentional discrimination and cannot be rebutted. Disparate effect is unintentional and may be rebutted by a business necessity argument. Most academic and policy-oriented research to date has focused on disparate treatment, as in the well-known Boston Fed study by Munnell and colleagues.[11]

In this chapter, we extend the discussion to the topic of disparate impact and consider how regulatory agencies might test for it and measure its magnitude, as well as how score developers might minimize its effect. Our work is not directed at any particular segment of consumer lending, though most of our experience is with mortgages. The default rates and intergroup differences we present should be viewed as broadly representative, not as examples of any particular line of consumer lending. Testing scorecards where protected class data is not available, as with non-HMDA reportable consumer credit, must rely on proxies, such as the composition

---

[9] Sandler, Andrew L., and Jonathan Biran. (1995). "The Improper Use of Statistics in Mortgage Lending Discrimination Actions," in Anthony Yezer, ed., *Fair Lending Analysis*. Washington, D.C.: American Bankers Association.

[10] See Chapter 4 for a discussion of omitted variable bias.

[11] Munnell, Alicia H., Lynn Browne, James McEnearney, and Geoffrey Tootell. (1996). "Mortgage Lending in Boston: Interpreting HMDA Data." *American Economic Review,* 86 (1):25-54.

of the census tract in which the borrower resides. While invariably less precise, similar methods were applied in the auto finance cases (i.e., borrower characteristics were inferred from place of residence).

We then define criteria for a good disparate impact test and for a good corrective action plan. We also describe the data used in this study and present the scorecards that will be the subjects of our disparate impact analysis. We evaluate two disparate impact testing procedures, univariate and multivariate, and show that the multivariate is superior. Following this we show how the standard corrective action of eliminating potentially problematic variables from scorecards does not actually correct disparate impact. We then present a new corrective action that does eliminate disparate impact. Retaining the original variables but adjusting scorecard weights by employing protected class status as a control variable during estimation.

Conceptually, the tests and corrective procedures can be combined to form three approaches to identifying and correcting disparate impact (1) univariate testing with variable elimination, (2) multivariate testing with variable elimination, and (3) multivariate testing with adjustment of scorecard weights.

Finally, we present a summary and recommendations.

PERFORMANCE CRITERIA AND DATA

Due to privacy concerns, rather than using actual data in this study, we generated an artificial data sample that is designed to mirror a typical pool of mortgage loan applicants. The data are generated separately for a protected and a nonprotected class, so that the loan and borrower characteristics of each group are retained.

In order to fully evaluate our tests and corrective procedures, we generate two data samples, Process 1 and Process 2, that have the same means for the variables but different patterns of correlation, which leads to different degrees of disparate impact in the estimated scorecards. (In fact, the data samples have been constructed so that scorecards estimated on the Process 2 data will not have disparate impact. This will allow us to see if any of the tests suffer from a false positive problem—finding disparate impact where there is none.)

The data samples consist of three variables (1) FICO score,[12] (2) DTI, and (3) income. The first two factors are widely viewed as important pre-

---

[12] FICO is a generic credit score marketed by Fair, Isaac. It takes on values from 300 to 900; every 20-point decrease doubles the odds that a borrower will default on any credit account.

dictors of credit risk. Income is a more questionable factor due to its correlation with protected group status, for which it may simply be acting as a proxy. In our presentation, income does not actually affect default, but it is included in the estimated models to provide an additional performance hurdle for the tests and corrective procedures. Variable means for the data samples are presented in Table 10.1.

TABLE 10.1 VARIABLE MEANS FOR THE DATA SAMPLES

Variable	Protected Class Mean	Non-Protected Class Mean
FICO score	667	712
Debt ratio	39%	37%
Income	$61,000	$95,000

Once the scorecards are estimated from the data samples, the worst 5 percent of loans will be rejected and the rest accepted. Our measure of disparate impact, Ψ, is the percentage of rejected protected-class members that would not have been rejected if there were no disparate impact. A good disparate impact test is one that differentiates between $\Psi>0$ and $\Psi=0$, and a good corrective action plan is one that achieves $\Psi=0$ (or at least close to it).[13]

ESTIMATED SCORECARDS

The estimated default models for each data sample from which we will derive scorecards are presented in Table 10.2. In the Process 1 model all variables are statistically significant at the 0.0001 level. In the Process 2 model, income is not significant. We included income in the model specification even though it does not belong there. This typifies actual modeling, in which the developer does not know in advance exactly which explanatory variables belong in the model and will very likely include some irrelevant ones at first.

Note than in Process 1, income erroneously appears to be significant. One of the side effects of disparate impact is that insignificant variables may appear significant.

---

[13] For a more technical description of the methodology, see Fortowsky, Elaine, and Michael LaCour-Little. (2002). "Credit Scoring and Disparate Impact." Paper presented at the 2002 Midyear Meeting of the American Real Estate and Urban Economics Association (AREUEA), Washington, D.C.

TABLE 10.2 ESTIMATED EQUATIONS (USING SAS PROC LOGISTIC)

Variable	Process 1 Estimated Coefficient	Significance	Process 2 Estimated Coefficient	Significance
Intercept	1.880	<.0001	-10.487	<.0001
FICO	-0.016	<.0001	-0.026	<.0001
Debt ratio	0.176	<.0001	0.519	<.0001
Income (00,000)	-0.336	<.0001	-0.030	<.3439

To derive the scorecards shown in Table 10.3 from Table 10.2 we transformed the coefficients so that the resulting scores would range from 0 to 100.[14] For the Process 1 model we added 70 base points and multiplied each variable coefficient by 2.5/ln(2). For the Process 2 model we added 50 base points and multiplied each variable coefficient by 1.2/ln(2).

Such transformations, which are standard practice in scorecard building, speak to the fact that only the ordinal ranking of the scores is important. Note that the predicted values from the transformed models have the property that the odds of default double for every 2.5 points in the Process 1 model and for every 1.2 points in the Process 2 model.

TABLE 10.3 SCORECARDS FOR PROCESS 1 AND PROCESS 2

	Scorecard 1 (Process 1)	Scorecard 2 (Process 2)
Base points	70	50
FICO score	-0.058	-0.045
Debt ratio	0.635	0.899
Income (00,000)	-1.212	-0.052
	$\Psi=25.6$	$\Psi=0.1$

TESTING FOR DISPARATE IMPACT

In Table 10.3 the last row gives the disparate impact measure for each scorecard. For Scorecard 1 it is 25.6, indicating that 25.6 percent of the protected class applicants who were rejected would not have been if there had not been disparate impact. For Scorecard 2 the disparate impact measure is 0.1, effectively zero.

For a test to be good, it should be able to make it clear that there is disparate impact in Scorecard 1 but not in Scorecard 2. (Recall that Scorecard 1 is characterized by $\Psi>0$ and Scorecard 2 is characterized by $\Psi=0$.) The

---

[14] See Chapter 4 for a discussion of scorecard scaling.

multivariate test correctly identifies both cases while the univariate test (see Table 10.4) erroneously concludes that Ψ>0 for Scorecard 2.

TABLE 10.4 RESULTS OF A UNIVARIATE TEST FOR DISPARATE IMPACT

		Scorecard 1		Scorecard 2	
Variable	*Difference in Class Means*	*Point Weight*	*Point Difference*	*Point Weight*	*Point Difference*
FICO score	-45	-0.058	2.16	-0.045	2.03
Debt ratio	2	0.635	1.27	0.899	1.80
Income (00,000)	-0.34	-1.212	0.41	-0.052	0.02
Mean score			51.05		51.17

In Table 10.4, the columns labeled Point Difference measure how much each variable boosts the protected-class score (higher scores are worse for the applicant). Entries in these columns are calculated as the difference in means across the protected and nonprotected classes, multiplied by the point weight.

In Scorecard 1, the point differences are fairly large for the FICO score and DTI ratio. Comparing them to the mean score of 51.05 for the nonprotected class, we see that the FICO score is responsible for an increase of 2.61/51.05 = 5.11 percent in protected-class score and debt ratio is responsible for an increase of 1.27/51.05 = 2.49 percent. Given the magnitude of these effects, both variables would generally be considered as having disparate impact and corrective action would have to be investigated. (Income, which is responsible for only a 0.81 percent increase in score, would generally not be so considered.) Because there was potential for disparate impact, the conclusion is that Ψ> 0 for Scorecard 1.

In Scorecard 2, the point differences for FICO and DTI are also large, with FICO responsible for a 3.96 percent increase in score (based on a mean score of 51.17 for the nonprotected class) and DTI for a 3.51 percent increase. Again, both variables would generally be considered as having disparate impact, indicating a conclusion of Ψ> 0 for Scorecard 2. This is a false positive finding of disparate impact when none exists.

The conclusion of Ψ> 0 for Scorecard 2 illustrates a broader property of the univariate test. It tends to characterize *every* scorecard as having disparate impact. This is because the test is largely driven by cross-class differences in scorecard-variable means, which are almost always sizable but which are not related to the value of Ψ.

In the multivariate disparate impact test, the model is re-estimated using a protected-class indicator as an explanatory variable. If the coefficient on the protected-class indicator is significant and positive, then there is potential for disparate impact ($\Psi > 0$). If the coefficient is negative or not significant, then $\Psi = 0$.

Re-estimating the models with a protected-class indicator yields the results presented in Table 10.5. Given the significance of the protected class indicator, we conclude $\Psi > 0$ for Scorecard 1 and $\Psi = 0$ for Scorecard 2. This is the correct conclusion.

By looking at the change in the estimated coefficients relative to the original equations, the multivariate test lets us identify which variables are producing disparate impact. The change in the coefficients is -56 percent for FICO, 190 percent for DTI, and 100 percent for income, indicating that the variables are all potential drivers of disparate impact. Note that the ordering of the variables by their importance is different than in the univariate case. From highest potential for disparate impact to lowest, the multivariate ordering is (1) debt ratio, (2) income, and (3) FICO. In the univariate approach FICO moved ahead of debt ratio and income. Such reorderings can usually be expected because, unlike the univariate approach, the multivariate approach takes account of cross-correlation among variables, which may amplify or attenuate the impact of any single variable on the scores.

TABLE 10.5 RESULTS OF A MULTIVARIATE TEST FOR DISPARATE IMPACT

	Scorecard 1		Scorecard 2	
Variable	*Estimated Coefficient*	*Significance*	*Estimated Coefficient*	*Significance*
Intercept	-10.33	<.0001	-10.52	<.0001
FICO score	-0.025	<.0001	-0.026	<.0001
Debt ratio	0.510	<.0001	0.519	<.0001
Income (00,000)	-0.003	<.9116	-0.028	<.3708
Protected	10.27	<.0001	0.04	<.6436

The usual way to correct disparate impact is to drop variables from the scorecard. Usually the decision to drop a variable is made by subjectively weighing its business relevance against its contribution to the average score difference across classes. We investigated how well this approach works by dropping each variable in turn from the scorecard and then recalculating the new value of Ψ.

Table 10.6 presents the results. The first column gives the value of Ψ when we re-score the applications using the original scorecard coefficients but omitting the variable. The second column gives the value of Ψ when we re-estimate the model after dropping a variable and then use the new coefficients to score the applications. In every case, Ψ is substantially greater than zero. From this, we can conclude that dropping variables is not an effective corrective action.

TABLE 10.6 EFFECT ON SCORECARD 1 OF DROPPING VARIABLES

Variable	Without Re-estimation	With Re-estimation
FICO score	$\Psi=12.1$	$\Psi=12.4$
Debt ratio	$\Psi=83.1$	$\Psi=83.3$
Income	$\Psi=22.9$	$\Psi=22.9$

WHAT TO DO IF YOU FIND DISPARATE IMPACT

The reason the corrective action of dropping variables does not achieve the desired objective is that disparate impact is due not to the mere presence of particular variables in a model but to the general correlation among all the variables, including the error term and the protected class indicator. Correcting disparate impact requires a more drastic solution than dropping variables. We propose the solution suggested by Table 10.5. As a standard practice, use protected class status as a control variable during model development but exclude it in the final scorecard. Effectively, this would amount to replacing the Scorecard 1 point weights with those from Table 10.5, appropriately transformed. The new scorecard would look like Table 10.7, which achieves $\Psi=0$ (no disparate impact).

TABLE 10.7 CORRECTED SCORECARD FOR PROCESS 1

Variable	Point Weight
Base points	70
FICO score	-0.090
Debt ratio	1.839
Income (00,000)	-
	$\Psi=0.0$

SUMMARY AND RECOMMENDATIONS

In this chapter, we defined a measure of disparate impact, Ψ, as the percentage of rejected protected-class members that would not have been rejected if there were no disparate impact. We then defined a good disparate impact test as one that differentiates between $\Psi > 0$ and $\Psi = 0$, and a good corrective action plan as one that achieves $\Psi = 0$. We set up two test scorecards, one in which $\Psi > 0$ (Scorecard 1) and one in which $\Psi = 0$ (Scorecard 2).

We then evaluated two tests for disparate impact, the univariate and the multivariate. Both procedures identified Scorecard 1 as a case where $\Psi > 0$, but only the multivariate test correctly identified Scorecard 2 as a case where $\Psi = 0$. (The false positive shown for Scorecard 2 typically characterizes univariate tests for disparate impact.) Next we demonstrated that the standard corrective action of eliminating variables does not actually correct disparate impact—the closest we got to $\Psi = 0$ was $\Psi = 12.1$.

In the final section we presented a new technique for eliminating disparate impact in scorecards. It consists of retaining the original variables but adjusting their scorecard weights by including protected class as a control variable in the regression.

We recommend the multivariate testing procedure described in this chapter to both score developers and regulators. We also recommend our new approach for controlling disparate impact to model builders, though we suggest they consult with legal counsel and perhaps the primary regulator for their institution before implementing this innovative technique.

To policymakers we would recommend safe harbor rules to protect institutions adopting our approach in a good faith effort to minimize any adverse effect of credit scoring upon loan applicants.

Section Three
SCORE IMPLEMENTATION, MONITORING, AND MANAGEMENT

Chapter 11
HOW TO SUCCESSFULLY MANAGE A CREDIT SCORE DEVELOPMENT PROJECT

Dana Wiklund
Vice President, Decision Solutions
Equifax

This chapter addresses project management issues in building and implementing credit-scoring models. These issues range from selecting a model developer to the organizational issue of model acceptance. Coordination with the systems team is crucial to a successful model development project—a scoring model is an installed computer program that needs appropriate systems prioritization and support.

Organizational interests can be divided among those departments that will interact directly and those that will interact indirectly with it. Departments that will have direct interaction are Risk Management and Originations or Underwriting. Departments like Legal, Compliance, Finance, Marketing, and Collections whose work will be affected by the new model have an indirect but legitimate interest in the project. Figure 11.1 outlines project constituencies.

SELECTING A MODEL DEVELOPER

The first decision in selecting a model developer is whether to use internal resources or an external vendor. Many mid-market and large organizations already have substantial investments in their own modeling and analytics departments.

FIGURE 11.1 PROJECT CONSTITUENCIES

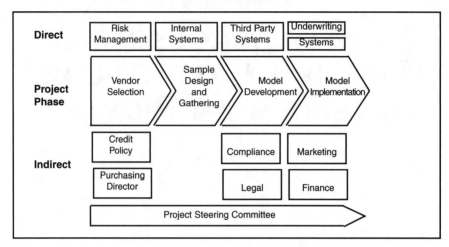

Internal model developers can offer cost advantages because usually these groups are already cost centers to the organization, and their expenses do not include the travel, data processing, and profit considerations of an external firm. Usually internal teams work with standard statistical software packages like SAS and S+ software. The techniques used to model populations may vary with the experience or background of the statistician. The scale of modeling activity within an organization is likely to be smaller than that of an external vendor but more flexible, allowing for the use of different techniques, because the internal team is not locked into scalable modeling processes for business reasons.

Using internal modeling resources has both advantages and disadvantages. Among the advantages of an internal team are more detailed knowledge of organizational data and products and quick turnaround if analysis shows it is necessary to validate or re-estimate a model. One disadvantage may be that an internal statistician may use a modeling technique that is not well understood by the line of business, one that is perhaps not consistent with risk modeling techniques used on previous projects. (The idea of business users understanding how a model was developed will be discussed later.) Important questions a modeling project manager must document with an internal model developer are statistical technique, sample integrity, and size and sufficiency of the development and hold-out or validation samples.

External model developers range from companies whose sole business is statistical models to the credit bureaus, which each maintain model development and analytic departments, to boutique firms specializing in statistical modeling. Engaging an external firm to build a model is a material economic investment. External models can cost from $30,000 to $100,000 and up.

Among the advantages of hiring an external vendor are process efficiencies in handling data, consistent statistical techniques, extensive auditing procedures, and experience developing models for different customers and product types. External developers may have a better understanding of potential development pitfalls in terms of sampling, validation, and choice of modeling characteristics because of their broad experience.

External modelers will manage the whole project, releasing the lender to manage the internal processes and business interactions that the model will bring. They also have many precoded processes for taking in data and creating modeling variables. For instance, they might take archived credit reports from a sample provided by the client and aggregate the modeling variable set for each credit bureau represented. Or they might take a list source of the data sample and obtain the underlying credit information at the point of observation. External modelers maintain many routines to find out quickly what characteristics are most predictive for a given business purpose.

As part of the engagement external vendors offer deliverables that include validation packages of both the development and the hold-out sample, documentation on how the modeling characteristics are aggregated, and specifications for programming the model into a decision platform.

The importance of characteristic aggregation programming specifications cannot be overstated. If the model is to be programmed into a mainframe decision support platform, characteristic specifications give the programmer a road map for coding each characteristic for each credit bureau, which is important because the method used by each credit bureau to calculate a characteristic will be slightly different. The final model scorecard or algorithm should also be documented in a way a programmer or systems analyst can understand and use.

SYSTEMS ISSUES

There are three important systems and programming issues that relate to managing scoring projects (1) scorecard installation, (2) connectivity with credit information, and (3) once the scoring process has been completed, scorecard tracking.

Scoring models can be installed in several ways. It is therefore advisable that a representative from systems and programming be on the project team from the very beginning. One option is to install them at a credit bureau or offsite intermediary. The benefit to this is that the programming hours necessary to install the model are incurred outside the organization. On the one hand, the company housing the model will charge for use of the model, either per name or by subscription. Still, if systems hours are at a premium within the organization, this installation alternative may be desirable. Usually, companies that house models—the three credit bureaus and companies that provide systems integration for credit bureau data—also have auditing capabilities.

There are two forms of internal systems platforms for credit scoring models. One is a traditional system where the model would be programmed in COBOL or a similar language within a mainframe-based applications processing system. Newer to the market are client-server-driven strategy management systems, which can manage score cut-offs and credit policy decision criteria. These systems are generally installed on a network server that is separate from the mainframe. Generally, client-server systems use mainframe data extracts of credit information to run the models, but a model can be implemented as an algorithm or a scorecard fairly efficiently.

Installing a model on a mainframe system requires the most organizational effort in terms of systems hours, auditing, and project management. A typical scorecard containing 12 characteristics may require 400 hours of systems programming resources. At a typical internal cost of $60 per systems hour, this would represent a $24,000 investment in addition to the development cost.

If mainframe installation is chosen, at the outset the project manager should work with the systems and programming representative to estimate the total systems hours that might be needed to install the model and prioritize programming resources. A systems manager should be on the project steering committee. If possible, a programmer who has worked on a scoring project or had exposure to credit information should be secured for the project (the prior experience might be programming done on a bureau link for the organization or on the applications processing system itself).

Installing the scorecard at a credit bureau or intermediary may cost between $10,000 and $25,000 in addition to model development. These organizations also have to cover the cost of programming and auditing, but the project manager may be able to negotiate the cost of implementation into model development.

Installing the model into a client-server system takes fewer systems hours but underlying programming for data feeds to the server may be necessary. If the client- server system is fed characteristics by an embedded or a foreign application, these characteristics may or may not account for what is in the new model. If at the outset of the project the client-server system supports a fixed number of credit information characteristics that cover a variety of risk or response indicators, it may be wise to limit the model to the variables in the system. Without necessarily affecting the potential power of the model, this will have a net savings on systems hours needed to program and feed new characteristics. As with any type of installation, a model installed on a client-server system will still need full auditing to assure that each characteristic is calculating correctly and that the model as a whole is delivering a correct score.

The systems and programming areas are also vital in scorecard monitoring—ensuring that appropriate data are fed through to the monitoring reports. A discussion with systems and programming about capturing scores and characteristic values should be part of score implementation. Once the systems hours have been assigned and a model coded and implemented, it may be difficult to get additional resources to capture this data. Storage space may also be a problem for some organizations.

PROJECT STEERING COMMITTEE

The fact that a project manager needs to consider both the direct and the indirect internal constituencies of the new model should be reflected in the makeup of the project steering committee. The committee should be established at the very outset of the project and should be composed of representatives with decision-making power from risk management, credit policy, systems, compliance, legal, marketing, underwriting, the line of business, and systems support. The committee, as the name implies, will steer the project, making major decisions through consensus as a team. Major decisions may include choice of vendor, approval of the contract, and scope and timing of the project plan. The steering committee is particularly valuable when things go wrong or when factions within an organization are putting up roadblocks to prevent the project from being successful.

When a project runs into problems like the developer (internal or external) missing deadlines, the steering committee should strengthen its support for the project manager. The departmental decision-makers on the steering committee not only give the committee more power within the organization but also can make things happen quickly within their own departments.

The goal of the project is usually to deliver a technology that enhances decision-making within the organization. The steering committee will make sure that the organization as a whole embraces the project and that it moves forward without problems with one department bringing it to a standstill. The committee environment is designed to foster issue resolution for the project.

The steering committee should meet at least once a month as well as at major milestones during the project. Its members should meet with the model developers at the capability presentation stage at the beginning of the project regularly through to delivery of the final model.

MACROECONOMIC ISSUES

In the 1990s, the United States economy experienced one of the longest sustained macroeconomic expansions in its history. It ended in 2001. A score developed during a period of expansion is at risk of being less predictive when the economy is contracting. That is why the economic environment is an important issue in a scorecard development project. Changes to applicant populations after the model is implemented can at the extreme lead to rapid deterioration of an empirically derived model.

During the sample design session with the scorecard developer it is important to make the economic environment an agenda item. Will your model be affected if the economy changes either for the better or for the worse? How can these effects be minimized?

The development sample for a credit risk model is typically drawn from a population of loans 18 to 36 months old. If the economy has gone through any significant upswings or downturns during that period, the modeler will need a plan to deal with it. A model developed during an expansionary economic period and installed in a recessionary or stagnant period may underestimate risk by inflating odds or deflating projected bad rates. Conversely, a sample taken from a recessive or stagnant period will result in a model that may overestimate risk or underestimate bad rate projections. The project manager will not want to install a costly new scorecard developed using a performance period that does not match well with the environment in which the model will be used.

Depending on the business that the model will support or the geographic dispersion of the product the model will be used for, issues of regional economic differences may surface. Loan products like bankcards and auto finance loans are becoming more generic across geographies. Sometimes a percentage of the business may be skewed towards a geography that has been in decline for several months during the performance period while other areas in which the lender is operating may be doing well. It is important to map out regional performance of credit products against geographic or regional economic performance early in the sample design discussions.

Sample sizes for scorecard development can be issues onto themselves, especially for smaller institutions. What can be done here to minimize the impacts of economic swings on scorecard developments? One option for discussion with the scorecard developer would be to augment the sample with loans whose performance over the time period sampled offsets trends during the same period that might be counter to the environment the model will be operating in. For example, if the national economy was doing well during the primary performance window, but the model will be implemented when the economy is stagnant, it might be wise to add to the sample records of loan performance during a recessive or stagnant period.

Another solution might be to look at regional economic differences if the sample is large enough and weight the sample by making use of a diverse economic sample. The developer may also be able to use loan trends and vintage analytics to adjust projected bad rates from a sample that has had no economic intervention. For example, if the model is projecting a bad rate of X and loans with that level of risk are known to be performing 20 percent worse recently, the bad rate projections for that score might be adjusted to X * 1.20. It is particularly essential, then, to monitor scorecard performance closely to affirm the bad rate projection adjustment strategy.

As was noted in Chapter 1, one of the current areas of research is how to make scores more robust across economic environments. Until best practices in this area can be determined, lenders should take great care in setting score policies when economic conditions are changing.

UNDERWRITING

Very few lenders have completely automated the underwriting or credit decision process. Behind most lending decisions there is likely to be a loan analyst or underwriter. Analysts and underwriters are often given authority to override a score-based lending decision in certain situations. A danger to successful scorecard deployment then is rebellion or nonacceptance by the underwriting department.

When models are brought into lending environments, they bring with them quantum leaps in efficiency that make it possible to reduce the number of people needed to make traditional judgmental loan decisions. For these reasons, the scoring project manager needs to take great care to educate staff of the underwriting department on scoring and how to interpret the specific model being installed, and to foster acceptance of any emerging technology that affects what they do.

Traditional or judgmental lending is based on the analyst's personal knowledge and experience within the industry segment being loaned to or with the specific product. Analysts making judgmental decisions on credit cards will think differently from those who are lending for the indirect auto channel. The underwriting decision on a credit card rests on the stability of the customers and how they have previously handled revolving debt, among other factors. The judgmental decision for an indirect auto loan will take into account other installment loan experience as well as how the monthly payment will affect the customer's debt burden.

The largest challenge in working with the underwriting team to gain acceptance of a new model is to teach them how a model can make an intelligent recommendation about credit risk based on limited information and nothing else, not even demographic or deal-related factors. (This statement assumes that most scoring models are based solely on credit information and have few master file characteristics.)

Early in the project, hold a training session with the underwriting team—even if the model being built will replace a model already in use. If, as is likely, it has been several years since the last model was installed, there are probably many new underwriters on the team. The training should cover three basic credit-scoring methodology (1) how samples are taken, (2) how independent variables are selected, (3) and what a dependent variable is. The training should survey the different types of statistics that can be used to predict outcomes and present examples of models and a sample scorecard. Reviewing a validation will demonstrate to the underwriters that a model does work and is fairly accurate in predicting risk.

Besides appointing a senior underwriting manager on the steering committee, make sure that project milestones are communicated to the underwriting department. For instance, when the preliminary model is developed, share with the underwriters some of the characteristics that are coming into the models. Specific characteristics will help them bridge the gap between judgmental and score-based decisions. An example would be Average Months in File. This characteristic calculates the aggregate age of all the tradelines in the credit file and then divides it by the number of trades in the file.

When the developer, whether internal or external, presents the preliminary models, make sure not only the underwriting manager but also a lead analyst is in the presentation meeting. The underwriting manager is already an internal business partner in the project, but a lead analyst will generate increased acceptance among the underwriters because that person can provide buy-in to the models and development process. One of the bigger arguments that has to be confronted is lack of understanding on how models are developed. Both analysts and underwriting managers can offset that kind of apprehension.

Once the final models have been tested and audited, conversion to the new model will need support from within the underwriting department. A member of the project team who knows the models being made available should actually be positioned in the underwriting department to answer questions and connect the judgmental "gut" decision an analyst feels with the score the model is applying to the loan situation.

An important point that has to be driven home with the underwriting team is that models are empirically developed using thousands of loan decisions and their outcomes. While judgment many contradict the score for certain loans, when all loans are viewed as a group score, models clearly can provide reliable evaluations of risk. Acceptance of these paradoxes is increased through support and coaching by a member of the project team as the model is rolled out.

MANAGING INDIRECT DEALERS

When risk models are introduced for the first time or new models replace current models, indirect dealer management is important. Direct lending is when the bank originates a loan directly with the consumer. Indirect lending is where the bank receives the application indirectly from a vendor of a consumer good. Indirect dealers are external parties like car dealers who submit applications to the bank via fax or electronic transmissions. The bank will then decide whether to underwrite the loan. If it does underwrite the loan, the bank assumes the receivable and the risk associated with the loan when closed.

When "push back"—disagreement on the decision a model is recommending—comes from an underwriting department, this is an organizational issue. The project team implementing the model and the underwriting department are ostensibly both on the team. Dealer pushback on new models is common, but indirect dealers usually know only the decisions that come back once loans are submitted, not the score produced by the new model.

Dealers pull credit bureau reports before submitting a loan application and can obtain a generic risk score. This will give the finance manager at the dealer an idea of the general risk the deal represents, but it may not completely agree with what the new model is recommending—the dealer's view of what is an acceptable risk may differ from that of the lender.

Indirect dealers view an approval as a deal made, and business closed. Usually the dealer does not have to assume the risk of a loan decision and therefore may be very sensitive when the approval environment changes. The approval environment is the perception built up by the dealer of what combination of risk and deal characteristics will be approved. (Deal characteristics are items like down payment, overall debt burden, value of the car, and what percentage of the purchase price is being financed.)

The sales and management team within the bank is sensitive to approval rates for each of their dealer channels. They are also sensitive to the business relationships between the bank and the dealer. The indirect lending business model has two sets of customers (1) dealers as business partners and (2) consumers as buyers of a product securing the loan, which may be a car, boat, appliance, tool, or any other good. Indirect channels as a whole pose higher risk to the financial services organization because the consumer is one step removed from it, and risk indicators can become disguised over time.

When a model is deployed or redeveloped, material aspects of identifying risk may change. Working with the indirect dealer sales department to prepare them for these changes will make model implementation easier. This can be done by having an indirect channel member on the steering committee for the project, training the indirect sales force on modeling and the modeling project life cycle, and discussing how the new model might affect lending decisions, and why. The usual change brought on by a new model is to create a more conservative lending situation, which in turn means lower approval rates and pressure to maintain market share.

Fraud in indirect channels has increased over time as the use of scoring technologies has increased. To guard against fraud stemming from use of automated decision tools, lenders should take on the role of fraud perpetrator by asking, "How could I manipulate this scorecard to raise the score?" Manipulations that are within the consumer's control would be transfers of revolving balances to new accounts that would not be reported to the credit bureau file for a month and changes in income information. While characteristics like income, age, occupation codes, and residence indicators are rarely used in scorecards today, lenders should always be on guard when using borrower reported information that can be falsified. The best defense against a scorecard being susceptible to fraud is to work with the developer to analyze how a score could be defeated or manipulated.

COMPLIANCE

A representative from the compliance department should be part of the project steering committee, because that department is concerned with how this model will affect fair lending practices and compliance with Regulation B. Most financial services organizations want to handle fair lending practices proactively, so the compliance officer will want to see that characteristics that could be construed as discriminatory are not included in the model. External vendors of scoring models are highly knowledgeable and generally do not include these types of characteristics in models, but if a model is being built internally, the developers may not be as familiar with compliance issues.

Compliance officers will also want to review the adverse action reasons that accompany turndown notifications. Adverse action statements specify what aspect of the credit score most negatively affected the overall score. They are ordered by various methodologies that rank a characteristic's impact on the final score. An example might be "historical derogatory payments on accounts." This would translate back into the model as a historical delinquency characteristic that has a negative impact on the final score.

TRAINING

The most successful scoring implementations give priority to training organizational constituencies and plan for it from the beginning of the project. Otherwise, training on scoring generally as well as on the specific modeling project at hand can often get lost in the congestion of programming, auditing, testing, and setting new credit policies for the model. If an organization is implementing a scoring model for the first time, training is even more crucial.

Training should be given to all business partners, direct or indirect. Indirect business partners include indirect lending channel representatives. A typical training presentation should include, but not be limited to:

* Goals of model development.

- General examples of common credit-scoring characteristics.[1]

- Modeling methodology.

- Plan for model implementation.

- Automated decisions the model might drive.

- Scorecard reporting.

- Scorecard validation.

- Adverse action statements.

- Support structure for the model within the organization.

MARKETING

The risk management department usually manages a credit risk modeling project because by definition risk management is responsible for limiting dollar losses to the organization. However, because the marketing department is tasked with the responsibility of attracting and retaining new customers, and it sets specific dollar targets for new originations and for managing attrition and early payouts, any new risk tool is going to intersect with the organization's marketing goals, starting with the rate of approval of new applicants—a new risk model will change the approval rate structure. One of the most sensitive tasks of a modeling project manager is to work with other risk managers and the marketing department to keep approval rates stable on the product line for which the model is being implemented.

Most model developments are undertaken for one of three reasons (1) There is no model in place, (2) the current model is not effectively ranking risk, or (3) while the model is ranking risk, newer technologies are available to build a model that does it better. The marketing department, which is probably not tuned into the current performance of a model, may assume that today's approval rates will and should continue under the new model.

The solution to this disconnect is to involve marketing business partners in the project at its outset. A representative from marketing should be on the project steering committee. Most outside model vendors can pro-

---

[1] The specific scoring characteristics that are in the model should be confidential to the risk management department or the department that is leading the project. The rationale for this is that if these characteristics are disclosed to the underwriting department, there is a risk that underwriters will manipulate the score by changing inputs to the applications system.

duce a report showing projected approval rates on the whole population at specific score cut-offs. This will enable the project manager to show marketing staff what an expected approval rate might be at a given cut-off and what projected risk is associated with that cut-off. This analysis offers a tool for compromise and management of expectations for the new decision environment.

SCORECARD MONITORING

Even as the model is being built, thought needs to be given to how performance will be evaluated once the scorecard is implemented. Because the information support structure to run monitoring reports should be in place at implementation, this will require coordination with the systems and programming department to assure that data for these reports is available. Chapter 13 describes a set of reports that permit active monitoring of applicant and booked populations, scorecard characteristics, and score performance. Monitoring reports are one of the most important elements of successful scorecard design and installation.

TIMELINES

Each modeling project will have its unique aspects, but there are three general phases to a scorecard development project (1) data gathering, (2) model development, and (3) model implementation. Most modeling projects, whether using internal or external resources, tend to take four to six months from design to conversion—though it must be acknowledged that data and business issues can extend the timeline significantly if the schedule is not managed carefully. Figure 11.2 shows an example of a project timeline Gantt chart showing the major project phases and task categories.

CONCLUSIONS

Communication with business constituencies within the organization during a modeling project is critical to successful development, installation, and acceptance of a new scoring model. Systems and programming are very important because a modeling project needs to be prioritized within the myriad of other operational demands placed on business today. In fact, the impact of credit scoring models on all aspects of the business side of the organization, not just systems, is so enormous that the project manager must handle it deftly.

FIGURE 11.2 TIMELINE GANTT CHART

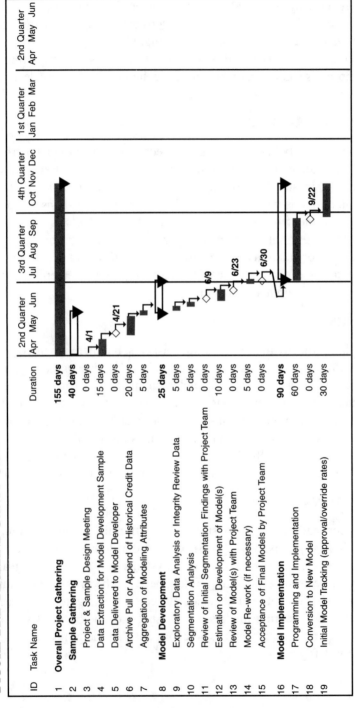

ID	Task Name	Duration
1	**Overall Project Gathering**	**155 days**
2	**Sample Gathering**	**40 days**
3	Project & Sample Design Meeting	0 days
4	Data Extraction for Model Development Sample	15 days
5	Data Delivered to Model Developer	0 days
6	Archive Pull or Append of Historical Credit Data	20 days
7	Aggregation of Modeling Attributes	5 days
8	**Model Development**	**25 days**
9	Exploratory Data Analysis or Integrity Review Data	5 days
10	Segmentation Analysis	5 days
11	Review of Initial Segmentation Findings with Project Team	0 days
12	Estimation or Development of Model(s)	10 days
13	Review of Model(s) with Project Team	0 days
14	Model Re-work (if necessary)	5 days
15	Acceptance of Final Models by Project Team	0 days
16	**Model Implementation**	**90 days**
17	Programming and Implementation	60 days
18	Conversion to New Model	0 days
19	Initial Model Tracking (approval/override rates)	30 days

A credit risk model, which directly affects the lending environment, can be undermined by an underwriting team that does not embrace the process and accept a new or updated model. The marketing department, too, is very sensitive to changes in the risk environment that directly affect approval rates on current product lines. Departments that manage indirect lending channels like auto or other durable goods financing can also be very sensitive. Because credit models are used in automated systems to make loan decisions, compliance and legal departments must take an active interest in the project. Educating each of these internal constituencies on credit scoring and the risk modeling process will enhance acceptance of this new or updated technology.

The decision on whether to use an internal or an external model developer may hinge on both how much experience the organization has with modeling and the economics of the project. The timing, when the model needs to be rolled out in terms of other organizational priorities, may also be a factor. The model developer should be conversant with sampling issues and data augmentation should internal data be insufficient for robust development. Lastly, once implemented, complete decision tracking and model stability monitoring and validation must be planned effectively.

Chapter 12
SCORECARD POLICIES: HOW TO USE YOUR SCORECARD TO YOUR BEST ADVANTAGE

Elizabeth Mays
Director of Retail Risk Modeling and Analytics
Bank One

INTRODUCTION

Did you hear about the lender who hired a vendor to build an acquisition scorecard, expended vast resources implementing it, invested staff time to create policy around use of the score, then ended up not using the scorecard—and not even realizing it? Unfortunately, mistakes lenders make can sometimes render their scorecards far less effective than they could be, or even totally useless. Lenders who think they are using their scorecards to best advantage in fact may be getting far less benefit from them than they might if they understood what mistakes to avoid. In this chapter we discuss three key scorecard policies that allow risk managers to make optimal use of their acquisition scorecards.

The first is adherence to a sound scorecard override policy. With a *low-side* override, an applicant is offered a loan even with a score that falls below the prescribed cutoff. Typically, this is done only after an underwriter or analyst has reviewed the application and found reason to believe that the borrower poses less risk than the score indicates. With a *high-side* override, the application is rejected even though it scores above the cutoff. In the next section we discuss how score overrides can sabotage a scorecard, and what a risk manager can do to prevent this.

The second policy tool for risk managers is having appropriate policies for which applications get turned down regardless of score. Lenders often impose policy limits to automatically reject even high-score applicants if they have extreme values of certain characteristics like low monthly income or a high DTI ratio. The use of limit policies not only is often appropriate, it can help lenders speed the loan decision process by not wasting time on applications they do not want to consider.

If these automatic limits are set at the wrong levels, however, they can reject good applicants whose profiles are completely within the risk tolerance of the lender and whose loans would turn out to be profitable. Such limits can choke off volume without decreasing risk, a combination that decreases profitability. How this can happen and how it can be avoided is the subject of the third section.

The last policy area on which risk managers should focus is formulating a rigorous cutoff analysis framework. A rigorous cutoff analysis looks at the profitability expected from loans at each value of the score and for the entire portfolio. Such analysis is time-consuming—it may involve numerous people throughout the organization—yet it is important that all components of profitability be properly accounted for so that cutoff scores can be set at the right level. That is the subject of the final section.

SCORE OVERRIDES

We will work here with an example of a case where too many low-side overrides caused a scorecard to be used suboptimally; in fact, low-side overrides—loans that score below the cutoff but are nonetheless approved—are our chief concern in this section.[1]

Permitting a limited number of overrides is good scoring policy, because it is always possible that good loans may be found among those below the cutoff. In practice, though, overrides should be kept to a mini-

---

[1] When discussing the override rate it is important to state explicitly how it is calculated. Some define the low-side override rate as the number of applicants with scores below the cutoff who are approved as a percentage of total applications *both above and below the cutoff*. Others define the rate as the number of applicants approved with scores below the cutoff as a percentage of total applications *below the cutoff only*. Clearly, the second percentage is always going to be much larger than the first given that the denominator (all applications below the cutoff only) is much smaller than that of the first (applications both above and below the cutoff). Still others define the low-side override rate as the number of *booked* loans with scores below cutoff as a percentage of *all booked* loans. All three measures serve a purpose and all should be tracked to understand the role overrides play in the portfolio.

mum.[2] If the score has been shown to do a good job of ranking risk, yet the override rate is high, there are two possible implications: (1) If the cutoff is set optimally to maximize profits, accepting loans below the cutoff will sabotage the scorecard and profitability will be lower than expected. (2) If analysts and underwriters are consistently finding good loans below the cutoff, it may be that the cutoff is not optimally set and should be lowered. In either case, a high override rate means the scorecard is not being used optimally.

To find out whether overrides are undermining the score, analyze the performance of overridden loans. In the portfolio of an actual lender who historically had a high override rate, about 85 percent of booked loans scored above the cutoff and the remaining 15 percent were the result of score overrides. The plot shown in Figure 12.1 was used to analyze the performance of loans accepted through overrides. To create the plot, we took loans that were two or more years old, ranked them by their origination score, and grouped them in 35-point score buckets. Then we calculated the good/bad odds[3] for each group and plotted it for each score range.

FIGURE 12.1 GOOD/BAD ODDS BY SCORE RANGE

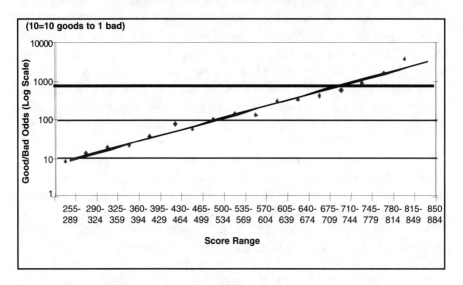

[2] A bank regulator once stated that he would "raise an eyebrow" if a lender were to accept more than 10 percent of all applications scoring below the cutoff.
[3] In this case a bad loan was defined as one that had gone 60 DPD two or more times in the two-year period.

When the score was developed it was scaled so that the expected good/bad odds would double for every 70-point increase in the score; the line drawn through the set of points has a slope consistent with that. Thus, because the line shows the expected good/bad odds at a given score, points too far off the line indicate that the actual observed odds differ from the expected odds. Overall, the points fit the line extremely well.

Our main interest is with the odds in score ranges below the cutoff of 500, the loans that were accepted as score overrides. When a loan is over-ridden, the analyst is saying there is reason to believe that the loan will perform better than the score would indicate—but our plot shows otherwise for this case. If the overrides truly performed better than the score would predict, the good/bad odds for the score ranges below the cutoff should lie well above the expected odds line, but here actual good/bad odds continue to decrease as scores decline and are very much in line with what the score predicted they would be.

If the lender wants to maintain volume at historical levels, it would be much better off to lower the cutoff slightly and accept all applications above it, but drastically reduce overrides below the new, lower cutoff. A significant number of this lender's overridden loans had very low scores, in the 250-400 range. Because the good/bad odds are higher in the 400-500 range than in the 250-400 range, it would be unambiguously better to lower the cutoff into the 400s to accept perhaps an additional 12 percent of loans. Overrides would then be limited only to special situations where a compelling case could be made that the score was not indicative of expected performance.[4] In fact, that was the strategy this lender adopted. The result of using the score to its full potential by relying more heavily on the score than on judgmental overrides is a lower bad rate at the same volume.

If, like this lender's, overridden loans perform no better than the score predicted they would perform, it is best to limit overrides and, if maintaining volume is a consideration, to also lower the cutoff score. The risk manager should carefully write policies detailing under what circumstances the scorecard may be overridden. The policy should list who in the organization has the authority to override the score. The authority may differ by loan size. Some loans may require approval from two or more reviewers.

---

[4] Note that though the good/bad odds are low at scores in the 250-400 range, there are still a number of good loans there, so overrides should not be completely prohibited. The challenge is to identify those with the highest likelihood of being good from among the low-scoring population.

A fairly short list of permissible reasons for overrides should be constructed and staff instructed to carefully annotate which of the permissible reasons applies in each case. Later, after the loans have aged and their outcome is apparent, the list can be used to analyze performance by override reason. If loans overridden for a particular reason do indeed perform better than the score predicted, the reason for the override can be incorporated either into future policy or into future versions of the scorecard.

POLICY LIMITS

Policy limits can help lenders avoid wasting time evaluating applications they clearly do not want. Common policy limits are to limit the payment to income ratio or the DTI ratio to levels that are consistent with the lender's risk appetite. If limits are not set carefully, however, too many good loans may be rejected, so analysis to determine the optimal levels of policy limits must be rigorous.

When setting policy limits, lenders sometimes look at bad rates for particular borrower or loan characteristics to see which appear to imply high risk. Figure 12.2 shows the percentage of loans in a particular consumer loan portfolio that went 90+ DPD within the first three years by DTI ratio. Clearly, higher debt ratios are associated with higher bad rates.

FIGURE 12.2 BAD RATE BY DEBT RATIO RANGES

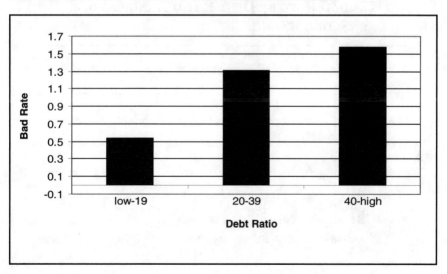

Say the lender has determined that the expected bad rate for any loan can go no higher than 1.3 percent if profitability hurdles are to be achieved with its current pricing. The lender may be tempted to limit debt ratios to below 40 to exclude a population of loans with high bad rates from its portfolio. What should be recognized, however, is that although the 40-high group has an *average* bad rate over 1.3 percent, many loans in that group have an expected bad rate well below 1.3 percent because compensating factors that lower the risk of the loan. Further, the custom score the lender uses is well equipped to identify such loans because although the score contains DTI ratio as one of its characteristics, it also weighs the effect of numerous other risk factors.

Dividing the population by score band and debt ratio as in Figure 12.3 shows that the score has already accounted for the risk of high-debt-ratio loans. We know this because within each score band the bad rates do not continue to increase with the debt ratio as they did in Figure 12.2. In fact, for the lowest score band, where most of the bad loans are found, the 20-39 debt ratio group actually has a higher bad rate than the 40+ debt ratio group. From this chart we can see that if we want only those applicants with low bad rates, we would be much better off cutting out low-scoring loans than cutting out high-scoring applicants with debt ratios at or above 40.

FIGURE 12.3 BAD RATE BY DEBT RATIO RANGE AND SCORE RANGE

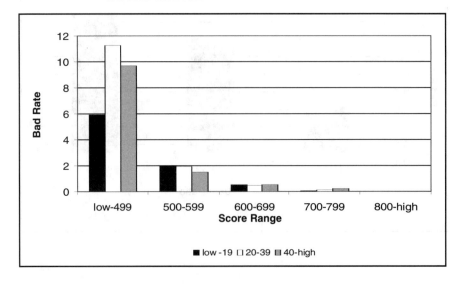

Debt ratio gives us only a small part of the risk profile of applicants. The statistical methodology used to build the scorecard, on the other hand, weighs the risk of having a high DTI ratio against all other risk characteristics and derives optimal point weights for each characteristic to best predict which loans will go bad. As a result, high-DTI loans are assigned fewer score points than low-DTI loans, but one or more compensating factors may allow them to score well above the lender's cutoff. Failing to book high-scoring loans because of the value of a single attribute may be a missed business opportunity.

Because the score already incorporates the risk effect of high debt ratios, what is an appropriate limit, if any, on the DTI characteristic? We need to look for guidance to the score itself and the data used to develop it. Because only about 2 percent of loans in the data sample used in our model had DTI ratios in excess of 50, the score is unlikely to be able to accurately evaluate their risk. Fifty is probably an appropriate limit in this case. The limit for any particular risk characteristic in the score should be set at the point beyond which there are too few loans in the score development sample to produce a reliable estimate of how the characteristic affects loan outcome.[5]

This example illustrates the importance of thorough analysis before setting policy limits. A custom score may already control the risk in question by penalizing individual risk attributes—and almost certainly in a much more effective way. While this is especially true of characteristics that are actually part of the score, it may also be true for characteristics not part of the score but correlated with characteristics that are.

In sum, to set appropriate policy limits on risk characteristics, those characteristics must be analyzed that pose incremental risk not measured by the scorecard. Producing charts like Figure 12.3 where the risk of a particular characteristic is analyzed at various score levels is very useful to see if the characteristic poses risk that is not already measured by the score.[6] If within a score the characteristic still appears to be related to the likelihood of loans

---

[5] This assumes that our main concern is controlling the portfolio bad rate at a given approval rate. In fact, if certain characteristics that are part of the score also affect profitability in other ways, say through different line utilization rates, attrition rates, or loss severity, these effects should also be incorporated into the analysis. As lending institutions move toward more detailed profitability models incorporating the effect of many characteristics on profitability, it may be that policy parameters will be set as part of an overall profit optimization plan that takes numerous constraints and interrelated effects of applicant characteristics into account.

[6] The only limiting factor to analysis is the number of loans in each cell of the matrix or chart. There must be enough loans in each cell (ideally several hundred or more) for the conclusions drawn about the relationships to be reliable.

going bad, a policy limit for that characteristic may be set at the point where losses become unacceptably high. If there is no apparent relationship between the characteristic and the likelihood of a bad outcome after the score is controlled for, a policy limit should be set at the level of the characteristic beyond which there is no representation in the score development sample.

SCORE CUTOFFS

There are a number of important considerations involved in setting a score cutoff, including how many loans will be approved and booked and what the expected return is on those loans. A lender must take operating capacity into account when setting the cutoff. Approving too many loans, or approving fewer loans than is optimal from a capacity point of view, could cause either overload of capital and resources or, just as important, underuse of resources. If the number of loans to be booked is to be changed, that must be planned for so that supporting staff and infrastructure adjustments can be made.

Table 12.1 is the kind of table risk managers might construct when doing cutoff analysis. It requires that the score to be implemented be calculated for a set of recent applications, in this case those received over the last 12 months. We use this set to produce measures of interest to the lender on the assumption that they will remain the same for future business. A description of each column follows:

1. Score range in descending order.

2. Number of applications in each score range.

3. Cumulative number of approvals.

4. Cumulative approval rate.

5. Booking rate in score range.

6. Cumulative number of loans booked.

7. Expected good/bad odds in score range.

8. Expected bad rate in score range.

9. Expected portfolio bad rate.

10. Return on assets (ROA) in score range.

11. Portfolio ROA.

TABLE 12.1 CUTOFF ANALYSIS

1	2	3	4	5	6	7	8	9	10	11
Score Range	Number of Applications	Cumulative Number of Approvals	Cumulative Approval Rate (%)	Booking Rate in Score Range (%)	Cumulative Number of Loans Booked	Expected Good/Bad Odds in Range	Expected Bad Rate In Range	Cumulative Expected Bad Rate	ROA in Range	Portfolio ROA
701-720	12000	12000	4	70	8400	1000	0.10	0.10	0.80	0.80
681-700	12000	24000	9	70	16800	875	0.11	0.11	0.80	0.80
661-680	12000	36000	13	70	25200	750	0.13	0.12	0.80	0.80
641-660	11000	47000	18	70	32900	625	0.16	0.13	0.85	0.81
621-640	11000	58000	22	70	40600	500	0.20	0.14	0.85	0.82
601-620	11000	69000	26	70	48300	438	0.23	0.15	0.85	0.82
581-600	11000	80000	30	70	56000	375	0.27	0.17	0.90	0.83
561-580	11000	91000	34	70	63700	313	0.32	0.19	0.90	0.84
541-560	11000	102000	38	70	71400	250	0.40	0.21	1.00	0.86
521-540	11000	113000	42	70	79100	219	0.46	0.23	1.10	0.88
501-520	11000	124000	46	70	86800	188	0.53	0.26	1.20	0.91
481-500	11000	135000	51	70	94500	156	0.64	0.29	1.30	0.94
461-480	11000	146000	55	70	102200	125	0.79	0.33	1.40	0.98
441-460	11000	157000	59	70	109900	109	0.91	0.37	1.50	1.01
421-440	11000	168000	63	70	117600	94	1.06	0.41	1.50	1.05
401-420	12000	180000	67	70	126000	78	1.27	0.47	1.50	1.08
381-400	12000	192000	72	70	134400	62	1.59	0.54	1.80	1.12
361-380	12000	204000	76	70	142800	54	1.81	0.62	1.90	1.17
341-360	12000	216000	81	70	151200	47	2.11	0.70	2.10	1.22
321-340	10000	226000	85	70	158200	39	2.52	0.78	1.90	1.25
301-320	10000	236000	88	70	165200	31	3.13	0.88	1.70	1.27
281-300	9000	245000	92	85	172850	27	3.57	1.00	1.50	1.28
261-280	9000	254000	95	85	180500	23	4.17	1.13	1.20	1.27
241-260	6000	260000	97	90	185900	19	5.00	1.24	1.00	1.27
221-240	3000	263000	98	90	188600	15	6.25	1.32	0.50	1.26
201-220	1000	264000	99	95	189550	13	7.14	1.35	0.10	1.25
181-200	500	264500	99	95	190025	11	8.33	1.36	0.00	1.25
161-180	400	264900	99	95	190405	9	10.00	1.38	-0.50	1.24
141-160	300	265200	99	95	190690	7	12.50	1.40	-1.00	1.24
121-140	300	265500	99	95	190975	6	13.79	1.41	-2.50	1.23
101-120	300	265800	99	98	191269	6	15.38	1.44	-4.00	1.23
81-100	300	266100	100	98	191563	5	17.39	1.46	-5.00	1.22
61-80	300	266400	100	98	191857	4	20.00	1.49	-7.00	1.20
41-60	300	266700	100	98	192151	4	22.22	1.52	-8.00	1.19
21-40	300	267000	100	98	192445	3	25.00	1.56	-10.00	1.17
0-20	300	267300	100	98	192739	2	33.33	1.61	-12.00	1.15

Column one shows the number of applications received in each score range, with the ranges listed from low risk to high so we can see the total number of loans that would be approved and booked and the expected portfolio bad rate at each possible cutoff. Columns two, three, and four show the number of applicants in each score range, the cumulative number of applicants at or below a given score range, and what the cumulative approval rate would be if the cutoff were set at the low end of each score range.

In column five we entered an assumption about the percentage of the approved applications in each range that will actually be booked. As we discuss below, we need this estimate in order to estimate bad rates and profitability for the entire portfolio. The booking rate assumption may be based on historical rates or it may not be if the lender believes circumstances will be different in the future from those of the past. Typically, booking rates (as a percentage of approvals) are very high in low score ranges because these applicants tend to have fewer choices in the loan market; higher-credit-quality borrowers can shop around for the best interest rate and may be bid away by other lenders. In Table 12.1 we have assumed that the booking rate varies from 98 percent for applications with the lowest scores to 70 percent in the highest score ranges.

The cumulative number of loans expected to be booked at or below each score is given in column six. Column seven shows the expected good/bad odds in each score range—the number of good loans expected for each bad loan in that range. A value of 15 would mean that for every 15 good loans, we expect to find one bad one. This 15 to 1 odds equates to an expected bad rate of 6.25 percent $(1/(1+15) = 6.25)$, as shown in column eight. (The derivation of the expected good/bad odds and the expected bad rate is explained in Chapter 4.)

The expected good/bad odds play an important role in the traditional method for setting cutoff scores. Traditional cutoff analysis sets the cutoff score as follows: Determine the amount of revenue expected from a good loan and the expected cost of a bad loan and calculate their ratio. If a bad loan costs the lender $10,000 and a good loan generates income over its life of $500, the ratio is 20:1 $(10,000/500=20)$. Then find the point on Table 12.1 where the expected good/bad odds are equivalent to this ratio. That is the cutoff—in this case at a score of about 260. The idea is that profit is maximized by finding the breakeven point where the last loan made would just cover the costs of bad loans made in that range. All other loans at scores above that score would be profitable.

Brown and Edelman[7] note at least three problems with this simplistic method:

1. It looks only at what happens at the margin (a single point in the score range) and fails to evaluate portfolio profitability, which is presumably the main concern.

2. The score definition of a bad account does not necessarily mean the loan would be unprofitable. It is common to define bad as serious delinquency, such as the likelihood of going 90 DPD but while some accounts that go 90 DPD proceed to charge-off and the outstanding principal is lost, others do not and the only expense incurred is for extra collections efforts.

3. It uses the same average revenue and cost assumptions for all the loans in the entire score distribution. As we discuss in covering the remaining columns in Table 12.1, expected revenue and expected cost can differ widely by score.

A better approach to setting cutoffs may be to estimate profits and profitability measures of interest, such as return on assets (ROA) or return on equity (ROE). To estimate either, we need a full accounting of all cash flows—both positive and negative—that are expected for the loans in each score range.

Besides estimating the amount of the cash flows, we need to estimate the period over which the cash will flow in. The length of time a loan stays on the books is likely to vary by credit score—not just because default rates vary by score but also because prepayment (attrition) rates are likely to vary as well. With installment loans, high-score borrowers often pay their loans off early, because they have more options than borrowers with poor credit for refinancing home or auto loans. They may also have higher incomes and be more likely to buy new vehicles sooner, paying off the old loan at that time. Similarly, low-risk credit card customers are likely to receive many more credit card offers from other lenders with advantageous terms and may switch balances more often than low-score borrowers.

Among income cash flows to the lender are interest income, origination fees, late fees, and early pay-off fees. Interest income cannot be known with certainty because coupons will vary with market conditions at the time the loan is made, but it is possible to make a reasonable estimate. The alter-

---

[7] Brown, Dawn, and David Edelman, "Some Views on Setting Scorecard Cut-offs." Paper presented at the September 2001 Credit Scoring & Credit Control VII conference sponsored by the Credit Research Centre at the University of Edinburgh.

native is to use the actual coupons on the previous year's loan originations. Income cash flows may also include income from other products associated with the loan, like credit insurance: If high-risk applicants are more likely to take credit insurance, this increases income to the lender and boosts the profitability of these accounts.

Cash outflows or costs include fixed costs, the cost of funding the loan,[8] and collection and default costs. Fixed costs like those for marketing, loan origination, and loan servicing may be somewhat difficult to allocate at the individual loan level, but the good thing for the purpose of this analysis is that they are likely to be the same for all applications (marketing and origination costs) or booked loans (servicing costs) and are not likely to vary by score.

Collection and default costs, of course, will be much higher in some score ranges than others. If the bad definition of the score happens to be charge-off, the expected probability of charge-off can be calculated using the method described in Chapter 4 for our profitability estimate. If the bad definition is something else, data on charge-off rates can be used to map scores for a specific probability of charge-off or loss. Similarly, estimated collection expenses can be allocated among score ranges using information on the number of times loans in each score range are delinquent during their lives.

The amount of the loss from a charge-off must be estimated in addition to the charge-off rate. For collateralized loans, the difference between the loan amount at default and the estimated value of the collateral is calculated and costs of repossessing and disposing of the collateral are added in. For both collateralized and noncollateralized loans we also need to estimate the amount of funds, if any, that can be recovered from the borrower after default.

Once we have derived the measures in Table 12.2 we are in a position to weight the tradeoffs involved in choosing the cutoff score from all those that are possible. There are at least three considerations that must be weighed here (1) approval rate, (2) number of bad loans that will be booked, and (3) portfolio profitability.

The approval rate matters most from a marketing point of view, especially for lenders who obtain their loans through indirect channels. Auto dealers, for example, are used to a certain percentage of applications being accepted by the lender; they are likely to be very disappointed by any

---

[8] As with future loan interest rates, the future cost of funds will not be known. The analysis can be based on past experience or on an estimate of the future cost of funds.

reduction in approval rates. Conversely, a lender that approves a higher percentage of these applicants than the competition may gain market share.

The approval rate also has important implications for loan underwriting and processing. Approving more applications than the lender has the capacity to efficiently and quickly underwrite and process causes delays that cause customer dissatisfaction.

The portfolio bad rate—the number of bad loans expected at a given cutoff—also has important implications for the collections, bad debt, and recovery areas. Even if loans within a given score range are believed to be profitable because their higher than average interest coupons make up for the increased delinquency and default rates, booking more bad loans may cause the lender to expand operations and thus substantially increase costs.

Finally, the estimated profitability of the portfolio is a prime consideration in setting the cutoff. Table 12.1 shows estimated ROA, but another lender may prefer a different metric. Whatever metric is chosen, the goal is to attain the highest possible profitability for the portfolio, taking into account other considerations that may be important to the lender, such as approval rate and portfolio bad rate.

Column 10, ROA in range, can be used to evaluate if the loans in a given score band pass the hurdle rate the lender has set for determining whether a particular investment meets its return requirements. Column 11, Portfolio ROA, gives an estimate of the return on the whole portfolio assuming the indicated number of loans at each score are booked. Even if the loans in a particular score band do not pass the hurdle rate, the lender may choose to set the cutoff at a particular point in order to maintain or gain market share by approving more loans. These are the types of tradeoffs that must be considered to establish an effective cutoff.

SUMMARY

Once a reliable, predictive account acquisition scorecard has been built, the risk manager's job is just starting. Three scorecard policy areas deserve in-depth attention and careful analysis (1) setting an appropriate score override policy, (2) setting policies for automatic rejection of applications regardless of score, and (3) cutoff score analysis.

If a lender's score is predictive, it should be overridden only rarely. Risk management policies should detail who in the organization has the authority to override the score and under what circumstances. Reasons for overrides should be carefully tracked so that they can be matched up with loan performance, to the benefit of future policies and scorecard development efforts.

Setting policies for automatic application rejection requires that the risk manager analyze whether a limit on a particular risk factor truly limits risk in a way the score cannot. Sometimes such policies reject high-scoring loans and unnecessarily limit volume with little or no corresponding decline in risk. Careful analysis of the risk factor in conjunction with the score should prevent this from happening.

Score cutoff analysis weighs competing goals of the lender to arrive at the best solution. Proper analysis requires estimating approval and booking rates, number of bad loans expected, and portfolio profitability at alternative cutoff scores. Measures of profitability should take all expected cash inflows and outflows into consideration and incorporate how they are expected to differ by score band.

Chapter 13
SCORECARD MONITORING REPORTS

Elizabeth Mays
Director of Retail Risk Modeling and Analytics
Bank One
Phil Nuetzel
Senior Economist, Risk Modeling Department of the Real Estate Group
Citigroup

INTRODUCTION

Once a scorecard has been implemented, its performance must be continually evaluated. In this chapter, we describe tracking reports for acquisition credit scorecards that let us answer important questions, such as:

- Is the scorecard being used as intended? Is the score cutoff being adhered to? Are score overrides being kept to a minimum? Are overrides being done for valid reasons? What are the most common reasons?

- Does the scorecard continue to rank the risk of loans as expected or has its performance deteriorated? Do the good/bad odds or bad rates match those that were expected when the scorecard was implemented?

- Have the characteristics of loan applicants changed? Are more low-score borrowers applying but being rejected? What are their characteristics?

- Has the score distribution of booked loans changed? Even if the proportion of booked loans scoring above the cutoff is constant, changes in the distribution, such as an increase in low-scoring accounts around the cutoff, could spell trouble.

In addition to its importance to the lender's credit quality and profitability, scorecard monitoring is important to bank regulators. The Office of the Comptroller of the Currency (OCC) has outlined its expectations about what national banks should do to monitor scores; OCC Bulletin 97-24 states that banks "must produce reports to monitor model accuracy and reliability."

The OCC distinguishes between *front-end* and *back-end* reports. Front-end reports may be generated soon after the score has been implemented; they do not report anything dealing with loan performance but are concerned with score distributions and the distribution of score characteristics. Back-end reports, which are designed to measure the scorecard's effectiveness, require that loans be at least somewhat seasoned so that it is clear whether the scorecard can distinguish good loans from bad. It takes at least a few months after a new score is implemented before these reports can be produced. The OCC states that the "frequency of reporting depends upon the bank's loan volume" and notes that "smaller volume banks may take six- to 12-months (or longer) to originate sufficient loan volume to perform valid statistical analysis."

Once a set of monitoring reports is designed, it should be fairly straightforward to generate them as often as needed. If volume permits, lenders that have recently implemented a new score will probably want to produce at least the front-end reports every month, though those that have been using the same score for a long time may feel that quarterly reports are sufficient.

Some lenders use custom scores designed specifically for their businesses; others use generic scores. The same tracking reports could be used for either except for the Characteristic Analysis report, which cannot be generated for generic scores because the characteristics are not available to the lender.

In the following two sections we describe in detail six monitoring reports that should make it possible to answer most questions about score use and performance. Adopting the OCC's terminology, the front-end reports that we will illustrate are:

- Population Stability and Approval Rate Report.

- Characteristic Analysis Report.

- Override Rate Report.

- Override Reasons Report.

The back-end reports are:

- Good/Bad Separation Report.

- Early Performance Score Report.

Besides providing a system to monitor a scorecard's performance, the reports make it much easier to formally validate a scorecard. They provide all the backup documentation typically required in a formal validation, as well as information that might be required in a standard regulatory filing.

The reports presented in this chapter are not based on actual lender data but are mocked-up versions of reports that we consider useful for score monitoring. No data from a particular institution should be compared with the numbers found in these reports.

Even though we have chosen to display the information in these reports as tables, it may be easier to review as graphs or charts. We encourage lenders to establish a reporting system for scorecard monitoring that is straightforward, easy to produce as needed, and structured as charts or graphs for user-friendly review. This will help ensure that score monitoring becomes an integral part of the risk management process and that scores are used to the greatest benefit of the lender.

FRONT-END REPORTS

POPULATION STABILITY AND APPROVAL RATE REPORT

The traditional Population Stability Report lists the score distribution of through-the-door applicants at several points, allowing us to monitor how the distribution is changing over time. This version of the report (Table 13.1) compares the score distribution of very recent applications (those taken in the last three months), older distributions (those taken in the last 12 months and in the 12 months before that), and the distribution of the development sample.

These comparisons give a good view of any changes in the distribution over time. Applicant distributions may change with the economic environ-

TABLE 13.1 POPULATION STABILITY AND APPROVAL RATES BY SCORE RANGE (THROUGH FEBRUARY 2002)

Score Range	Population Stability: Cumulative Distributions Through-the-Door Population				Withdrawn as % TTD Pop. in Range			Approved as % Decisioned in Range			Booked as % of Approved in Range		
	Past 3 Mos.	Past 12 Mos.	Yr. Ago 12 Mos.	Development Sample	Past 3 Mos.	Past 12 Mos.	Yr. Ago 12 Mos.	Past 3 Mos.	Past 12 Mos.	Yr. Ago 12 Mos.	Past 3 Mos.	Past 12 Mos.	Yr. Ago 12 Mos.
MISSING	1.06%	0.96%	0.77%	1.13%	0.00%	0.00%	0.25%	30.00%	28.00%	31.00%	100.00%	100.00%	99.75%
500-	3.53%	4.78%	6.45%	3.70%	0.00%	0.00%	0.50%	35.00%	36.00%	33.40%	100.00%	100.00%	99.50%
500-519	8.34%	10.13%	12.29%	12.43%	1.00%	0.00%	1.00%	37.00%	35.90%	39.34%	99.00%	100.00%	65.00%
520-539	16.92%	18.89%	21.08%	19.74%	2.00%	2.00%	2.00%	38.66%	39.19%	41.00%	65.00%	98.00%	98.00%
540-559	29.74%	31.21%	32.76%	28.40%	5.00%	4.00%	6.00%	73.34%	71.78%	73.56%	65.00%	65.00%	94.00%
560-579	45.76%	46.11%	46.44%	44.69%	7.00%	6.00%	8.00%	93.97%	93.22%	92.87%	65.00%	94.00%	92.00%
580-599	62.52%	61.56%	60.56%	56.92%	5.88%	5.11%	6.92%	95.00%	95.13%	94.71%	65.00%	94.89%	93.08%
600-619	77.18%	75.37%	73.40%	79.00%	7.06%	6.38%	8.65%	97.65%	98.00%	97.96%	65.00%	93.62%	91.35%
620-639	87.91%	85.95%	83.70%	83.81%	9.46%	8.56%	11.60%	98.06%	98.74%	98.44%	65.00%	72.20%	75.00%
640-659	94.48%	92.92%	90.98%	93.20%	11.35%	10.27%	13.92%	98.90%	98.60%	99.01%	87.52%	83.00%	86.08%
660-679	97.84%	96.87%	95.51%	99.48%	12.48%	11.29%	15.31%	99.45%	99.43%	99.39%	67.20%	65.00%	65.00%
680-699	99.28%	98.79%	98.00%	99.81%	13.73%	12.42%	16.84%	99.68%	99.55%	99.47%			83.16%
700+	100.00%	100.00%	100.00%	100.00%	15.10%	13.66%	18.52%	99.89%	99.92%	99.83%	72.25%	86.34%	81.48%
Total					9.79%	8.74%	11.90%	88.78%	88.76%	88.13%	76.61%	87.10%	87.41%
% Below Cutoff	16.92%	18.89%	21.08%	19.74%	0.75%	0.50%	0.94%	42.80%	42.17%	43.66%	91.00%	99.50%	90.56%
% Passing Cutoff	83.08%	81.11%	78.92%	80.26%	9.67%	8.63%	11.75%	98.31%	98.31%	98.20%	68.55%	79.89%	84.57%
	TTD			Sample	Withdrawn			Approved			Booked		
Number of Apps/Loans	7,439	31,967	29,063	56,031	728	2,480	3,047	7,351	31,428	28,539	7,631	27,372	24,948
AVG Score	600	596	591	611	660	655	661	650	644	639	640	633	639

ment, as a result of marketing initiatives, or because new markets have been opened through mergers and acquisitions. Making sure that distributions in recent periods are similar to development sample distribution can also create confidence that the score remains effective; if there have been large shifts in the population, rebuilding the scorecard might be worth considering—though that decision should not be made before a more thorough analysis.

We have listed *cumulative* TTD distributions to show the percentage of all applications that lie at or below a given score, but the marginal distribution (percentage of total applications in each score range) could just as well be shown instead.

One advantage of reporting the cumulative distribution is that from it we can calculate a measure of population stability directly. The KS statistic is often used to evaluate the ranking ability of scorecards by comparing the cumulative score distribution of good loans to the cumulative distribution of bad loans. It also can be used to compare the cumulative score distributions of applications taken over different periods to determine whether there has been a significant change. For example, if we want to see whether the population of applicants that applied over the last year is different from the population of applicants the year before, we can calculate the KS, which is simply the maximum difference between those two cumulative populations. The biggest difference (the KS) is in the score range 620-639, where the difference is 2.25. In this case, the KS is low, indicating very little difference between the two distributions.[1]

The dashed horizontal line in the table is used to show the cutoff score, which is 560. In the most recent three-month period, 29.74 percent of the applicants were below the cutoff and thus failed to qualify.

Populations of interest besides applicants are the withdrawn, approved, and booked populations. Our Population Stability and Approval Rate Report examines these ratios in the three right-hand panels:

- *The Withdrawal Rate.* Withdrawals of applications as a percentage of all TTD applications in that score range. An application can be withdrawn either before a decision is made or after approval.[2] A

---

[1] To determine whether the difference between the distributions of two populations is statistically significant, we compare the KS statistic to its critical value. The critical value at the 95 percent confidence level is calculated as FACTOR*sqroot((M+N)/MN), where M is the sample size of one population, N the sample size of the other population, and FACTOR equal to 1.22 for a one-sided test of significance.

[2] Some lenders define a withdrawal as something that takes place only after approval; withdrawals before a decision is made are simply considered unapproved applications.

change in the pattern or number of withdrawals may reflect competitive pressures, as when applicants in certain score ranges find alternatives with lower fees and rates or lenders that require less documentation. It might also reflect a slowdown in the underwriting process as applicants lose patience and move elsewhere to open accounts.

However, an increase in the withdrawal rate might not always be either bad or avoidable. For example, a withdrawal might be the most efficient outcome for some loans in low score ranges that are likely in any case to be rejected. A withdrawal may also occur when an applicant is unwilling to provide documents verifying income and employment.

• *The Approval Rate.* Approvals as a percentage of applications in that score range on which decisions have been made. If the lender is indeed depending on the credit score to properly evaluate applicant risk profile, the approval percentage should be near 100 among the highest-scoring applications. An approval rate of less than 100 percent for score ranges above the cutoff suggests that either the lender is using policy screens that reject applicants regardless of score or underwriters are subjectively overriding the score. The Override Reason Report discussed later helps determine which is the case.

• *The Booking Rate.* Booked loans as a percentage of approved applications in that score range. The same forces that affect withdrawals will tend to push the booking rate in the opposite direction. If an approved loan is not booked, either it is withdrawn or it is still in the pipeline. Low booking rates in high score ranges could indicate that the lender's product is not competitively priced.

All these ratios should be tracked to see how the applicant population is behaving and how the score is being applied in the current business environment.

The choice of time periods over which to measure the ratios is important; it will vary by both product and managerial preference. Products like mortgages that take time to underwrite and book will tend to have a relatively large percentage of recent applications in the pipeline at any given moment.[3] Measured over a short time, such as three months, the ratios will

---

[3] This will not be very important for products like credit cards and auto loans, which are underwritten more quickly than mortgages and have short pipelines.

appear low relative to those measured over longer periods, such as 12 months. For these products, the 12-month columns should probably be relied on more heavily. Because of possible seasonal effects, it is in any case always good to compare any ratio to one covering the same time period a year earlier, though calculating the ratios over periods longer than 3 months can minimize the impact of the underwriting delays.

Though the report emphasizes the distribution of applications *across* score ranges in the far left column, the ratios shown in the three panels at the right reflect the impact of underwriting practices and booking performance *within* each score range. The row labeled Totals at the bottom of the columns does not sum each column but instead gives the ratio across all score ranges (i.e., it is a weighted average of each ratio across the score ranges).

CHARACTERISTIC ANALYSIS REPORT

The Characteristic Analysis Report (Table 13.2) shows what percentage of the population fell into each range for each characteristic in the scorecard. For characteristics with more than two possible attribute values, the mean and median values are listed in the row below the frequencies. The sample report shows two examples of dichotomous indicator variables (DLQ12 and IQ) with two possible values and one example of a continuous variable (CLTV).

For continuous variables that were not binned into attribute ranges for score development, the choice of ranges is somewhat arbitrary. There may be business reasons for choosing certain ranges. For example, in the case of first lien mortgages, a combined LTV ratio of 80 percent may be used as the top of one range because 80 percent is typically the highest LTV at which mortgage insurance is optional for the borrower. Alternatively, the ranges might be set at equal quantiles of the development sample. However the choice is made, there should be enough ranges that significant shifts in the population over time can be detected.

The report has two major sections. The first shows the frequency distribution of the TTD population and the difference in frequency from the development sample. The second treats the distribution of the booked population. The distribution for the development sample is shown in the column at the far right.

Where there are significant shifts in distribution of the TTD population across the bands of an attribute, it is important to examine the booked population for similar shifts, and vice versa. If these shifts are comparatively small, or if shifts are observed in the opposite direction, it might indicate a conflict between marketing initiatives and underwriting policy or practice.

TABLE 13.2 CHARACTERISTIC ANALYSIS REPORT (THROUGH FEBRUARY 2002)

Charac-teristic	Value	Through-the-Door Population						Booked Population						Develop-ment Sample
		Frequency Distribution			Difference from Development			Frequency Distribution			Difference from Development			
		Past 3 Mos.	Past 12 Mos.	Yr. Ago 12 Mos.	Past 3 Mos.	Past 12 Mos.	Yr. Ago 12 Mos.	Past 3 Mos.	Past 12 Mos.	Yr. Ago 12 Mos.	Past 3 Mos.	Past 12 Mos.	Yr. Ago 12 Most.	
DLQ12	MISSING	1.26%	0.70%	0.90%	0.22%	-0.34%	-0.14%	0.20%	0.14%	0.31%	-0.84%	-0.90%	-0.73%	1.04%
	0	98.33%	73.67%	70.82%	-0.50%	-25.16%	-28.01%	62.68%	62.17%	62.46%	-36.15%	-36.66%	-36.37%	98.83%
	1	0.41%	25.63%	28.28%	0.28%	25.50%	28.15%	37.12%	37.69%	37.23%	36.99%	37.56%	37.10%	0.13%
IQ6	MISSING	0.47%	0.51%	0.63%	0.08%	0.12%	0.24%	0.35%	0.28%	0.16%	-0.04%	-0.11%	-0.23%	0.39%
	0	81.29%	86.58%	54.22%	0.36%	5.65%	-26.72%	91.76%	64.43%	50.06%	10.83%	-16.50%	-30.88%	80.93%
	1	18.24%	12.91%	45.15%	-0.44%	-5.77%	26.48%	7.89%	35.29%	49.78%	-10.79%	16.61%	31.11%	18.68%
CLTV	MISSING	0.00%	0.00%	0.00%	0.00%	0.00%	0.00%	0.00%	0.00%	0.00%	0.00%	0.00%	0.00%	0.00%
	1-60	3.03%	1.77%	0.66%	-1.51%	-2.76%	-3.88%	9.60%	14.90%	0.11%	5.06%	10.36%	-4.43%	4.54%
	61-70	2.32%	6.19%	7.96%	-7.35%	-3.48%	-1.71%	14.28%	19.39%	6.13%	4.61%	9.72%	-3.54%	9.67%
	71-80	5.76%	7.56%	18.33%	-3.31%	-1.51%	9.26%	30.25%	30.22%	21.48%	21.18%	21.16%	12.42%	9.07%
	81-90	29.34%	22.36%	15.00%	9.57%	2.58%	-4.77%	36.75%	40.28%	18.49%	16.97%	20.50%	-1.29%	19.78%
	91-100	55.13%	59.77%	54.33%	1.48%	6.13%	0.68%	6.26%	-5.47%	53.02%	-47.38%	-59.12%	-0.63%	53.65%
	>100	4.42%	2.35%	3.73%	1.12%	-0.95%	0.42%	2.86%	0.68%	0.76%	-0.44%	-2.62%	-2.54%	3.30%
	Mean	90	88	85	3	1	-2	84	83	81	-3	-4	-6	87
	Median	95	90	89	6	1	0	85	84	83	-4	-5	-6	89

It might also be a signal that certain opportunities are not being exploited. Suppose that the product type, say an adjustable-rate mortgage (ARM), is one of the characteristics used in a scorecard. If a shift in applications for ARM rather than fixed-rate mortgages is observed in the booked population but not in the TTD population, this might suggest that the pricing of these products is attracting more low-risk applicants to ARMs and high-risk applicants to fixed rate loans.

Although the Characteristic Analysis report in Table 13.2 does not do so, another option is to list the number of score points assigned for each attribute value. This would help the reviewer to assess the impact on the score distribution of any shifts in the distribution of values for any particular characteristic.

Finally, it is possible to calculate population stability measures from the information in this report—for example, KS statistics to test for differences in the distributions of recent applicants relative to the development sample. Such a calculation should be done using a relatively large number of ranges (10-20) chosen to ensure that the frequencies are not too concentrated within particular ranges. Note that here the hope is that the KS will be as small as possible, the opposite from when the KS is used to compare distributions of goods and bads. A small KS here indicates that the distribution of the characteristic within the validation sample is similar to that of the development sample, which indicates scorecard stability.

OVERRIDE RATE REPORT

The Override Rate Report (Table 13.3) provides a number of ratios that quantify the proportion of cases in which applications score below the cutoff but are approved (low-side overrides) or above the cutoff but are declined (high-side overrides). In sum, it shows the extent to which a policy of score-based approval is overruled.

Scores can be overruled either because automated policy rules reject applicants if they demonstrate certain characteristics (such as a recent bankruptcy) even if they score above the cutoff or because underwriters have made judgmental overrides. Policy and judgmental overrides should be tracked separately to make quite clear the reasons for the overrides so as to determine whether they are being used appropriately.[4]

In general, a high percentage of overrides in either direction is undesirable if a score is effective at ranking credit risk. An increasing tendency

---

[4] See Chapter 12 for a discussion of how lenders can analyze low-side overrides to determine whether underwriters have made wise decisions.

TABLE 13.3 OVERRIDE RATE REPORT (THROUGH FEBRUARY 2002)

Category	As % of Applications In Range			As % of Total Booked Loans		
	Past 3 Mos.	Past 12 Mos.	Year Ago 12 Mos.	Past 3 Mos.	Past 12 Mos.	Year Ago 12 Mos.
Low-Side Approvals	392	2,237	2,336	392	2,237	2,336
% Approved	35.17%	34.77%	36.19%	8.52%	13.26%	11.17%
Low-Side Booked	294	1,678	1,752	294	1,678	1,752
% Booked	30.80%	25.82%	30.87%	7.46%	9.85%	9.53%
High-Side Declines	4	26	350	4	26	350
% Declined	0.08%	0.10%	1.53%	0.12%	0.13%	2.08%

to override the score might reflect either a failure to understand how to apply a score or a shortcoming in other policy rules.

The ratios on the Override Rate Report use TTD overridden applications, not approved applications or booked loans, as their numerator, with one exception: the "% booked" line in the Low-Side Booked section, which uses the number of low-side loans booked.

In the first column, the numbers in the rows labeled % Approved and % Booked are calculated by dividing the numerator by the number of TTD applications in the category for the time period. For example, 35.17 percent is obtained by dividing all low-side approved applications by all TTD low-side applications.

The percentages in the last three columns are calculated by dividing approved and booked loans by the total number of booked loans across all categories (not the number of loans in the category). For example, 7.46 percent is obtained by dividing all low-side loans booked by the total number of booked loans in all categories.

Some lenders may find it desirable to track application referrals on the override report. For example, a number of applications might be referred to a separate affiliate specializing in lending to subprime borrowers. These referrals might otherwise have been high-side overrides or low-side declines, so an accounting of how often they happen may be of separate interest to management.

OVERRIDE REASONS REPORT

Another report dealing with overrides lists the top reasons for both low-side and high-side overrides and their frequency. The reason codes are usually stored in a lender's loan application database and can be useful with the Override Rate Report. The frequencies of the various codes may make it easier for managers to understand the reasons for changes in the number of overrides or to diagnose possible shortcomings in credit policy.

TABLE 13.4 OVERRIDE REASONS REPORT (THROUGH FEBRUARY 2002)

	Past 12 Months		Year-Ago 12 Months	
	Number of Loans	% of Total Overrides	Number of Loans	% of Total Overrides
Low-Side Overrides				
Reason 1	432	19.3%	530	22.7%
Reason 2	286	12.8%	315	13.5%
Reason 3	172	7.7%	77	3.3%
Reason 4	136	6.1%	168	7.2%
Reason 5	121	5.4%	119	5.1%
High-Side Overrides				
Reason 1	12	46.6%	151	43.2%
Reason 2	8	31.1%	112	32.0%
Reason 3	7	27.2%	97	27.7%
Reason 4	5	19.4%	55	15.7%
Reason 5	4	15.5%	68	19.4%

In Chapter 12 we discuss how to analyze whether loans booked as a result of low-side overrides perform better then their score would indicate. If there are enough overridden loans in each reason category in the Table 13.4 report, once the loans have aged sufficiently the same analysis may be done separately for each override reason category. If certain reasons for overriding the score result in good loans, that factor might be incorporated into future scorecards or adopted as one of the standard policy rules for all applications.

BACK-END REPORTS

GOOD/BAD SEPARATION REPORT

The Good/Bad Separation Report (Table 13.5) evaluates how well a score-card distinguishes loans with a good outcome from those with a bad outcome. If the model's separation ability has deteriorated, it may be time to build a new model. The definition of bad and the performance period should be the same after implementation as during development because the intent of this report is to determine whether the score is still doing what the lender expects it to do.

The Good/Bad Separation Report here compares the ability of the score to separate good loans from bad for three different samples. The panel on the left shows results for the current validation period. Assume that the original outcome period for the score was 18 months, the validation sample is made up of loans that have been on the books at least 18 months, and performance data is available up through the current month. The second panel of the report would show the results from a past validation sample, perhaps one performed a year ago.

TABLE 13.5 GOOD/BAD SEPARATION REPORT: BAD—EVER 60+ DPD DURING PERFORMANCE WINDOW (THROUGH FEBRUARY 2002)

Score Range	Current Validation Sample				Validation Sample One Year Ago				Development			
	Cumulative % Goods	Cumulative % Bads	Separation Bad-Good	% Bad in Range	Cumulative % Goods	Cumulative % Bads	Separation Bad-Good	% Bad in Range	Cumulative % Goods	Cumulative % Bads	Separation Bad-Good	% Bad in Range
500-	7.2	13.2	6.0	3.07%	7.2	13.2	6.0	3.25%	7.2	15.2	8.0	2.29%
500-519	14.6	28.7	14.1	1.78%	14.6	28.7	14.1	1.88%	14.6	33.7	19.1	1.37%
520-539	23.0	40.2	17.2	0.84%	22.0	40.2	18.2	0.93%	23.0	44.1	21.1	0.49%
540-559	31.6	50.6	19.0	0.55%	29.0	50.6	21.6	0.64%	31.6	57.8	26.2	0.47%
560-579	37.5	61.9	24.4	0.51%	37.5	59.9	22.4	0.44%	37.5	68.3	30.8	0.31%
580-599	44.4	70.7	26.3	0.33%	44.4	70.7	26.3	0.43%	44.4	78.7	34.3	0.26%
600-619	49.9	78.5	28.6	0.26%	49.9	78.5	28.6	0.28%	49.9	87.0	37.1	0.18%
620-639	55.0	85.0	30.0	0.20%	55.0	84.0	29.0	0.18%	55.0	89.0	34.0	0.04%
640-659	67.7	89.8	22.1	0.12%	67.7	89.8	22.1	0.15%	67.7	89.8	22.1	0.01%
660-679	78.4	93.2	14.8	0.07%	78.4	93.2	14.8	0.08%	78.4	93.2	14.8	0.05%
680-699	91.3	96.4	5.1	0.06%	91.3	96.4	5.1	0.06%	91.3	96.4	5.1	0.04%
700+	100.0	100.0	0.0	0.06%	100.0	100.0	0.0	0.06%	100.0	100.0	0.0	0.04%
KS Statistic			30.0				29.0				37.1	
Total Loans	48,677	842	49,519	1.70%	46,780	857	47,637	1.80%	34,615	385	35,000	1.10%

Though those loans would now have been on the books for 30 months, only the first 18 months of performance would be used in the comparison with the sample in the first panel. (It is useful to compare these two sets of numbers to see how the model has been performing since the last validation.) Finally, the third panel uses data from the development sample. This lets us see whether the score is still performing as well as it was when it was first implemented.

Each panel lists the cumulative percentages at or below a given score of loans with a good outcome and of loans with a bad outcome. The difference between these two percentages is the scorecard's degree of separation at that score level. The largest value of the separation among the score ranges is the KS statistic, which is also listed on the report. [5]

Two things that can happen after scorecard implementation can undermine portfolio performance (see Chapter 6). The first is a diminution in the scorecard's ability to rank risk. Whether this has happened can be judged by looking at the separation columns across the three panels and comparing the KS statistics.[6]

The second problem is that, even though the score may continue to rank risk well, the odds/score or bad rate/score relationship can shift so that a given score range now has a higher or lower odds or bad rate than before. To evaluate that possibility, look at the "% Bad in Range" column (number of bad loans in that range as a percentage of all loans in that range) and compare it across the three panels.[7] If the current bad rate within a particular score range is significantly different from earlier periods, it is time to evaluate possible changes in either the cutoff score or other booking strategies.

If indeterminate accounts were excluded from the development sample (see Chapter 4 for a discussion of indeterminates), they should be exclud-

---

[5] The KS statistic is the maximum separation achieved across the entire distribution of the score. Loans for which the score is missing should be excluded from this table because including them would result in an incorrect calculation of separation and thus an incorrect KS statistic.

[6] It is also useful to plot on a single graph the log of the good/bad odds against the score for each sample. The log odds should be linear when plotted against the score. This type of chart makes it very easy to see whether the slope or level of the odds/score relationship has changed.

[7] Note that here we are showing the marginal bad rate within each score range, while the discussion in Chapter 6 illustrated the concept by using the odds/score relationship. It makes no difference whether the good/bad odds or the bad rate at each score range is tracked because each is just a transformation of the other—the conclusion about any shifts in performance should be the same. It may be easier to make this assessment, however, by plotting the log odds rather than the bad rates since the plot should be linear with respect to the score

ed in this analysis as well. Since the score is used on *all* accounts, however, and the KS statistic can vary substantially depending on whether indeterminate accounts are in or out of the sample, we recommend generating a third report that does include the indeterminate accounts.[8]

Typically, the development sample has more observations in low score ranges than the validation sample if the lender has been honoring the cutoff score established at implementation. Thus, even if the bad definitions and outcome periods are identical, the data in the first and second panels may show less separation than the score achieved in the development data set. Thus, the seeming deterioration of the score's ability to risk-rank loans may in fact be due to the change in the score distribution of loans between the development and validation sample rather than the score's inability to evaluate risk. Chapter 7 explains how to determine whether the score has indeed deteriorated or whether the decline in the separation and ranking statistics is due to the change in the distribution of scored loans.

EARLY PERFORMANCE SCORE REPORT

The Good/Bad Separation report is designed to evaluate performance using the same bad definition and outcome period as was used for score development. We also need a shorter-term view of score performance if we are to do something promptly about a deteriorating score or higher-than-expected bad rates. The purpose of the Early Performance Score Report (Table 13.6) is to get an idea of how well the score is ranking risk based on the short-term performance of loans booked relatively recently.

The Early Performance Report lists Ever 30+ DPD and Ever 60+ DPD rates by score band for loans booked in the last three months, six months, and 12 months. More precisely, the bad rates are calculated by dividing the number of loans booked in each score band that were delinquent within the performance window by the total number booked in the same score band. For comparison purposes, the percentages generated for the same categories a year ago are included. For example, for a report dated Through February 2002, the Past 3 Months column would contain the delinquency rates and performance of loans booked from December 1, 2001, though February 28, 2002, and the column headed Year Ago 3 Months contains the delinquency rates of loans booked from December 1, 2000, though February 28, 2001. As with some of the other reports, the dashed horizontal line shows the cutoff score for loan decisions. Loans booked in the bands above this line (scores below the cutoff) are low-side overrides.

---

[8] We leave open the question of whether indeterminates should be included as goods or bads, which can be addressed separately for each business.

TABLE 13.6 EARLY PERFORMANCE SCORE REPORT: BAD RATES BY SCORE RANGE
(THROUGH FEBRUARY 2002)

Score Range	Bad: Ever 30+ DPD Loans Booked In:						Bad: Ever 60+ DPD Loans Booked In:					
	Past 3 Mos.	Yr. Ago 3 Mos.	Past 6 Mos.	Yr. Ago 6 Mos.	Past 12 Mos.	Yr. Ago 12 Mos.	Past 3 Mos.	Yr. Ago 3 Mos.	Past 6 Mos.	Yr. Ago 6 Mos.	Past 12 Mos.	Yr. Ago 12 Mos.
MISSING	4.28%	5.03%	4.28%	5.03%	37.05%	30.84%	4.28%	3.81%	11.25%	15.67%	11.90%	15.67%
500-	2.27%	1.62%	7.76%	9.44%	7.76%	18.23%	0.49%	1.62%	8.71%	1.62%	10.71%	5.24%
500-519	1.40%	1.93%	2.77%	3.37%	2.77%	3.37%	0.47%	0.91%	5.30%	4.54%	5.30%	4.54%
520-539	2.19%	0.61%	2.86%	3.04%	6.36%	5.40%	0.41%	0.30%	5.34%	0.30%	5.34%	0.30%
540-559	0.85%	0.56%	1.19%	4.57%	6.73%	6.68%	0.85%	0.56%	1.78%	3.38%	2.28%	5.56%
560-579	0.74%	1.82%	3.17%	3.14%	7.56%	7.25%	0.47%	0.19%	1.36%	4.07%	8.30%	8.86%
580-599	1.38%	0.31%	1.38%	2.69%	3.46%	2.69%	1.00%	0.27%	2.50%	1.40%	3.86%	1.40%
600-619	1.44%	1.04%	1.44%	1.04%	3.05%	3.72%	0.24%	0.01%	0.24%	1.78%	3.66%	1.78%
620-639	1.08%	0.01%	1.08%	0.15%	1.94%	4.02%	0.16%	0.01%	0.16%	1.02%	4.42%	1.54%
640-659	0.37%	0.98%	1.86%	2.19%	4.61%	2.19%	0.24%	0.25%	0.97%	2.12%	1.73%	2.27%
660-679	0.68%	0.26%	0.68%	1.19%	2.99%	1.78%	0.45%	0.26%	1.06%	1.15%	3.58%	2.61%
680-699	0.43%	0.51%	0.43%	0.55%	1.65%	1.52%	0.22%	0.15%	1.00%	0.93%	1.93%	2.01%
700+	0.26%	0.50%	0.49%	0.86%	0.49%	0.86%	0.05%	0.05%	0.24%	0.92%	0.24%	1.13%
Average Bad Rate	0.81%	0.89%	1.30%	1.60%	3.70%	3.96%	0.28%	0.38%	1.71%	1.47%	3.67%	4.22%
Number of Total Loans	7,631	6,437	13,508	12,659	27,372	24,948	7,631	6,437	13,508	12,659	27,372	24,948

The delinquency rates in the right-hand panel labeled Bad: Ever 60+ DPD will be relatively low for loans booked in the past 3 months. These are shown in the first two columns of the panel. Only a few of these loans will have had their first payment due date within a month of the booking date, and only those few have any chance of going 60 days delinquent within this period. It might therefore be preferable in some cases to show 60-day delinquency rates for loans booked within the past four or five months, with the other columns to the right also redefined using longer performance windows. As with any of the other reports, the precise column definitions can be changed to suit the needs of the business.

Changes in bad rates may indicate the need for some action, such as rescaling the score or adjusting the cutoff. For example, a shift toward higher bad rates in low-score bands might give an early hint of a need to increase the cutoff score, assuming that management wants to limit credit risk to a particular level. If the report shows that the original score/odds relationship is not preserved, then rescaling the score may be appropriate, but because it is possible that other policy changes or marketing initiatives might have caused the shift, the analyst should be cautious about recommending changes.

SUMMARY AND CONCLUSIONS

Continuous evaluation of a scorecard after it is implemented is sound risk management as well as responsive to regulators. Acquisition scorecard tracking reports can answer basic questions about how a scorecard is being used and its accuracy and reliability. These are important considerations no matter whether lenders use scores designed specifically for their businesses or generic scores that use a broader bad definition. In the final analysis, either type of score must be effective in ranking risk and predicting portfolio performance for the lender. These reports allow risk managers to continually assess whether this is happening.

Among the tracking reports were four front-end reports that looked at score distributions and the distributions of score characteristics and two back-end reports that measured how effective the score was in distinguishing good loans from bad. While it was outside the scope of this chapter, tracking reports can also be produced for behavior scores that risk-rank seasoned loans for collections purposes. These would include a report showing stability of the scored accounts across score bands, a Characteristic Analysis Report, and a Good/Bad Separation Report.

Once a set of monitoring reports is designed, the process should be automated so that the reports can be produced as often as desired. The reports allow more frequent monitoring of scorecards and they also make the process of formally validating a scorecard much simpler because they provide all the backup documentation that is typically required.

Chapter 14
CREDIT SCORING AND RISK BASED PRICING: AN INCOME STATEMENT APPROACH

Dana Wiklund
Vice President
Equifax

INTRODUCTION

The primary challenge of risk management is to balance risk and reward. This balancing must be a cooperative effort between the risk manager and other constituencies in the organization, such as marketing, finance, underwriting, and collections. This chapter describes how to deploy a pricing model that uses an income statement approach within the context of a discounted cash flow analysis. An important component of the pricing model is estimating losses for loans of differing credit quality.

The interest rate charged for a loan product and the amount of credit risk assumed when its price is set are the two determinants of how financially successful a loan product or vintage of loans will be. Success is measured over time as interest income accumulates and is then eroded by expenses. Very small changes in pricing can make a loan vintage a financial failure. Often these failures can remain hidden because an organization can operate in disparate ways depending on different objectives. Risk management and marketing may be in different divisions. Or they may be separated by geography, or by organizational culture.

Successful lending organizations keep both customer and product in mind when analyzing risk for pricing purposes. Higher prices bring in more income but may also attract borrowers whose credit risk is higher, driving up the losses that will be incurred by the vintage over its lifetime.

Credit losses are by far the most difficult expense item to predict with precision. Expenses like those for marketing a product, servicing the loan vintage, collections, and reserving for future losses are all well-defined and at least somewhat predictable. Credit losses fluctuate over the life of a loan depending on changes in consumer behavior and economic conditions as well as the future marketing efforts of competitors aiming to bid away your customers and cause early payoffs. Within your product line there may be differences in both regional economic conditions and repayment behaviors. Pricing a product is very closely tied to the risk inherent in the product, the population it is being marketed to, and the risk the organization is willing to accept. Credit scores are highly useful in predicting potential losses for both portfolio segments and individual loans. Potential income, expense, and profit from lending activities are most often estimated at the portfolio level, but can also be considered loan by loan.

This chapter describes a financial model based on monthly estimated cash flows over the life span of a loan vintage. Each month begins with a given amount of dollars outstanding. The income statement describes how income is generated and then eroded by expense items. The analysis looks at the net present value (NPV) loan vintage that is fully amortized over 36 months. We show how losses based on credit scores can be incorporated into the pricing analysis and walk through a sensitivity analysis that demonstrates how changes affect pricing strategies while expenses are held constant. We examine how pricing and expense components can affect the financial success of the loan vintage over its life span.

INCOME STATEMENT APPROACH

In constructing the income statement approach to risk-based pricing, we make a number of assumptions. Each month begins with a given amount of dollars outstanding. These dollars—$50 million in our example—are amortized over the life span of the vintage, in this case 36 months. Gross interest yield is calculated by applying a monthly interest rate to the dollars outstanding. As the outstandings amortize, the amount of monthly income for the vintage declines.

Table 14.1 shows the income statement for the first month in the life of the loan vintage. The top portion includes fee income, the charges for late fees and miscellaneous services to the account. It is calculated as a percentage of outstanding balances. One expense item, the cost of funds, is also in the top part of our income statement, because cost of funds is a direct function of outstandings and is necessary to calculate *net interest margin.* Net interest margin is income less the cost of funds to generate that income.

TABLE 14.1. INITIAL INCOME STATEMENT

	CF Month 1
Balances	
Gross outstandings	$50,000,000
- Balance amortization	$1,388,889
= Net balances	$48,611,111
Income	
Gross interest yield/income	$729,167
+ Fee income	$121,528
- Cost of funds	$101,273
= Net interest yield/income	$749,421
Expense	
Marketing expense	$12,153
Servicing expense	$72,917
Collections expense	$48,611
Charge-off expense	$64,815
Total expenses	$198,495
Profit/Net Contribution Margin	$550,926

Core expenses in the bottom half of the income statement are for marketing, servicing, charge-offs, and collections. Generally, these expenses can be calculated as a function of outstandings at any given point in the vintage's life span.

Net interest margin less expenses equals *net contribution margin.* Net contribution margin is the profit resulting from a month's cash flows that can be contributed back to business activities.

Other assumptions for how expenses are incurred for this loan vintage *not necessarily accrued* are as follows:

- **Charge-off expense.** Because 80 percent of total loan losses are expected in the first 24 months, this amount is amortized evenly over these months. The remaining 20 percent of losses are amortized and applied during the last 12 months of the vintage's lifespan. This is a simplifying assumption. In practice, lenders should carefully analyze the timing of losses from previous vintages and build appropriate timing assumptions into their pricing models.

- **Early pay-off** is ignored in this example but the likelihood of early pay-off for loan products deserves careful attention.

- **Marketing expenses** incurred before the vintage is on the books are amortized as a function of outstandings, though often large marketing expenses are incurred as negative cash flows before the first month of amortization. This is done to simplify the analysis.

- **Servicing and collections expense** is applied as a percentage of outstandings.

- **Loan loss reserves** are assumed to be held by the organization but are not an integral part of our example.

The loan vintage can be analyzed over its lifetime by calculating its NPV over its lifespan of 36 months using balance amortization, expense application, and loss assumptions. NPV is the sum of all future cash flows discounted to the present day at an expected rate of return. If the sum of discounted cash flows is positive, the financial objective is being attained. A negative NPV for the vintage indicates that the expected return on investment (ROI) has not been achieved.

NPV is a method applied in financial scenarios to help financial managers make capital budgeting and investment decisions. NPV analysis assumes that an investment constitutes upfront negative cash flow and the return of capital plus a premium for the use of the capital comes in as future cash inflows. Applying NPV concepts to a loan vintage implies that the cash outflow is in the form of expenses for launching and maintaining a loan vintage and the cash inflows come in as interest and fee income. Mathematically, the NPV of a loan vintage can be viewed as follows:

$$\text{Net Present Value} = \sum \left[\frac{\text{Monthly Contribution Margin}}{(1 + k)^t} \right]$$

where   k = Rate of return
             t = Time period

The NPV equation may be used in a number of ways. First, if we assume a given coupon on the loan vintage (used to calculate gross interest income) and a given required rate of return, we may solve for NPV. Alternatively, if we assume a given rate of return, we may solve for the coupon that would be required to give rise to these values. Thus, risk-based coupons can be set so that all costs, including expected credit losses, are covered and the return expected by shareholders is earned.

Table 14.2 is a spreadsheet showing the cash flows expected in the first and last 3 months of a sample loan vintage.

TABLE 14.2. INITIAL AND TERMINAL CASH FLOWS COMPARED

	First Three Months			Last Three Months		
	CF Month1	CF Month2	CF Month3	CF Month34	CF Month35	CF Month36
Balances						
Gros s outstandings	$50,000,000	$48,611,111	$47,222,222	$4,166,667	$2,777,778	$1,388,889
- Balance amortization	$1,388,889	$1,388,889	$1,388,889	$1,388,889	$1,388,889	$1,388,889
= Net balances	$48,611,111	$47,222,222	$45,833,333	$2,777,778	$1,388,889	$0
Income						
Gross interest yield/income	$729,167	$708,333	$687,500	$41,667	$20,833	$0
+ Fee income	$121,528	$118,056	$114,583	$6,944	$3,472	$0
- Cost of funds	$101,273	$98,380	$95,486	$5,787	$2,894	$0
= Net interest yield/ income	$749,421	$728,009	$706,597	$42,824	$21,412	$0
Expense						
Marketing expense	$12,153	$11,806	$11,458	$694	$347	$0
Servicing expense	$72,917	$70,833	$68,750	$4,167	$2,083	$0
Collections expense	$48,611	$47,222	$45,833	$2,778	$1, 389	$0
Charge -off expense	$64,815	$62,963	$61,111	$1,852	$926	$0
Total expenses	$198,495	$192,824	$187,153	$9,491	$4,745	$0
Profit/Net Contribution Margin	$550,926	$535,185	$519,444	$33,333	$16,667	$0

Net Present Value	$3,521,219
Assumptions	
Gross outstandings	$50,000,000
Gross interest yield rate	18.0000%
Gross monthly interest yield	1.5000%
Fee income rate	0.2500%
Cost of Funds	2.5000%
Required rate of return	12.0000%
Marketing expense	0.0250%
Servicing expense	0.1 500%
Collections expense	0.1000%
Charge -off expense	4.0000%

✓ wrong

In Table 14.2, the NPV of the loan vintage using our assumptions is $3,521,219. This value assumes an 18 percent coupon and lifetime credit losses that total 4 percent of original dollars outstanding. The risk manager has to evaluate the criteria for credit risk being used with a given product and estimate how much risk is inherent in the approved and booked population. This risk assessment is used in conjunction with information from marketing, product development, or lending to arrive at pricing that will both meet customer needs and produce a reasonable financial result.

In this example, our loan vintage has an NPV of $3,521,219. Setting the interest rate at 18 percent is reasonable because our required rate of return is 12 percent and our expected gross dollar losses are 4 percent. The risk manager has control over pricing and most expenses but can only estimate credit losses, which are the most volatile of expenses. The next section describes how credit scores can be used to estimate these losses.

When we say that the NPV for our vintage is $3,521,219, what does that mean? We are saying that the sum of the 36 monthly cash flows for net contribution margin is worth $3.52 million in today's funds. Financial theory holds that cash flows in the future are worth less than their nominal amount by a factor equal to the expected rate of return. Discounting future cash flows takes into account the cost of capital to the firm. Figure 14.1 shows how nominal periodic cash flows from our vintage and the discounted value of those future cash flows varies over time. It shows relative month-to-month differences in future cash flows better than 36 months of income statements could.

NPV of residual income

FIGURE 14.1. PROJECTED MONTHLY CASH FLOWS COMPARED WITH DISCOUNTED CASH FLOWS

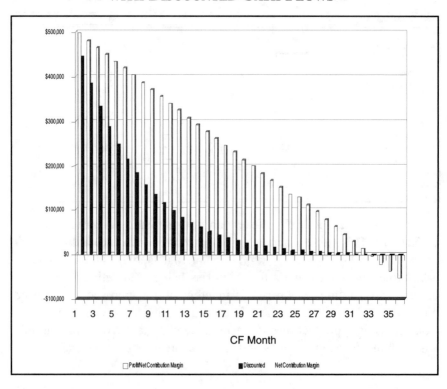

The sum of cash flows over the lifespan of our vintage totals $9.97 million, but we do not have access to those funds today because they have not yet arrived. Calculating the current valuation of those funds using a 12 percent discounting factor produces our NPV of $3.52 million.

NPV can also be calculated for a segment of the portfolio or even for an individual loan. Consider the following example. As a risk manager or lending officer you have to price a $30,000 personal loan to a long-standing customer. You have always considered this customer's credit and character to be of high quality, but your custom model generates a credit score for the customer of 525, which corresponds to a projected 36-month bad rate of 3 percent. Table 14.3 is the pro forma income statement for this loan.

TABLE 14.3. PRO FORMA INCOME STATEMENT FOR AN INDIVIDUAL LOAN

	First Three Months			Last Three Months		
	$CF_{Month\,1}$	$CF_{Month\,2}$	$CF_{Month\,3}$	$CF_{Month\,34}$	$CF_{Month\,35}$	$CF_{Month\,36}$
Balances						
Gros s outstandings	$30,000	$29,167	$28,333	$2,500	$1,667	$833
- Balance amortization	$833	$833	$833	$833	$833	$833
= Net balances	$29,167	$28,333	$27,500	$1,667	$833	$0
Income						
Gross interest yield/income	$438	$425	$413	$25	$13	$0
+ Fee income	$73	$71	$69	$4	$2	$0
- Cost of funds	$61	$59	$57	$3	$2	$0
= Net interest yield/income	$450	$437	$424	$26	$13	$0
Expense						
Marketing expense	$7	$7	$7	$0	$0	$0
Servicing expense	$44	$43	$41	$3	$1	$0
Collection s expense	$29	$28	$28	$2	$1	$0
Charge -off expense	$29	$28	$28	$1	$0	$0
Total expenses	$109	$106	$103	$5	$3	$0
Profit/Net Contribution Margin	$340	$331	$321	$20	$10	$0
Net Present Value	$2,174					
Assumptions						
Gross outstandings	$ 30,000					
Gross interest yield rate	18.0000%					
Gross monthly interest yield	1.5000%					
Fee income rate	0.2500%					
Cost of funds	2.5000%					
Required rate of return	12.0000%					
Marketing expense	0.0250%					
Servicing expense	0.1500%					
Collections expense	0.1000%					
C harge -off expense	3.0000%					

Pricing this loan at 18 percent produces a 36-month NPV of $2,174. Is this optimal? Optimal pricing depends on the goals of the organization. According to capital budgeting theory, if the sum of a series of cash flows discounted at a required rate of return exceeds $0, the undertaking is acceptable, so income and expense over the life of this loan are acceptable. A sensitivity analysis shows that if the rate charged for this loan is decreased to 3.99 percent, the NPV given our assumptions falls to 0, which though not optimal is still acceptable.

What would happen if we have underestimated the risk of this long-standing customer? Using a coupon of 18 percent, what loss probability could we tolerate before our loan has a zero or negative NPV? Scenario analysis shows that when we solve for a $0 NPV varying the charge-off expense, the threshold is a charge-off probability of 38 percent (see Table 14.4).

TABLE 14.4. LOSS PROBABILITY VARYING CHARGE-OFF EXPENSE

	First Three Months			Last Three Months		
	CF Month 1	CF Month 2	CF Month 3	CF Month 34	CF Month 35	CF Month 36
Balances						
Gros s outstandings	$30,000	$29,167	$28,333	$2,500	$1,667	$833
- Balance amortization	$833	$833	$833	$833	$833	$833
= Net balances	$29,167	$28,333	$27,500	$1,667	$833	$0
Income						
Gross interest yield/income	$438	$425	$413	$25	$13	$0
+ Fee income	$73	$71	$69	$4	$2	$0
- Cost of funds	$61	$59	$57	$3	$2	$0
= Net interest yield/income	$450	$437	$424	$26	$13	$0
Expense						
Marketing expense	$7	$7	$7	$0	$0	$0
Servicing expense	$44	$43	$41	$3	$1	$0
Collection s expense	$29	$28	$28	$2	$1	$0
Charge -off expense	$372	$361	$351	$11	$5	$0
Total expenses	$452	$439	$426	$15	$8	$0
Profit/Net Contribution Margin	-$2	-$2	-$2	$10	$5	$0
Net Present Value	$0					

Assumptions	
Gross outstandings	$30, 000
Gross interest yield rate	18.0000%
Gross monthly interest yield	1.5000%
Fee income rate	0.2500%
Cost of funds	2.5000%
Required rate of return	12.0000%
Marketing expense	0.0250%
Servicing expense	0.1500%
Collections expense	0.1000%
Char ge -off expense	38.2377%

According to capital budgeting theory, if a series of cash flows discounted at a required rate of return exceeds $0, then the undertaking is acceptable. In this example, the level of income and expense over the life of this individual loan are acceptable. A sensitivity analysis shows that if the rate charged for this loan is decreased to 3.99 percent, the NPV given our assumptions falls to 0. This low interest rate may not produce an optimal scenario in terms of value, but it is still acceptable from a theoretical sense.

ESTIMATING CREDIT LOSSES USING CREDIT SCORES

We described in Chapter 4 how the expected odds or bad rate could be calculated for each score range in a lender's portfolio. If an account was opened with a risk score of 500, Table 14.5 tells us that over the performance period of the score, 3 percent of accounts scoring between 500 and 524 are expected to go bad.

TABLE 14.5. PROJECTING EXPECTED BAD RATES

Sample Credit Risk Score						
A	B	C	D	E	F	G
Interval	Interval Bad Rate	Interval Count	Unit Loss Vector	Average Loan Amount	Dollar Loss Vector	Descending Cumulative Dollar Losses
575-600	0.25%	5,000	13	4000	$50,000	$50,000
550-574	0.50%	3,000	15	3500	$52,500	$102,500
525-549	1.00%	2,000	20	2500	$50,000	$152,500
500-524	3.00%	1,500	45	2000	$90,000	$242,500
475-499	6.00%	750	45	1900	$85,500	$328,000
450-474	12.00%	200	24	1500	$36,000	$364,000
425-449	24.00%	50	12	1000	$12,000	$376,000
400-424	50.00%	10	5	500	$2,500	$378,500
100-399	75.00%	0	0	0	$0	$378,500

A bad is any account that reaches a level of delinquency that matches the definition used to develop the model. For example, if model development defines a bad as any occurrence of a 90+ days past due delinquency, once a booked loan becomes 90 days past due, it is considered a bad. If the bad definition used for model development is that an account be charged off, we can use the expected bad rate to estimate the number of charged-off loans to expect in each score range.

If the bad definition is something other than charge-off, we must map the scores to an expected charge-off rate to construct what is termed the *unit loss vector* in the table. A unit loss vector is a projection of how many loans will be charged off during a specified time period. The unit loss vector at a given score interval can be converted into a dollar loss projection by multiplying unit losses by the original loan amount. Knowing the expected loss amount for the loans in each credit score range permits us to use this analysis to calculate the coupon that would be needed for each score segment to achieve the institution's hurdle rate.

In addition to estimating the lifetime loss expected from loans in the various credit score ranges, we must also estimate *when* losses will take place so that we can slot them into the appropriate month in our pro forma income statement. Lenders can draw their own loss timing curves using internal data on the timing of losses from well-seasoned loan vintages or, as was suggested in Chapter 8, they may borrow one from a published source.

CONCLUSION

Drawing up a pro forma income statement allows the risk manager set risk-based prices that bring the lender the required ROI. Credit scoring is a fundamental component of this analysis. Scoring allows the risk manager to estimate one of the most volatile expenses, credit losses. Because credit losses can destroy the financial value of an individual or a group of loans very quickly, integrating credit scoring into this analysis is critical to successful decision-making. The tools needed to conduct these analytics are spreadsheet software, an expected odds chart, and good communication between the risk manager and other constituents in the organization, such as the marketing, corporate finance, and loan-servicing teams.

INDEX